Nations of Emigrants

Nations of Emigrants

Shifting Boundaries of Citizenship
in El Salvador and the United States

Susan Bibler Coutin

Cornell University Press
Ithaca and London

First published 2007 by Cornell University Press

Printed in the United States of America

Library of Congress Cataloging-in-Publication Data

Coutin, Susan Bibler.
   Nations of emigrants : shifting boundaries of citizenship in El Salvador and the United States / Susan Bibler Coutin.
        p. cm.
   Includes bibliographical references and index.
   ISBN 978-0-8014-4574-3 (cloth : alk. paper) — ISBN 978-0-8014-7396-8 (pbk. : alk. paper)
   1. Citizenship—El Salvador.   2. Citizenship—United States.
3. El Salvador—Emigration and immigration.   4. United States—Emigration and immigration.   I. Title.

   JV7423.C68 2007
   323.6'3—dc22

                                                          2007014445

Cornell University Press strives to use environmentally responsible suppliers and materials to the fullest extent possible in the publishing of its books. Such materials include vegetable-based, low-VOC inks and acid-free papers that are recycled, totally chlorine-free, or partly composed of nonwood fibers. For further information, visit our website at www.cornellpress.cornell.edu.

Cloth printing   10   9   8   7   6   5   4   3   2   1
Paperback printing   10   9   8   7   6   5   4   3   2   1

To Raphael and to Curt

Contents

Acknowledgments

I am deeply indebted to the individuals and organizations that provided me with interviews and other material for this book. I promised interviewees anonymity, so I will not list them by name. I would, however, like to thank the institutions and individuals that in some way facilitated the research process. I should note that by naming an institution, I do not mean to imply that that institution in any way officially endorsed this project or the analysis that I present here. My debts are great, so this list will be long, and those who, for reasons of confidentiality, remain unnamed should know that their efforts are remembered and deeply appreciated.

For providing information or facilitating the research process, I am grateful to the *American Baptist Churches v. Thornburgh* class counsel, the American Immigration Lawyers Association, Asociación Adentro Cojutepeque, the Association of Salvadorans of Los Angeles, the Asylum Division of the U.S. Immigration and Naturalization Service, the Banco Central de Reserva de El Salvador, CARECEN Internacional, Cáritas de El Salvador, Casa de la Cultura de El Salvador, Catholic Relief Services—Programa de El Salvador, the Central American Resource Center (Los Angeles, San Francisco, and Washington, D.C.), the Centro Binacional de Derechos Humanos in Tijuana, Centro Hispano Cuzcatlán, Centro Latino Cuzcatlán, the Centro Salvadoreño, Citizens and Immigrants for Equal Justice, the Coalition for Humane Immigrant Rights of Los Angeles, the Citizenship

Assistance Campaign of Los Angeles County, COFESAL (Comité de Festejos Salvadoreños), the Comisión Nacional de Desarrollo, Comité Pro-Mejoramiento San Miguel Tepezontes, Comité Propaz y Reconstrucción de Cacaopera, Comité Unión Salvadoreña, Comunidad Salvadoreña en Los Angeles, COMUNIDADES (Comunidades Unificadas de Ayuda Directa a El Salvador), COMUNIDADES Federal Credit Union, Dirección General de Atención a la Comunidad en el Exterior of the Ministerio de Relaciones Exteriores de El Salvador, *El Salvador Día a Día*, the Embassy of El Salvador in Washington, D.C., El Espinal, the Facultad Latinoamericana de Ciencias Sociales in San Salvador, the Fundación Centroamericana para el Desarrollo Humano Sostenible, the Guatemalan Unity Information Agency, Homies Unidos, the Immigrant Legal Resource Center, the Immigrants' Rights Project of the American Civil Liberties Union, the Instituto de Derechos Humanos de la Universidad Centroamericana, Instituto de Estudios Jurídicos de El Salvador, the Los Angeles Asylum Office, Los Angeles City Council, the National Immigration Forum, the Northern California Coalition for Immigrant Rights, the Organización Internacional para las Migraciones office in El Salvador, *La Prensa Gráfica*, Programa Nacional de Competitividad of the Ministerio de Economía de El Salvador, the Proyecto de Cooperación Técnica sobre Derechos Humanos de El Salvador of the Oficina del Alto Comisionado de las Naciones Unidas para los Derechos Humanos, El Rescate, the Salvadoran American National Association, the Salvadoran American National Network, the Salvadoran Consulate in Los Angeles, the Salvadoran-American Leadership and Educational Fund, the Service Employees International Union, Southwest Voter Registration, the Universidad Centroamericana José Simeón Cañas, the U.S. Embassy in El Salvador, the U.S. Department of Justice, and the offices of several U.S. senators and congressional representatives.

The following individuals also provided invaluable assistance in the course of my research: Jesús Aguilar, Susan Alva, Katherine Andrade-Eekhoff, Carlos Ardón, Sergio Barahona, Sylvia Beltran, Caroline Berver, Patty Blum, Sergio Bran, Meredith Brown, Sandra de Castillo, Oscar Chacon, Juan Carlos Cristales, Carlos Dada, Robert Foss, Randy Jurado, Edgardo Mira, Esther M. Olavarria, Jaime Peñate, Luis Perdomo, Gilma Perez, Gaspar Rivera, Eduardo Rodriguez, Angela Sambrano, Greg Simons, and Rick Swartz. Silke Kapteine generously provided housing, advice, friendship, and a bit of German instruction when I was in El Salvador. I have fond memories of the days that we spent together.

My research was supported by grants from the Law and Social Science Program at the National Science Foundation (awards #SES-0001890 and

#SES-0296050) and a research and writing grant from the John D. and Catherine T. MacArthur Foundation. The Office of Research and Sponsored Programs at California State University, Los Angeles, and the Social Ecology Research Office at the University of California, Irvine, provided assistance in managing my research funds. Susan Hyatt and Susan Garcia, in particular, were very helpful. The Executive Vice Chancellor's Office at the University of California, Irvine, provided funding for research assistants. The Grant Seed Money fund of University Auxiliary Services at California State University, Los Angeles, provided the financial support that first enabled me to seek funding for this project. I was a visiting scholar at the International Institute for the Study of Law in Oñati, Spain, as I was preparing to embark on research. Some of the resulting manuscript was written while I was a Resident Fellow at the University of California Humanities Research Institute.

I was fortunate during this research project to have an abundance of very capable research assistants who helped gather secondary documents, transcribe audiotapes, and organize my research data. Thank you to Gisela Castro, James Daza, Lee Franklin, Ester Hernandez, Jose Herrerias, Ana Larios, Andrés Salcedo, Janet Salinas, Rosaura Tafoya-E., Sylvia Valenzuela, Gabriela Vega, and Lucero Zamudio. You were all wonderful, and I have thought of you many times as I worked with the data. In addition to helping gather and organize data at UC Irvine, Ester Hernandez accompanied me on one of my research trips to El Salvador and assisted with numerous interviews there. My conversations with her inform this account.

Unless otherwise noted, all translations of Spanish sources (whether written or oral) are mine, so I bear responsibility for any translation errors.

Many, many colleagues have shared ideas, read drafts, and provided advice. My analysis is indebted to collaborations with Bill Maurer and Barbara Yngvesson, both of whom have gone far beyond the normal bounds of colleagueship in providing advice, guidance, and moral support. My analysis of deportation is indebted to my collaboration with Barbara Yngvesson on our coauthored article, "Backed by Papers: Undoing Persons, Histories, and Return" (*American Ethnologist* 33, no. 2:177–190). Beth Baker-Cristales, Ester Hernandez, and Ana Patricia Rodriguez have been invaluable colleagues, sharing interview experiences and exchanging ideas. In particular, my analysis of remittances draws on ideas developed in my exchanges with Ester Hernandez as we wrote our coauthored article, "Remitting Subjects: Migrants, Money, and States" (*Economy and Society* 35, no. 2:185–208). Tom Boellstorff pointed out that this book is an ethnography of departures—I am indebted to him for suggesting this line of thinking.

Conversations with Justin Richland helped me to better articulate the book's argument. Daniel Goldstein provided detailed comments on chapter 6. Cecelia Lynch and Victoria Bernal were extremely supportive throughout the writing process, and Victoria Bernal helped to devise the book's subtitle. Conversations with Elana Zilberg provided insight into transnational youth cultures. Cheryl Maxson and Diego Vigil provided information about gangs in El Salvador. The following people read and commented on chapters in earlier incarnations: Rick Abel, Beth Baker-Cristales, Victoria Bernal, Michelle Bigenho, Tom Boellstorff, Teresa Caldeira, Lisa Catanzarite, Antje Ellerman, Daniel Goldstein, Inderpal Grewal, Setha Lowe, Cecelia Lynch, Bill Maurer, Sally Merry, Nancy Reichman, Justin Richland, Annelise Riles, Austin Sarat, Stu Scheingold, Susan Sterrett, Susan Terrio, Finn Yngvesson, Barbara Yngvesson, and Mei Zhan. I would also like to thank my colleagues at UC Irvine and in particular Kitty Calavita, whose work has been an inspiration. Early drafts of chapters were presented at the University of British Columbia, the University of Denver, UCLA, UC Irvine, and the Universidad Centroamericana "José Simeón Cañas," as well as at meetings of the American Anthropological Association, American Ethnological Society, Latin American Studies Association, Law and Society Association, and Pacific Sociological Association. I am grateful to session and conference organizers, panelists, and audience members for their critical feedback on these drafts. A version of chapter 4 appeared in *American Anthropologist* 107, no. 2: 195–206. Portions of this work are reproduced here with permission of the American Anthropological Association and the University of California Press. Portions of the material in chapter 2 appear in the chapter "Cause Lawyering and Political Advocacy: Moving Law on Behalf of Central American Refugees," in *Cause Lawyers and Social Movements*, ed. Austin Sarat and Stu Scheingold, 101–19 (Stanford: Stanford University Press, 2006). This material is reproduced here with the permission of Stanford University Press, copyright © 2006 by the Board of Trustees of the Leland Stanford Jr. University.

I am grateful to Dr. Ana E. Miranda Maldonado for permission to reprint her poem "Ni de aquí, ni de allá." Ana Miranda Maldonado was born in San Salvador, El Salvador, and is currently an internal medicine resident at UC San Francisco Medical Center.

I am also grateful to Homies Unidos, El Salvador, for permission to reprint the song "Fruits of War" by Marvin Alexander Novoa, aka Bullet. Bullet was a talented artist and performer who was a founding member of Homies Unidos. He was working with deportees and to prevent violence in El Salvador, when, tragically, he was killed. Through reprinting his song,

I hope to honor his memory and the spirit of his work. I am grateful to Luis Romero Gavidia of the San Salvador office of Homies Unidos for sending me his transcription of the Spanish lyrics to "Frutos de la Guerra." I am also indebted to Elana Zilberg for checking the Spanish version of "Frutos de la Guerra" against her audio recording of Bullet performing the song and for sending me a corrected copy of the lyrics. She also generously provided an English translation that she and Bullet created prior to his death.

I also owe a debt of gratitude to the photographer Alfonso Caraveo Castro and to the Archivo Colef for permission to reproduce the photograph that appears as figure 1.

I am grateful to Becky Rice and George Tsamaras of AILA and to Maria Elena Durazo of Immigrant Freedom Workers Ride/UNITE Here for their assistance in obtaining permission to reproduce images as illustrations.

I thank Peter Wissoker for being a perceptive editor. His comments and suggestions helped to improve the manuscript in the final stages. I am also grateful to Susan Specter, Karen Hwa, John Raymond, and other staff at Cornell University Press for their assistance.

Finally, I am grateful to Curt, Jesse, Jordy, and Raphael, all of whom had to put up with my absences during interviews scheduled on weekends and evenings, travel to research sites or to conferences, and late-night writing sessions. Each child's birth has coincided with a book project, and this one is Raphael's. My son Casey, who was born as I was completing the manuscript, reminded me of the importance of play. Thank you, Curt, for your loving support and for keeping life interesting.

Abbreviations

ABC	*American Baptist Churches v. Thornburgh*
AEDPA	Anti-Terrorism and Effective Death Penalty Act
AILA	American Immigration Lawyers Association
ARENA	Alianza Republicana Nacionalista (Nationalist Republican Alliance)
ASOSAL	Association of Salvadorans of Los Angeles
BCIE	Banco Centroamericano de Integración Económica (Central American Bank for Economic Integration)
BCR	Banco Central de Reserva (El Salvador)
BID	Banco Interamericano de Desarrollo (Interamerican Development Bank)
CASA	Central American Security Act
CIEJ	Citizens and Immigrants for Equal Justice
COMUNIDADES	Comunidades de Ayuda Directa a El Salvador (Communities of Direct Assistance to El Salvador)
COPRECA	Comité Propaz y Reconstruccion de Cacaopera (Committee for Peace and Reconstruction of Cacaopera)
DED	deferred enforced departure
DGACE	Dirección General de Atención a la Comunidad en el Exterior (General Directorate of Attention to the Community Living Abroad)

DOJ	Department of Justice
DUI	Documento Único de Identidad (Unique Identity Document)
EAD	employment authorization document
EVD	extended voluntary departure
FAIR	Federation of Americans for Immigration Reform
FISDL	Fondo de Inversión Social para el Desarrollo Local (Social Investment for Local Development Fund)
FMLN	Frente Farabundo Martí de la Liberación Nacional (Farabundo Martí National Liberation Front)
IIRIRA	Illegal Immigration Reform and Immigrant Responsibility Act
IMF	International Monetary Fund
INA	Immigration and Nationality Act
INS	Immigration and Naturalization Service
IRCA	Immigration Reform and Control Act
IWFR	Immigrant Workers Freedom Ride
LIFA	Latino and Immigrant Fairness Act
LIFE	Legal Immigration Family Equity Act
NACARA	Nicaraguan Adjustment and Central American Relief Act
NCLR	National Council of La Raza
NGO	nongovernmental organization
OECD	Organisation for Economic Co-operation and Development
OIM	Organización Internacional para las Migraciones (International Organization for Migration)
PDH	Procuraduría de Derechos Humanos (Human Rights Ombudsry)
PNC	Policía Nacional Civil (National Civil Police)
SOLVE	Safe, Orderly Legal Visas and Enforcement Act
TPS	temporary protected status
UNHCR	United Nations High Commission for Refugees (Alto Comisionado de las Naciones Unidas por los Refugiados)
USAID	United States Agency for International Development
USCIS	United States Citizenship and Immigration Service

Prologue

"Ni de aquí, ni de allá" by Ana E. Miranda Maldonado

Ni de aquí, ni de allá

"Guatamalan tribal children"
don't speak Spanish
county nurses insist they do
"SEÑORA, OIGA SEÑORA . . ."
cinnamon moon faces,
ash glass eyes stare
Accused:
Malnutrition, neglect, child abuse
"no, not Mexican,
INDÍGENAS, hablan *quiché*."
Ni de aquí ni de allá

"Not *Mexican*, then what?"
SALVADOREÑA
"What's that?"
CENTRO AMÉRICA
"Mexican, Spanish, Chicana
same thing, we're all AMERICANS now"

NEITHER.
Ni de aquí ni de allá

M-16s protecting DEMOCRACY
neighborhood tanks, decorative bullets,
mundane corpses, methodical desapariciones
"war made las salvadoreñas psychos"
Beware the Salvi Chick:
daily revolutionary
nightly disco bunny.
Ni de aquí ni de allá

Vos sos
"Se dice *tú eres*"
un cipote, cerote,
bichito pasmado.
"That's not *real* Spanish"
Vaya pue, I'm down.
Ni de aquí ni de allá

Vamos por la Olympic
comamos pupusas, frijoles molidos,
plátanos fritos, Kolashanpan.
Perhaps cute café on Melrose
eat California wraps:
you know,
teriyaki grilled chicken, olives,
buttermilk Ranch, in like, a burrito!

Soy de aquí *y* de allá

Introduction

The title of this book is a play on the familiar claim that the United States is a nation of immigrants. This claim is appealing because it combines two seemingly incompatible ideas. A nation is supposed to be a primordial entity comprised of people who share a common history, heritage, culture, territory, language, and perhaps even blood (Anderson 1983; Hobsbawm 1990; Hobsbawm and Ranger 1992). In certain regards, "nation" and "race" can even be used interchangeably (Williams 1996). "Immigrants," in contrast, are by definition uprooted, disconnected from their places of origin, culturally alien, perhaps unable to communicate with one another or their host society, precariously positioned within their countries of residence, vulnerable to being sent away, present only by the good graces of their hosts, rather than by right (see Kanstroom 2000), and, in a U.S. context, presumed to be nonwhite (Haney López 1996; Ngai 2004; Perea 1997; Sánchez 1997). Combining these two constructs in the phrase "nation of immigrants" stakes a powerful and expansionist claim. To be a nation of immigrants is to be capable of consuming and transforming alien others, producing generic citizens (Coutin 2003; Greenhouse 1996). The nation becomes the pot capable of melting and remolding those who pass through it. To become citizens, aliens undergo a death of sorts, in that the legal being that was born through their originary citizenship is destroyed only to be reborn as a U.S. citizen.[1] In the process, individual histories of migration are reconstituted as recapitulations of the history of the nation, fresh "blood" enters national veins, "law" (which reconstitutes this "blood") proves superior to "natural ties," and alien origins become "backgrounds" or "heritages" and thus something that everyone has (Coutin 2003). In this fashion, the nation of immigrants becomes capable of absorbing others, expanding in population and territory, subsuming difference within the "American way of life," and continually being reinvented. Internationally, it can claim to be an example of tolerance, a (modern) community that has moved beyond the divisiveness of ethnic strife, a beacon for the disaffected of other (presumably inferior) nations.

In contrast, the phrase "nations of emigrants" highlights both the interconnectedness of nations and the fact that immigrants come from somewhere else. As a nation of emigrants, the United States, like other so-called receiving countries, is made up of people who once had and may still have ties to other countries. Immigration does not simply entail absorbing immigrants; in addition, it connects countries in regional and transnational labor, social, familial, and political networks. So-called sending countries are also nations of emigrants with dispersed populations whose loyalty and obedience these states may, to some degree, claim. Given such connections, ethnic and national differences may not be as generic or commensurable as the nation of immigrants construct suggests. If both "sending" and "receiving" countries are regarded as nations of emigrants, then it is no longer clear which migrant movements consist of going and which of coming, and legal definitions of belonging need not be privileged over other ties. The term "nations of emigrants" also highlights the ways that, through migration, nations themselves become multiple. For example, the Salvadoran population in the United States has been conceptualized as the fifteenth department of El Salvador (Baker-Cristales 2004), and El Salvador can be conceptualized as existing in U.S. as well as in Salvadoran territory. Instead of legitimizing expansionism, the phrase "nations of emigrants" therefore points to reverse colonization, the ways that the territories of receiving nations are being colonized by those who need access to these nations' resources (Coutin, Maurer, and Yngvesson 2002, 830; see also Sassen 1989).

By focusing on ways that the United States and El Salvador are nations of emigrants, in this book I interrogate the constructs and apparatus through which immigration is conceptualized. Terms such as nation, citizen, and immigrant presume a certain coherence—that nations are distinct, boundaries are clear, membership is complete, citizenship is singular, and movement is unidirectional. This coherence is belied by the social realities—nations can be interspersed, boundaries can be relocated, membership can be partial, "citizenship" can be multiple, and movement can be multidirectional or even, at times, stationary—that migration entails. In drawing attention to gaps between immigration as a conceptual system and as a social reality, I do not mean to suggest that if we revise our immigration categories or make some policy adjustments, then these gaps would be closed. Rather, I argue that the immigration system *creates* the very disjunctures that seem to undermine it and that, moreover, these disjunctures can be key to the immigration system's coherence. For example, territorial integrity demands excluding unauthorized migrants; otherwise nations would not be bounded. The exclusion (through denials of work authorization, housing, social services, and so forth) of the unauthorized creates "holes" within national territories, through the space taken up by those who are in some ways located "elsewhere." Territorial *integrity* is thus made possible by territorial *disruptions* (Coutin 2005a). My point is not that the constructs through which immigration is conceptualized are false but rather that they are ephemeral, that their very solidity requires the production of other realities and constructs within which this seemingly solid system suddenly appears unreal. The movement between what might be termed official and unofficial realities produces a shimmering quality, like a holographic image that appears and disappears when a surface is tilted slightly.

To describe the paradoxes that characterize the current social order, immigration scholars have coined such terms as "transmigrant," "denationalized nation-states," and "denationalized citizenship" (Basch, Schiller, and Szanton Blanc 1994; Bosniak 2000; Schiller, Basch, and Szanton Blanc 1995). My contribution to this effort is to draw attention to ways that incompatible realities are true simultaneously. Thus, individuals are defined in terms of nationality (e.g., when being naturalized or deported) even as in many ways nationality is irrelevant (e.g., when providing emergency health care) (Coutin 2003, Soysal 1994). Sovereignty remains important even as nations can advocate that their expatriate citizens be granted immigration rights in other countries (Mahler 2000a, Hansen and Stepputat 2005). Citizenship rights, as Hannah Arendt argues, remain critical to individual well-being and in some sense take precedence over other rights (Arendt 1966). Yet, the right to citizenship is only meaningful in a world in which states can guarantee citizens' rights (Moodie 2006). Therefore, in this book, I seek to move between realities, privileging first one, then another, in order to demonstrate that traditional immigration categories can be both deadly and fleeting, both powerful and irrelevant. Defined as prohibited persons, unauthorized migrants can be hit by cars while fleeing across a freeway, but they also can live for decades as members of communities where their presence is officially forbidden.

Capturing the "shimmering" quality of incompatible realities that are true simultaneously requires juxtaposing multiple accounts, taking up one while not entirely letting go of another. These multiple accounts are often produced by the same actors. States define immigration and citizenship in traditional terms and new ways *at the same time*. Migrants live multiple accounts of their lives *at the same time*. Narratives of progress can be interspersed with accounts of exploitation, and former adversaries can also be allies (Nelson 1999). In this book, I have tried to juxtapose such accounts. I draw on the perspectives and experiences of migrants not only out of interest in migrants themselves but also as a means of explicating the state policies that these migrants live. Similarly, I have quoted state officials not only out of an interest in their worldview but also to shed light on forces that shape migrants' lives. I incorporate accounts from news articles, government reports, and documents produced by international agencies, as these define and reflect public discourse regarding migration. I examine how immigration law is produced, interpreted, and enacted, but I also take up related policies, regarding violence, crime, and finance. I try to look at the United States in light of El Salvador and vice versa, always keeping multiple nations in focus. By juxtaposing and interweaving accounts of lawmaking and transgression, the official and the unofficial, individuals and nation-states, inclusion and exclusion, I seek to show how nations are made complete by emigrants who, often tragically, must be absent.

In describing ways that official and unofficial accounts are true simultaneously, I treat persons, space, and nations as physical, legal, and social entities. For instance, individuals can be defined within legal categories, they exist as social beings, and they are made to embody particular qualities (such as deportability; see de Genova 2002). Space is made up of legal jurisdictions, social interactions, and physical territory through which people travel. Nation-states are legal formations, products of social imagination, and entities that can occupy territory, claim or reject members, and go to war. I draw attention to these multiple "dimensions" or "levels" not to examine how they interact but, rather, to account for the violence, mundaneness, and excess or pleasure linked to migration. Migration can entail exile, dismemberment, suffocation within a locked boxcar, but it also can produce wealth, emotional investments, and even enchantment (e.g., with particular nations, identities, or relationships). The latter are not "fictitious," to be juxtaposed to the materiality of the former. Rather, the physical can realize the legal or the social and vice versa, as when migrants who are pulled between the clandestine and the aboveboard are literally dismembered (see chapter 4). Such realizations are often counterintuitive. For instance, there are senses in which people are "owned" by their papers, in that individuals can be deported to their countries of citizenship or can be reborn as citizens of a new country (see chapter 1 and Yngvesson and Coutin 2006). Yet such realizations can also be partial, as when deported individuals seek to re-create something of their former (and now forbidden) lives within the country to which they have been deported.

I first encountered the idea that El Salvador is a nation of emigrants in August 2000, when I began the research for this book. Speaking at a conference organized in San Salvador by the Association of Salvadorans of Los Angeles (ASOSAL), a high-level Salvadoran official stated, "We have become an emigrant people."[2] In fact, according to the Salvadoran Ministry of Foreign Affairs website, "One of every four Salvadorans is abroad; of this total, at least 94% have gathered in the United States (2.3 million) with a high concentration in the state of California, where approximately 1.3 million Salvadorans reside" (Ministerio de Relaciones Exteriores n.d.[c]). This population dispersal—the Ministry of Foreign Affairs website also lists Salvadoran communities in Canada, Mexico, other countries in Central America, South America, Europe, Asia, Africa, and Oceania—has enormous implications for the country of El Salvador. In the year 2002 alone, Salvadorans living in the exterior sent $1,935,200,000 to family members in El Salvador, an amount that was equivalent to 13.6 percent of El Salvador's Gross National Product and that made up for more than 90 percent of the country's trade deficit (Banco Central de Reserva de El Salvador 2003). By 2005, the amount of remittances had grown to over $2.8 billion (Banco Central de Reserva de El Salvador 2006). The Salvadorans who sent these remittances began migrating to the United States in large numbers in the early 1980s, due to the political violence, human rights violations, and economic devastation of the 1980–1992 Salvadoran civil war (Baker-Cristales 2004; Hamilton and Chinchilla 1991; Menjívar 2000). After peace accords were signed in 1992, migration continued, as Salvadorans sought jobs, security, and to be reunited with family members. Migrant remittances are credited with enabling El Salvador to stabilize its economy and remain solvent in the postwar years (García 1994, 1997). Although Salvadoran authorities were, in many cases, responsible for abuses that led Salvadorans to flee the country during the 1980s (Commission on the Truth for El Salvador 1993; Hamilton and Chinchilla 1991; Menjívar 2000), by the mid-to-late 1990s the Salvadoran government began to court expatriate

Salvadorans, building a monument in their honor, creating a government office dedicated to Salvadorans in the exterior, and lobbying the U.S. government on their behalf (Baker-Cristales 2004). U.S. immigration policies have become critical to El Salvador, given that mass deportations or even cutting off the flow of new migrants could have devastating effects on the country.

Although emigration has become both an individual and in some respects national strategy within El Salvador, Salvadorans have not always been welcomed within the United States. During the 1980s, when the Salvadoran population in the United States grew to between five hundred thousand and nine hundred thousand (Aguayo and Fagen 1988; Montes Mozo and García Vasquez 1988; Ruggles et al. 1985),[3] the U.S. government adopted the position that these migrants—most of whom had entered the country without authorization—were economic immigrants who deserved to be deported to El Salvador rather than persecution victims who deserved political asylum in the United States. As U.S. support for the Salvadoran government in its war against guerrilla insurgents grew, a solidarity movement that opposed U.S. intervention in Central America and sought refugee status for Salvadorans and Guatemalans was formed (Coutin 1993; C. Smith 1996). In 1985, members of this movement sued the U.S. government, charging that the asylum process was biased against refugees from "friendly" countries, such as El Salvador. In 1991, this case, known as *American Baptist Churches v. Thornburgh* or "ABC," was settled out of court, permitting some three hundred thousand Salvadorans and Guatemalans to apply for political asylum under rules designed to ensure fair consideration of their case. At the same time, the 1990 Immigration Act created temporary protected status (TPS) and designated Salvadorans as its first recipients. TPS and the ABC settlement secured Salvadorans temporary legal status in the United States, but, due to delays in adjudicating their pending asylum claims, it rarely led to permanent residency. In 1996, the passage of the Illegal Immigration Reform and Immigrant Responsibility Act (IIRIRA) made it more difficult to obtain legal permanent residency and led Salvadoran activists (with the involvement of the Salvadoran government) to campaign for exemption from certain provisions of IIRIRA. This campaign resulted in the passage of the Nicaraguan Adjustment and Central American Relief Act (NACARA) in 1997 and a series of administrative concessions guaranteeing that the vast majority of ABC class members would eventually gain permanent residency. Salvadorans who, during the 1980s, had been regarded as undesirable and deserving of deportation came, in the late 1990s and early 2000s, to be defined as deserving immigrants, "people we knew" (to quote one asylum official interviewed), and future citizens. Nonetheless, bureaucratic delays in processing their applications for residency resulted in lengthy waits for permanent residency for many of these migrants.

In this book I analyze the degree to which Salvadorans who, during the 1980s, were directly or indirectly excluded from both El Salvador and the United States came, in the 1990s, to be a recognized presence in both nations. Doing so requires considering ways that individuals can be physically present but legally absent, existing in a space outside of society, a space of "nonexistence," a space that is not actually "elsewhere" or beyond borders but that is rather a hidden dimension of social reality (Coutin 2000, 2005a; Menjívar 2006). Individuals can also be physically absent but socially, emotionally, and politically "present," living political realities, fulfilling economic obligations, and experiencing overwhelming nostalgia keyed to places they no longer actually know (Baker-Cristales 2004). Such positionings are potentially violent, as they disconnect being and presence, producing ghostlike renderings of clandestine persons. Prohibited migrants regularly die crossing the U.S.-Mexico border and come to be memorialized as names on a cross, or sometimes merely as "no identificado" (unidentified). Law, which is powerful enough to cause these deaths, is also sometimes not powerful at all. In fact, prohibited presences can become so powerful that law itself changes in accordance with the very reality that it forbids (Bauböck 1994; Calavita 2005; Hammar 1990). Such transformations occurred in the case of Salvadorans, who were eventually largely guaranteed legal status precisely for engaging in practices (working, living in the United States) that were originally prohibited to them. When law legitimizes the prohibited, the space occupied by the legally nonexistent and the physically absent is temporarily acknowledged by nations that otherwise claim jurisdiction over all space. Belonging and exclusion are therefore complex and incomplete. That which is excluded takes shape "elsewhere," and "belonging" belies its official measures.

Analyzing forms of inclusion and exclusion speaks to contemporary debates on immigration policymaking in the United States. The mid-2000s have given rise to sharp divisions over whether unauthorized immigrants are an economic drain or boon, security risks or community members, an irreversibly alien element or the lifeblood of the United States. Though possible solutions to the "problem" of illegal immigration—ranging from making unauthorized entry a felony to creating a guest worker program—are under debate, there appears to be a political consensus around the idea of stiffening border enforcement, targeting aliens who have been convicted of

Fig. 1. Crosses placed along the U.S.-Mexico border to mark migrants' deaths. Photograph by Alfonso Caraveo Castro. Reprinted with permission of Alfonso Caraveo Castro, Archivo Colef.

crimes, and increasing the penalties associated with reentry after deportation. The human costs of such policies are documented in this book. Stiffened border enforcement can lead to increased suffering as would-be migrants pay smugglers higher fees and resort to more deadly methods of clandestine entry (Andreas 2000; Nevins 2002), while increased reliance on prosecution and deportation can create a permanent underclass of unauthorized residents. Temporary legal statuses can also situate individuals in a legal limbo, leading to painful and lengthy separation from family members and making it harder for migrants to pursue futures (Mountz et al. 2002). Current debates over immigration have also tended to focus on migrants' impact on the United States, rather than their impact on migrants' countries of origin (Sassen 1989). By treating both the United States and El Salvador as nations of emigrants, I seek to highlight migrants' transnational significance and thus broaden this focus beyond U.S. borders.

The case of emigration from El Salvador to the United States is both typical and atypical. Like El Salvador, many nations are reaching out to their expatriate citizens. Mexico has created the National Council for Mexican Communities Abroad, Haiti created the Ministry of Haitians Living Abroad, numerous Central American countries focus on migrants' rights during Immigrant Week, and Italy has granted legislative representation for Italians living abroad (Instituto de los Mexicanos en el Exterior 2006; Mahler 2000b; Povoledo 2006; Schiller, Basch, and Szanton Blanc 1995). Migrant remittances have become a worldwide phenomenon, with countries, such as the Philippines, relying on migrants as a significant source of national income (Menjívar et al. 1998). The case of El Salvador exemplifies such general trends, but it is more extreme in magnitude. The Salvadoran civil war produced a sudden, large-scale migration, such that an estimated one out of every four citizens now lives outside the country. Given the scope of emigration, remittances are exceptionally important to El Salvador (Díaz-Briquets and Pérez-López 1997; Garcia 1994; Menjívar et al. 1998; Orozco, de la Garza, and Baraona 1997; Rivera Campos 1996). Further, Salvadorans' experiences are also unusual in that the civil war gave rise to a U.S.-based solidarity movement that won them temporary legal statuses, such as TPS and pending asylum applications. The ambiguity of their presence, as initially unauthorized but temporarily permitted, has therefore been more pronounced than that of many migrants. The scope of emigration from El Salvador and the ambiguity of unauthorized Salvadoran migrants' status in the United States thus make this a particularly telling case through which to assess migrants' transnational significance.

This book is based on three sources. First, between 2000 and 2002, I conducted interviews in San Salvador; Washington, D.C.; Los Angeles; New York; San Diego; and Tijuana with forty-three policymakers (congressional staff members and officials in the former Immigration and Naturalization Service, Department of Justice, Department of Homeland Security, Clinton administration, first Bush administration, State Department, Salvadoran consulate and embassy, Salvadoran Ministry of Economy and Ministry of Foreign Affairs, U.S. embassy in El Salvador, and the administration of Salvadoran President Francisco Flores), sixty-three advocates (members of migrant and human rights nongovernmental organizations [NGOs] in El Salvador, attorneys involved in class-action suits on behalf of Salvadoran immigrants, members of Salvadoran community organizations in the United States, participants in immigrant-rights coalitions), and twenty-two Salvadoran immigrants with pending immigration cases. These groups overlapped, as over half of the advocates were themselves Salvadorans, many of whom had been directly affected by U.S. and Salvadoran policies. Interviews, which lasted from one to four hours, examined interviewees' experiences formulating, attempting to influence, or being affected by policies that the U.S. or Salvadoran government adopted toward Salvadoran migrants between 1980 and the early 2000s. Interviews were audiotaped, if the interviewee consented. Nonaudiotaped interviews were transcribed from notes immediately after the interview. In 2004, I had the opportunity to make follow-up research trips to San Salvador and Washington, D.C. I interviewed an additional two current or former officials, two NGO members, and one journalist in El Salvador and three current or former officials and one NGO member in Washington, D.C. I also reinterviewed six people.

Second, interview accounts have been supplemented with secondary documents, including news articles (particularly from the Los Angeles Spanish-language newspaper *La Opinión* and the Salvadoran papers *La Prensa Gráfica* and *El Diario de Hoy*), excerpts from the Congressional Record, policy papers written by Salvadoran analysts, memos issued by advocates or by government officials, drafts of legislation or regulations, and documents posted on government and other websites. Some of these secondary documents were obtained through personal contact with interviewees and are not easily accessible through public databases.

Third, I draw on my prior research within the Central America solidarity movement and within the Salvadoran community in Los Angeles (Coutin 1993, 2000). Between 1986 and 1988, I conducted fifteen months of fieldwork in the San Francisco East Bay and in Tucson, Arizona, within the U.S. sanctuary movement, a network of congregations that had declared themselves "sanctuaries" for Salvadoran and Guatemalan refugees. During fieldwork, I participated in the sanctuary activities of three congregations, volunteered with the movement, and interviewed one hundred movement participants.[4] I heard numerous accounts of human rights violations and political violence; I learned about the controversies surrounding U.S. Central American and refugee policies; I spoke with Central American and U.S. activists regarding strategies for achieving peace in El Salvador and refugee status for Salvadorans and Guatemalans; and I became aware of the ways that U.S. immigration policies affected the lives of migrants and those who aided them. Between 1995 and 1997, I did the research for a second project, an analysis of Salvadoran immigrants' efforts to obtain permanent legal status in the United States. For that project, I observed the legal services programs of three Central American community organizations in Los Angeles; attended immigration court hearings; participated in rallies, meetings, and community events; and interviewed ninety legal-service providers, activists, and immigrants with pending applications for political asylum or other immigration remedies. Through this research, I became familiar with Salvadoran immigrants' understandings of U.S. immigration law, political advocacy and policymaking regarding the Salvadoran immigrant community, shifts in advocates' and immigrants' strategies over time, the nature of political violence, rationales for conferring permanent legal status, and changes in U.S. immigration law. The knowledge acquired through these two earlier projects informs my analysis in this book.

Conducting the research for this book required forays into new ethnographic contexts. My research was geographically dispersed and potentially huge in scope. I had to learn about regional governmental efforts to formulate migration policies, migrants' experiences en route to the United States, negotiations between congressional representatives and the White House, the processing of NACARA applications, public debates over remittances in El Salvador, depictions of street crime in Salvadoran newspapers, what it is like to be deported as a criminal alien, Salvadoran officials' advocacy on behalf of Salvadoran emigrants, how NACARA applicants were affected by delays in processing their applications for residency, and other diverse topics. I learned about some of these things directly, through observations or interviews, and about others indirectly, through secondary accounts such as news articles, government reports, or even scholarly literature. I treat all of these sources as ethnographic, as ethnography is not synonymous with interviews and participation, but rather is a particular way of seeing, in which social realities both disappear and become visible (Coutin 2005a). In other words, the "holding in juxtaposition" that is key to my account of migration between El Salvador and the United States is also key to ethnography more generally, as ethnographers often have to temporarily suspend certain interpretations of cultural reality in order for others to materialize.

Doing the research for this book was a heady experience. I met people, such as a Salvadoran émigré who was physically ill due to fear that her son could be deported, a Department of Justice official who had been peripherally involved in the sanctuary movement, and a Salvadoran official who had had to reconceptualize his duties in transnational terms, all of whom I would otherwise never have had the opportunity to meet. I heard extraordinary stories about historic (but seemingly almost accidental) policy breakthroughs; personal experiences that created deep commitments to Central American issues; and the tragedies, fears, and accomplishments of individual migrants. I realized that although, given the scope of my current research, a fieldwork-based methodology was not feasible, I had lived through many of the policy changes that are described in this book. I knew Tucson-based sanctuary activists on whose behalf (in part) the ABC case was filed; I observed asylum hearings prior to the ABC settlement; I completed asylum applications for Salvadorans late into the night on the last day that these could be filed under the terms of the ABC settlement agreement; I served as a volunteer interpreter during some of the first ABC asylum hearings in 1997; I helped to complete NACARA applications in the late 1990s; and I attended numerous rallies organized by Central American immigrants and community groups from the mid-1980s into the 2000s. Although I did not do fieldwork in the diverse contexts in which interviewees operated, I did follow Salvadoran activists' and other networks to locate the people I interviewed. Therefore, although interviewees may not have known one another, they were connected through the policy-making processes that are the subject of this book.

One of the challenges that I faced in writing this book was demonstrating that seemingly disparate immigration-related phenomena, such as remitting, political violence, deportation, and legislative histories, are in certain respects all facets of one another. My strategy in meeting this challenge has been to tack back and forth, moving between exclusion and inclusion, individual narratives and national accounts, phenomena that I came to know through fieldwork and those that I encountered in more distanced ways. In this way, I hope to convey an increasingly complex picture, giving the reader a sense of "and yet . . ." In short, the phenomena that I depict in this book are not tidy—they spill outside of their boundaries, such that immigration is about violence, which is about financial exchange, which is about law, which is about family, which is about nations, which are about individuals. The book's chapters are intended to interrupt one another, such that the book itself enacts the partiality, disjuncture, and convergence that migration entails.

In chapter 1, "Los Retornados (Returnees)," I analyze the most extreme form of exclusion, namely the de facto exile of longtime U.S. residents who were deported to El Salvador following criminal convictions. The chapter situates narratives of individual deportees, interviewed in El Salvador, within a broader account of shifts in U.S. policies regarding removal. Theoretically, the chapter addresses the inaccessibility yet necessity of clear origins or endpoints, the irony of deporting people "back" to a place that they are not fully "from," the ways that people come to embody legal constructs, and the senses in which nations or places are set in motion through the movement of people.

In chapter 2, "La Ley NACARA (Nicaraguan Adjustment and Central American Relief Act)," I move from an analysis of how people are affected by policies to an account of the policies themselves, often as narrated by actors who were key in making these policies. The focus of this chapter shifts from El Salvador to the United States, and to ways that Salvadorans increasingly came to be included in the U.S. polity, ultimately, through the passage of NACARA. Juxtaposing this chapter with the one on deportees suggests that there are limitations to inclusion, and that even the seemingly deserving and accepted immigrants described in chapter 2 can face the sudden abductions experienced by deportees quoted in chapter 1. Theoretically, this chapter develops the notion that legalization entails traversing the paths and demarcations created by law, such that, over time, law can retroactively incorporate and redefine illegality.

In chapter 3, "Atención a la Comunidad en el Exterior (Attention to the Community Living Abroad)," I continue with the focus on government policies but shift from the United States to El Salvador. Theoretically, the chapter develops the notion of "transnational nationalism," that is, ways that the Salvadoran state seeks to cultivate Salvadoran identity among emigrants, and to thus incorporate Salvadorans living abroad within the nation of El Salvador. But, as with chapter 2, the figure of the deportee haunts this picture of increasing national inclusion. Furthermore, the chapter points out that the very claiming of the citizen-as-migrant entails exclusion in that one has to *migrate* to be so claimed, and the claiming itself constructs migrants in particular ways.

In chapter 4, "En el Camino (En Route)," I move from the two forms of inclusion described in chapters 2 and 3 to the exclusion experienced by unauthorized migrants who enter clandestine spaces, risk their lives, and encounter an exploitation that prevents them from fully "arriving" at their destination. Like chapter 1, this chapter draws on individual stories of migration experiences and focuses on the interstitial—on movement between places, identities, and legal categories. Although migrants and deportees travel in opposite directions, there are striking similarities in their experiences, and the undocumented, like the deportee, exposes the limits of the more inclusive policies described in chapters 2 and 3. Theoretically, the chapter argues that clandestinity is a dimension of the aboveboard, which suggests that as people move through geographic space, they also move in and out of clandestinity. Chapter 4, like the earlier chapters, also demonstrates ways that, through migrants' movements, nations and national law are set en route.

In chapter 5, "Las Remesas (Remittances)," I turn again to a rationale for inclusion, namely, the remittances that migrants send home to their family members in El Salvador. In contrast to the individual narratives presented in chapter 4, chapter 5 moves to an analysis of public discourse about remittances and to the accounting practices that permit remittances to become visible. Analytically, the chapter examines various paths through which informal monetary transfers come to be reclaimed and incorporated into national and international financial reports. In this sense, the chapter picks up on themes key to chapter 2 (about accounting for time, presence, and deservingness) and chapter 3 (in that remittances are a key basis for reclaiming emigrant citizens). Chapter 5 is also implicitly juxtaposed with chapters 1 and 4 in that the figures of the deportee and the migrant en route challenge celebratory hailings of the remitting migrant as the savior of the nation.

Chapter 6, "Productos de la Guerra (Products of War)," returns to exclusion, focusing on how political violence led Salvadorans to flee their country and how migrants are partially blamed for the current criminal violence experienced by El Salvador. The chapter uses both individual narratives about the Salvadoran civil war and more distanced material, such as United Nations reports about rising criminal violence in El Salvador. Theoretically, the chapter attends to ways that the past (the civil war) haunts the present (criminal violence), even as the present is depicted as having broken sharply with the history of human rights violations that characterized the civil war period. The chapter also details ways that the structural violence that migrants experience (e.g., the sorts of deprivations depicted in chapter 4) are reinscribed in migrants themselves, making them appear to be agents of a broader violence.

In chapter 7, "¡Sí, se puede! (Yes, it can be done!)," I return to the United States and to government policies, focusing on the paradoxical way that efforts to prohibit unauthorized migrants can make such migrants increasingly visible, enabling them to claim legal rights. Chapter 7 picks up the story that was being told in chapter 2, bringing it up to date with accounts of the efforts to obtain a broad-based legalization program in 2000, more restrictive immigration policies adopted after September 11, 2001, and the 2006 debates over immigration policies. By showing how migrants' significance to their countries of origin and residence can mobilize powerful entities on their behalf, this chapter reiterates the notion that both the United States and El Salvador are nations of emigrants.

In the book's conclusion I discuss ways that the analysis speaks to new forms of ethnography. Many of the subjects of this ethnography are in motion, not necessarily from a clear origin point to an ultimate destination but rather along paths that end abruptly, double back, and begin again in a new spot. An ethnography of emigration requires a certain open-ended quality and a kind of doubling back, just as migrants who depart may or may not be able to reach their destinations. The book's form therefore restages the juxtapositions, disjunctures, and relocations that emerge in the data and are central to the book's argument.

CHAPTER 1

Los Retornados (Returnees)

The noncitizens and their families who bear the brunt of our current harsh laws are the canaries in the coalmines of our legal system. We do not "cry wolf" when we give voice to their concerns, for their concerns are ultimately ours, as they are ultimately us.

Daniel Kanstroom, "Crying Wolf or a Dying Canary?"

Greg Michaels, a young man who was born in El Salvador, adopted by a U.S. family at age two, raised in Ohio, convicted on fraud charges in his early twenties, and deported to El Salvador, described what it was like to "return" to his country of origin:

> When I went from Houston to El Salvador, I said to myself, "This really isn't happening." It's sort of like if I took everything from you, threw you on a plane and said, "Here, you're going to Africa, and this is where you're living—now do it!" You'd say, "What?"
>
> It's like trying to put a puzzle together when you don't have all the pieces. It's tough. I can put the corner pieces together and some of the outside pieces together, but I can't put the rest together.
>
> It's sort of like trying to climb up a glass mountain. You can get up a little, but, whoosh, you go right back down. I never thought I'd say [it], but I firmly believe that I would rather be in prison or homeless in the United States.[1]

As an adoptee who was raised by non-Salvadoran parents but who never was naturalized, Greg was more legally vulnerable than many adoptees and more culturally alienated than many deportees. In fact, after Greg was deported, U.S. law changed so that foreign-born adopted children automatically acquire U.S. citizenship.[2] At the same time, Greg's experience was also routine. U.S. immigration law regularly sorts out legal residents and those who lack the right to remain in the United States, and this sorting process regularly privileges legal definitions of belonging over other measures. Such sortings displace and misplace people, reduce complex connections to a single strand, and give this strand the power to pull people "back" to an "origin" that they may not even remember or recognize (Yngvesson and Coutin 2006; Zilberg 2007b, forthcoming). To downplay the stigmatizing nature of this pull "back" (to an exile, of sorts), immigrant advocates in El Salvador coined the term *retornados* or "returnees" to refer to deportees. "Retornados" highlights the fact of return and leaves the returning person's "choice" in the matter face-savingly indeterminate. Nonetheless, the alienation experienced by retornados haunts legal determinations of membership.

Removal, which is the current legal term for deportation, is supposed to merely situate individuals in the place of their legal citizenship. Individuals are removed from the United States because they lack the legal right to be present there, and they are sent to a particular country because that is where they legally belong. Of course, there are instances in which an individual is rejected by both the United States and the individual's country of origin. Cases in point include the Marielitos, who were expelled from Cuba but due to their prior criminal convictions not permitted to reside in the United States, and intercountry adoptees who, in their countries of origin, became noncitizens at the moment of their adoption (Hamm 1995; Levine 2000). Such individuals, whose state of legal citizenship is contested, sometimes experience lengthy detentions.[3] In most cases, however, removal is legally conceptualized as merely locating a person in his or her proper place. Despite its resemblance to the now-defunct penalty of transportation, removal is not deemed to be a punishment, and cannot be imposed as a penalty following a criminal trial (Harwood 1986; Kanstroom 2000).

Although it is supposed to simply sort people according to preexisting identities and characteristics, removal transforms those who go through this process. Through removal, people who have complex belongings to multiple communities are stripped of certain memberships and, simultaneously, of relationships, plans, and futures. Retornados undergo a rite of passage in which they discover that they are "owned," in a sense, by the legal constructs that document their existence (Yngvesson and Coutin 2006). In fact, through detention and deportation, they actually become the physical beings that correspond to these legal constructs, and they are barred from the United States, the country with which they may most closely identify. If they return, they must live as prohibited beings, individuals who lack the right to legalize, who can be federally prosecuted if apprehended, and who may well be removed again. Like other rites of passage, removal erases and endows statuses, identities, and rights.

Although removal transforms individuals, these transformations are incomplete, a fact that allows deportation to relocate not only individuals but worlds (Zilberg 2004, forthcoming). Although retornados become, in a material sense, Salvadoran citizens who are barred from reentering the United States, retornados may also retain their prior affiliations and may seek to re-create the world that they supposedly left behind. Such re-creations may take many forms—forming particular social groups, speaking English, pursuing activities that they would have pursued in the United States, reconstituting spaces to be "like Los Angeles" or another U.S. city. Such practices reconstruct and relocate retornados' prior social worlds, however ethereally, and thus bring some of the United States to El Salvador, transforming (in some minimal sense) national territories and making the boundaries and classifications that are the basis for removal indistinct. Retornados are removed because they are Salvadoran, yet when they are in El Salvador they may be seen as "from the United States." At the same time, many returnees do not stay in El Salvador, but return to the United States illicitly (Heyman 1999). As barred subjects, they bring with them the alienness that is produced by law and that law cannot overcome. The presence of prohibited aliens creates pockets of foreignness within the United States as well. Thus, retornados are situated outside of both the United States and El Salvador and, in this way, their presence can interrupt the territory of each nation (Coutin 2000; see also Maurer 1997).

In transforming individuals and altering national territories, deportation defies the very realities that it is supposed to affirm. If national territories are not mutually exclusive, and if national populaces are not clearly bounded, then at least some individuals have messy affiliations that prevent them from being sorted solely according to legal categories. Removal can only be morally justified if particular fictions are maintained. These fictions include the ideas that nations are sovereign and mutually exclusive, that borders can be controlled, that individuals are citizens of only one nation, that legal citizenship is the basis for other forms of social connections, that papers authenticate identities, and so forth. Of course, these are not merely fictions: nations *are* sovereign, borders *are* controlled, papers *do* authenticate identity—individuals are removed, after all, so these things are "true." Nonetheless, when nations make claims on citizens (such as claiming citizens' loyalty or encouraging remittances), these claims must be juxtaposed to the legal abandonment that is removal and—however euphemistically it is stated—return.

Removal

In 1996, U.S. immigration law changed dramatically with the elimination of deportation and exclusion—the two preexisting methods of keeping someone out of the United States—and the creation of removal. The distinctions between deportation and exclusion had been legally significant but, in certain respects, difficult to fathom. *Deportation* consisted of forcibly removing someone from U.S. territory, whereas *exclusion* referred to preventing him or her from entering in the first place. "Entry" and "presence," however, were legal constructs, making this seemingly clear-cut distinction more complex. For example, suppose that a person was allowed in at a U.S. port of entry and told to return in two weeks in order to be inspected and admitted, and then simply failed to reappear for the inspection. Such an individual might live in the United States undetected for years but legally would be deemed to be outside of the country seeking admission. If apprehended, this individual would be placed in exclusion proceedings rather than deportation proceedings. In contrast, someone who entered the United States without inspection (e.g., by crossing the U.S.-Canadian border) and then was apprehended would be placed in deportation proceedings. The distinction between deportation and exclusion was nonetheless important, as certain remedies were only available to individuals who were in deportation proceedings.

In 1996, IIRIRA replaced both deportation and exclusion with the single process of removal. A glossary posted on the Bureau of Citizenship and Immigration Services (n.d.) website defines "removal" as "the expulsion of an alien from the United States. This expulsion may be based on grounds of inadmissibility or deportability." Indeed, post-1996 editions of the Statistical Yearbook of the Immigration and Naturalization Service (INS) have listed numbers of "Aliens Expelled" instead of "Aliens Deported," as in earlier editions. Although removal sounds like a benign procedure, expulsion conveys something of the violence of this process for those who experience it.

The creation of removal was linked to other policy changes designed to make deportation a more efficient process, increase the numbers of unauthorized immigrants removed from the United States, prioritize the removal of aliens who had been convicted of crimes, and prevent immigrants from prolonging their legal proceedings in ways that bought aliens additional time in the country and, some alleged, the ability to avoid deportation altogether.[4] To these ends, IIRIRA and the 1996 Anti-Terrorism and Effective Death Penalty Act (AEDPA) expanded the range of criminal convictions for which an alien became deportable; applied this expanded definition retroactively; eliminated waivers—known as "212(c)"—that had permitted aliens to argue that, despite their criminal records, they deserved to remain in the United States; dramatically reduced judicial review of decisions in immigration cases; imposed mandatory detention on most criminal aliens who were in removal proceedings; and created "expedited removal" proceedings, through which immigration officials could remove unauthorized entrants without a court hearing, as long as these individuals did not express a credible fear of persecution—as such fear could be grounds for granting political asylum (Isgro 1997; Morawetz 2000; O'Callaghan 2002). In the words of one analyst, these changes "brought about a rather complete convergence between the criminal justice and deportation systems" (Kanstroom 2000, 1891). Acts that, under criminal law, were neither aggravated nor felonies became "aggravated felonies" for immigration purposes—and thus offenses that made noncitizens deportable. Such acts included driving under the influence (in Texas), simple battery, shoplifting, and selling small amounts of drugs. The effects of such changes in immigration law were exaggerated by trends in criminal justice, such as the war on drugs and truth-in-sentencing laws, that gave larger numbers of noncitizens records and sentences that made them deportable (Morawetz 2000).

The legal changes associated with removal were not uncontroversial. Retroactive application of the 1996 immigration laws struck many as unfair. Some have argued for a return to the earlier waiver system, in which criminal aliens had the opportunity to argue that their equities (such as relatives, lengthy periods of residence, property, work histories) in the United States, the circumstances of their crime, and their subsequent rehabilitation weighed against their deportation (Morawetz 2000). Critics argued that it was unconstitutional to shield executive actions from judicial scrutiny (Kanstroom 2000). Expedited removal proceedings were challenged for failing to provide adequate recourse to victims of persecution who were in need of political asylum (O'Callaghan 2002). Mandatory detention has been denounced as a violation of immigrants' civil liberties (Hafetz 1998). The expanded definition of crimes that make individuals deportable has been criticized for imposing disproportionately harsh penalties for minor offenses (Morawetz 2000). These criticisms have given rise to a number of legal challenges to specific provisions of IIRIRA and AEDPA, as well as to legislative proposals to reform these laws.[5]

Not surprisingly, the 1996 immigration acts transformed immigration enforcement practices, increased the detention center population, altered the proportion of convicted criminals among deportees, increased the overall numbers of individuals expelled from the United States, and reverberated within the immigrant community more generally. According to the conventional wisdom regarding immigration law enforcement, apprehensions and removals along the U.S.-Mexico border do no more than delay immigrants, who may successfully evade U.S. immigration agents in subsequent attempts (Harwood 1985; Heyman 1998). This situation is changing, as individuals are increasingly prosecuted and incarcerated for immigration violations, such as entry without inspection and reentry following deportation or removal. A Bureau of Justice Statistics report attributes 14 percent of the growth in the federal prison population between 1985 and 2000 to increases in the incarceration of immigration offenders (Scalia and Litras 2002). Improved apprehension and record-keeping techniques are giving larger numbers of illicit border crossers criminal and immigration records (Heyman 1999). Increases in funding and personnel have enabled immigration agents to heavily patrol popular border crossing corridors, forcing undocumented immigrants into more difficult—and therefore, more deadly—terrain (Nevins 2002). The number of aliens expelled has increased dramatically, from 50,924 in 1995, prior to the passage of IIRIRA and AEDPA, to 69,680 in 1996, 114,432 in 1997, and 186,391 in 2000 (U.S. Department of Homeland Security, Office of Immigration Statistics 2006, see table 1.1). The 1996 laws' targeting of criminal aliens is responsible for much of this growth, as the number of criminal aliens removed more than doubled from 33,842 in 1995 to 72,523 in 2000. The most dramatic increase, however, occurred in the number of noncriminals removed, a figure that grew from 17,082 in 1995 to 113,868 in 2000 (INS 2000; U.S. Department of Homeland Security 2006). Most likely, the availability of expedited removal proceedings and the formalization of what previously would have been informal "administrative removals" are responsible for this increase. Although the risk of being apprehended within U.S. borders and removed from the country may still be statistically low for the estimated 7–10 million undocumented immigrants in the United States,[6] "the perception of risk for noncitizens has surely changed dramatically" due to these changes in deportation policies (Kanstroom 1999, 463).

TABLE 1.1.
Aliens expelled, 1991–2005

Year	Number
1991:	33,189
1992:	43,671
1993:	42,542
1994:	45,674
1995:	50,924
1996:	69,680
1997:	114,432
1998:	173,146
1999:	181,072
2000:	186,194
2001:	178,207
2002:	150,788
2003:	189,856
2004:	202,290
2005:	208,521

Source: U.S. Department of Homeland Security, Office of Immigration Statistics, 2005 *Yearbook of Immigration Statistics*.

Increases in the number of aliens removed from the United States provoked alarm on the part of nations, such as El Salvador, that have large populaces in the United States and that depend on immigrant remittances and fear the influx of large numbers of unemployed and often criminal compatriots. In 2005, the vast majority of deportees (144,840 out of 208,521) were sent to Mexico, the second largest number (14,556) went to Honduras, the third (12,529) to Guatemala, and in fourth place was El Salvador, with 7,235 deportees (Dougherty, Wilson, and Wu 2006). The numbers of aliens deported to El Salvador has fluctuated over time and did not increase as dramatically as overall trends in removals would predict (see table 1.2). The numbers of individuals deported to El Salvador in 1983, 1989, 1997, and 1999 were almost the same; and the number of individuals deported between 1980 and 1989 was actually larger than the number deported between 1990 and 1999—a surprising fact, given that during the 1980s El Salvador was wracked with political violence and widespread human rights violations. Several factors may be responsible for this pattern. Due to the Salvadoran civil war, the 1980s were peak years of emigration from El Salvador, therefore the numbers of Salvadorans apprehended along the U.S.-Mexico border may also have been higher. This was also a period when, despite a strong Central American solidarity movement (Coutin 1993; C. Smith 1996), the U.S. government regarded Salvadorans as "economic immigrants" undeserving of political asylum

TABLE 1.2.
Aliens expelled to El Salvador, 1980–2005

1980:	1,774	1993:	2,117
1981:	2,724	1994:	1,900
1982:	2,067	1995:	1,932
1983:	3,398	1996:	2,493
1984:	2,616	1997:	3,900
1985:	3,218	1998:	5,348
1986:	3,481	1999:	4,048
1987:	2,508	2000:	4,617
1988:	2,780	2001:	3,808
1989:	3,984	2002:	3,902
1990:	2,470	2003:	5,108
1991:	1,496	2004:	6,405
1992:	1,937	2005:	7,235

Sources: Immigration and Naturalization Service and U.S. Citizenship and Immigration Services statistical yearbooks.

(Bach 1990; Churgin 1996; Coutin 1993; C. Smith 1996; Zolberg 1990). By the early 1990s, the ABC settlement agreement, TPS, and other temporary remedies reduced the numbers of deportable Salvadorans. By 1996, with the passage of AEDPA and IIRIRA, removal figures began to creep up, peaking at 5,348 in 1998 then jumping to 6,405 in 2004 and 7,235 in 2005; however, in contrast to the steady increase in overall removals from the United States, the number of Salvadoran deportees fluctuated, decreasing slightly after 1998 and again after 2000. These decreases reflected the United States's temporary suspension of deportations to El Salvador following Hurricane Mitch in 1998 and the award of temporary protected status for Salvadorans in the wake of the 2001 earthquakes. Still, the average number of individuals deported to El Salvador between 1996 and 2005 was 4,686, almost double the average number (2,525) deported annually between 1980 and 1995.

The rationales for removing aliens, particularly long-term legal residents convicted of crimes, provide insight into the notions of citizenship and alienage that are central to the U.S. deportation system. The term "removal" connotes a technical, even scientific, process designed to eliminate something unsightly, dangerous, or polluting. For instance, trash, warts, and asbestos are "removed." The idea that deportation can have a "cleansing" effect on society derives from what Kanstroom (2000) describes as the conflation of two sorts of deportation: border control and social control. Border control is intended to regulate movement across U.S. borders and through ports of entry. As social control, in contrast, deportation provides an opportunity to rid society of the undesirable, particularly criminals. Such "cleansing" can only be justified, Kanstroom points out, by regarding even legal permanent residents as "guests" who are continually "on probation." If their conduct fails to meet with the approval of their host society, then the probation is terminated, and even supposedly "permanent" legal residents lose status. Despite the fact that, in certain countries (including the United States), legal aliens have been granted many of the same rights as citizens (Hammar 1990), the citizen-noncitizen distinction remains sharp, and is cited to justify denying respondents in immigration proceedings the basic rights (e.g., to counsel) that criminal defendants enjoy. For instance, Kanstroom (2000, 1909) points out that "federal deportation laws based on postentry criminal conduct require a theoretical explanation for why banishment is a punishment when applied to citizens, but is not a punishment when applied to lawful resident aliens. This explanation . . . derived from the status of alienage being seen as an increasingly tenuous claim to any rights against deportation." Similarly, in ruling that a legal permanent resident who was being detained did not have the right to a bail bond hearing, U.S. Supreme Court Justice John Paul Stevens wrote, "In the exercise of its broad power over naturalization and immigration, Congress regularly makes rules that would be unacceptable if applied to citizens" (*Demore v. Kim* 2003, 2, quoting *Mathews v. Diaz*, 426 U.S. 67, 79–80 [1976]). National sovereignty is commonly cited as grounds for giving the U.S. Congress and the executive branch broad discretion in making such distinctions (Kanstroom 2000).

In addition to "cleansing society" of undesirable noncitizens, the 1996 laws are often credited with "restoring credibility" to U.S. immigration law (Kanstroom 2000; U.S. Department of Justice, n.d.). The notion that denials of various sorts are evidence of accountability, standards, and "credibility" is widespread. For instance, in academia, journals that have the highest rejection rates are deemed the most prestigious. Even U.S. sanctuary activists, who were assisting Central Americans in crossing the U.S.-Mexico border, cited the fact that they denied assistance to certain would-be refugees as evidence of the fact that these border workers "had standards" (Coutin 1993). The credibility of U.S. immigration laws could, of course, be measured in other ways. For instance, laws could be assessed according to whether they achieved justice, united families, and respected migrants' rights. Other standards seem to have been used historically. For instance, in the late 1800s and early 1900s, deportation laws limited postentry expulsion to individuals who were caught or exhibited undesirable conduct within a year of entry. As recently as 1953, a presidential commission recommended that aliens who had lived in the United States for twenty years or who were lawfully admitted prior to sixteen years of age should not be deportable for criminal convictions, as "their countries of origin . . . certainly are not responsible for their criminal ways" (quoted in Morawetz 2000, 1961). By making noncitizens' residency "probationary" and by prioritizing legal alienage over other assessments of belonging, responsibility for aliens' criminal ways becomes irrelevant to the technical process of removal.

When they are removed, aliens simultaneously become completely illegal beings and completely constituted by law. It could be said that they *embody* legal categories.

Embodying Law

Retornados were deported because their presence in the United States was illegal. Juridically, they were positioned *outside* of the United States, even though many retornados had lived within U.S. borders for years. Their existence in this country was therefore multidimensional. While they were socially and physically in U.S. territory, retornados, particularly those who were undocumented, were legally clandestine, and therefore were simultaneously present but absent (Coutin 2005a). They lived in the United States but in a twilight zone–like other dimension, alongside, but in certain key respects entirely apart from, other residents. Even retornados who were legal permanent residents and therefore legally recognized in the United States remained aliens and were therefore vulnerable to losing this recognition. The illegality of deportable aliens is the necessary counterpart (and "outside") to the legality of U.S. citizens. There is thus a sense in which illegal aliens bring law, sovereignty, and the nation into being. At the same time, deportable aliens, who are the very essence of illegality, are created by law. It is law that defines them as deportable and that constitutes them exclusively as citizens of El Salvador and as noncitizens (aliens) vis-à-vis the United States. Through detention and deportation, prohibited aliens become the physical beings that correspond to their legal identities as Salvadoran citizens. Their legal identities are no longer disembodied but rather materialize through their removal, first to a detention center and then through deportation itself. Law *removes* retornados, constructing them as bodies from which law is absent and yet who are nonetheless totally physically bounded by law. The space vacated by deportable aliens' presence is not unlike the outline of a recently removed body at a crime scene, or the silhouettes of the disappeared that haunted Buenos Aires during the political protests that ended the dirty war.[7] The illegality that suffuses the bodies of deportable aliens also bounds law.

Among those who eventually became retornados were de facto U.S. citizens who had complex ties to U.S. communities. As Fernando Tovar, a member of a Salvadoran NGO that worked with deportees, explained, "Actually, [deportees] are not so Salvadoran. More in a legal sense, but in regards to their personality, often they think more like [people from] the state where they have developed." Greg, who was adopted by U.S. parents and whom I met through Salvadoran NGOs, considered himself to be "a person of the United States because that's all I've ever really known or could remember." Once, when he was filling out an application, he was asked for naturalization papers. Although he did not have these, Greg still regarded himself, in essence, as a U.S. citizen. He commented, "Maybe they were just asking for something I didn't have or most people didn't have. Sort of like asking you for clearance to go into the Pentagon. It's a once-in-a-lifetime thing." Puppet, who immigrated to the United States from El Salvador at age four and who I also met through Salvadoran NGOs, regarded himself as more from Los Angeles than El Salvador.[8] He explained:

> I knew that I was from El Salvador, but I didn't feel that I was from there. It was like, it was just like a dream to me, you know? It was this place that existed in my mind, but that I had like faint memories of. And they didn't start asking me where I was from until like, you know, I guess I don't really remember, maybe like in the fourth grade. And they made like a little map [of] where everybody in the class was from, and then I was from El Salvador. There was these other kids that were from El Salvador. But they didn't know how to speak English, and they had just got to the States, and I thought to myself, "I'm not like these kids, you know? How could I be from there, you know? I dress different, I talk different, my friends are different, you know?" So I always thought, "Damn, am I from there?" But I feel more like from L.A., you know?"

Although eventual retornados may have had complex ties, regarding themselves as being from El Salvador but also, in key ways, from the United States, their alienage lurked as a hidden (or in some cases, not so hidden) fact able to overpower other elements of their existence. King, who became a legal permanent resident of the United States in 1988 but who was eventually deported due to criminal convictions, recalled that his mother continually warned him that he was "different" from his peers:

> She says, "Son. Be careful! You're not like the rest of them. They'll take you. They won't take them. They were born here." And I'm like, "Yeah, Mom!" You know, I like would want to understand her and then I'd just forget about it, you know what I mean? And then, as time went by, she was always telling me and telling me. Came high school and she reminded me, and I got suspended a few times. She was telling me, "Look son, you'd better be careful. I've told you a million times, you're not like the rest of them." You know, the rest of my friends, they were all born over there [in the United States]. . . . I went to juvenile hall for a week. She goes, "Look son, you'd better be careful now. That was a close one, you know? They're going to take you. I'm telling you man, there's nothing I'm going to be able to do."

As this passage suggests, alienage makes individuals vulnerable to abduction, to being pulled through the hole that illegal personhood creates within legal jurisdictions, and to being forced to remain outside in the "elsewhere" that hitherto may have been "like a dream."

Luis Manzano, a legal permanent resident from Mexico whom I met through an immigrant advocacy group in Los Angeles, experienced such an abduction. He recounted:

> The whole family, including my nine-year-old daughter and my sisters, my nephews, my parents, we all went back to Mexico to visit my grandparents and other people. You know, like a family trip. And we're driving back and I'd somehow forgotten my green card at home. So they held us there in Texas for about four hours. They're doing all this computer stuff, and I'm sitting there and I don't know what's going on. And they said, "Well, we'll let you in. We'll furlough you in." I didn't know what the hell that was. "We'll furlough you in. But you have to report to Immigration when you get into town, you know, on such-and-such a date." And I was like, "Yeah, sure, no problem," you know? They said, "For an interview." So that's what I did. When I went to the "interview" [as] they called it, they started asking me if it was true that in '91 I sold weed and this and that. And I was like, "Yeah, you know, that happened. That was a long time ago. I took care of it. I didn't run off." And they said, "Okay, well, we're going to deport you for that offense. "And they handcuffed me and took everything away—my phone, everything I had.

Through detention and deportation, individuals who had previously had complex ties to the United States actually became the physical beings that corresponded to their legal identities as foreign citizens whose presence in the United States was forbidden. Such transformations did not follow a criminological logic, as King, who was transferred to an immigration detention center immediately on being released from prison, noted:

> We did time in the state prison. And their own [the U.S.] government says, "Okay, you're rehabilitated, you're able to go back to society." And then INS turns around and says, "No! You're a threat to society. You're a terrorist threat and you're a flight risk!"[9] I mean, that confused me, because, you know, it's the same government, or what?

Mandatory detention and ineligibility for bail treated detainees as aliens subject to "rules that would be unacceptable if applied to citizens" (*Demore v. Kim* 2003, 2). In detention centers, noncitizens were removed from society, not as punishment, but simply to hold them until the sorting process was completed and they reentered U.S. society or were removed beyond U.S. borders.

When they underwent deportation, noncitizens discovered that they were "owned" by the "papers" that authenticated their legal identities, and that they had to become exclusively "Salvadoran" (or another foreign nationality) and therefore fully alien and prohibited (Yngvesson and Coutin 2006).[10] They were reconstituted as bodies from which U.S. legal status had been erased, leaving only a physical being that had to be removed to its site of legal existence. King described this alienating process:

> We went to an airport right there in Arizona, waited for a plane, got on the plane with the marshals—a government plane—and the marshals shackled us up, our feet, hands. We took off to Houston. [There,] they took us through a little INS tank thing, and from there they processed us. They took us to a county jail, in one of the counties in Houston, far. A messed-up jail. We were there, and they wouldn't let us buy nothing at the store, so we didn't have no deodorant, no razor, no toothbrush. They were treating us lower, like, "you're getting deported anyways, you don't need none of that."
> So we were like, "you know," that wasn't right. They put us in these holding cells, like these dorms, with no air conditioner. No air at all. It was

like hot, moisture. Like everything starts sweating, you know, with the body heat. And the water was no good. There was no drinking water, only a shower. The toilets were messed up, there was no pressure. All kinds of messed-up things.

And we were there for four days. They were giving us like the blues, [as] they call it. They weren't giving us no deodorant, like I said, nothing. No hygiene.

So then *finally*, a sergeant came, and I go, "Look, sergeant, man, what's going on? We don't get rec, yard, nothing. You know? You're treating us like animals, man!

Finally, one day, they showed up, and he says, "Alright, everybody!" Calling out names. "Get ready! Leaving!" And finally we all got our stuff, turned it in, and we went into [a] basketball gym and waited there a few hours, and they processed us, they handcuffed us, and we waited for the bus, and then we went to get our personal property. By the time we left, it was nighttime. So we went back to the INS center, and waited *all night* for the plane, for the morning, with no food, no nothing. All bunched up in a little room.

So we were awake, awake. And then finally, it was four in the morning, and he says, "Alright, get ready! Call you by names! Come up!" You know, and shackle you up. Ch-ch-ch-ch-ch [the sound of being shackled]. And then from there we got on the bus, went to the airport a few blocks away from the INS facility. We waited on a bus, and finally the plane came, another one of the oldest planes I ever seen in my entire life.

And then from there, we waited, we boarded it, we got ready. And we took off. Fshshshshs000000000000! [sound of airplane taking off]. All shackled up. T-t-t-t [sound of shackles]. And then, like, they give us, like, a tore-up sandwich and stuff to eat up there. You know, I wasn't hungry. I didn't eat nothing. That's the least thing I had on my mind was food after leaving, you know, the country you were raised in.

They think they can treat you like you don't know your rights. Even if you're deportable, you still got rights, human rights.[11]

As de facto or probationary U.S. legal identities were drained from their bodies, these deportees became animal-like, "lower," people who could be denied hygiene, food, physical comfort, information, and rights. This process was akin to death, as the person who they were in the United States was being destroyed. In fact, an NGO member who works with deportees in El Salvador explained that one of his tasks was to convince retornados that "you have not ended your life with a return." Removal can cost retornados their relatives, possessions, jobs, homes, habits, and anticipated futures.

King lost his fiancée, who had visited him throughout his imprisonment but who ended their relationship when he was deported. He commented, "Before I found out that I got deported, I had a whole life ahead of me, you know? I was going to work hard, buy a home, somehow, marry this girl and have kids and live happily ever after." Mario Nolasco, a retornado I met in El Salvador, lost one of his daughters to adoption and could not fight the adoption process, which was occurring in the United States, from El Salvador. Just their bodies were sent to El Salvador, as a member of a Salvadoran NGO that received deportees explained: "They were dumped in the airport, without money. Only with a cardboard box with a change of clothes, without a belt, without shoelaces. Sometimes with clothing appropriate for Alaska, thick, thick, thick clothing, because that's what they were given there in prison." Surprisingly, deportees even lacked identity documents. In order to travel to El Salvador, deportees were issued a provisional passport, which was then taken from them at the airport when they arrived. They were, in the words of one Salvadoran NGO member, "doblemente mojados," doubly illegal, deported from the United States as illegal aliens but lacking proof of citizenship in El Salvador. They embodied legal categories.[12]

In order to be removed from the United States, retornados first had to be claimed by their country of origin. In many cases, this was a straightforward process, as an official at the Salvadoran consulate in Los Angeles described:

> We provide assistance to deportees, by going to their deportation centers to provide them with a travel document so that they can have no problems returning to their country.
>
> We have a unit in El Salvador called Attention to the Community, where we immediately take down the person's name, their date of birth, the place they are from, the name of the father and mother. Immediately, we send a memo to this unit, and they in a matter of a day or two, at most three, verify the birth of this person, and they, by fax, send us their birth certificate, [and] we give it to them. Automatically we find out whether this person specifically is Salvadoran or not.

In some cases, documentation of an individual's birth was missing. In such instances, the Salvadoran consulate interviewed individuals about cultural knowledge, tourist sites, historical facts, and geographic regions to determine whether they were Salvadoran. A Salvadoran official gave examples of questions asked during this interview: "They check the person's speech. If they use words like 'zipote' [child; also spelled 'cipote'] that are peculiar to

El Salvador, then that helps to verify their national identity. Or, if they know key facts about El Salvador. So they ask them, 'What is the most important river? What are the TV channels?' Something that everyone would know if they are Salvadoran." This interviewee presumes that legal identity and cultural knowledge correspond, which may not be the case when an individual emigrated to the United States at a very young age. During a radio interview in El Salvador, one deportee recalled:

> They said, "What's the national anthem?" I was like, "Man, I don't know." "What's the biggest railroad?" I was like, "What?" I told him, "Look, man, I don't know nothing about El Salvador. I've been in this country [United States] for over, you know, twenty years. I don't know nothing about that country." He was all pissed off 'cause I didn't know what the biggest river was. I mean, I grew up in L.A. The longest river there is the L.A. River, you know? (Richman 1999)

Removal is, perhaps, the moment of deportees' greatest legal specification, when they are claimed by El Salvador and when they are definitively named as deportable aliens by the United States. It is also, however, a moment when they are abandoned.

Abandonment

There is a sense in which retornados, particularly those who have lived much of their lives in the United States, do not have a country. Legally exiled from the country where they were raised, they find themselves in what is, in many ways, an alien land. They are denied or stripped of legal status in the United States, made ineligible for visas to reenter the United States, and sent back to El Salvador not as heroic citizens whose remittances saved the country from financial ruin, but rather as failed émigrés likely to enter the ranks of the unemployed, the impoverished, and the criminal. They are considered by many to be a burden on their country of origin (though advocates have disputed this notion), and, according to a U.S. official I interviewed in San Salvador, the United States does the Salvadoran government a favor by pacing deportations to prevent too many deportees from arriving at one time. Although retornados are deported because they are Salvadoran, and although the removal process constitutes these individuals as the embodiment of their legal identities, retornados have, of course, been shaped by the lives that they have led. As a result, in El Salvador, they experience a disjuncture between their legal and social selves, *much as they did in the United States before they were deported*. Although they receive some governmental and NGO assistance on reentering El Salvador, retornados often remain, in certain key ways, alien, sometimes leading them to be rejected by relatives, officials, and community members. Deportees may be abandoned, arriving at the airport with no friends or relatives to meet them, no money or possessions, no home, and no source of livelihood. As alien beings, they retain something of their previous social locations as de facto U.S. citizens. As a result, they both move through and transform geographic spaces, creating holes occupied by, to paraphrase Greg, "people of the United States."

Being deported, particularly after living in the United States or being granted permanent residency, is a strong form of rejection, a withdrawal of rights, connections, and services—in short, an abandonment. As an immigrant advocate in El Salvador explained, "Upon being deported, there is a tremendous rejection and huge impact against their persons." Some retornados argued that deportation violated an implicit contract between the state and legal residents. Greg pointed out that when he had lived in the United States, he had been eligible for public services, a recognition that implicitly defined him as a legal subject within the United States. He commented, "What I don't understand is working all my life, you're entitled to welfare and Social Security and all this other stuff, which I was entitled to because I had worked there, lived there all my life. So I don't understand how, now, I am not considered a citizen." Noting that he had been brought to the United States by his parents, Puppet suggested that he had never chosen to grow up in the United States and therefore ought not to be subsequently removed to a place that was, to him, alien. Puppet commented, "I thought 'residency' meant permanent residency, you know? 'Permanent' means forever! It doesn't mean 'temp.' " The withdrawal of legal status, and hence the privilege of presence, is enforced through harsh penalties on those who reenter the United States. The crime of reentry following deportation is punishable by up to two years in prison, or up to ten years for a person with a criminal history (1952 Immigration and Nationality Act [INA], section 276).

Although their Salvadoran citizenship made them deportable in the United States, in El Salvador many deportees were regarded as foreign (see also Duany 2000; Zilberg 2007b). The identity documents that pulled them out of the United States did not necessarily assume material form when deportees arrived in their "native" land. When Puppet applied for a Salvadoran passport, hoping to once again journey north, Salvadoran officials were not eager to issue him one: "They didn't even think I was from here when I spoke to them. I could barely speak Spanish, and I spoke Spanish weird." Similarly, Greg described his frustration in attempting to get identity documents in El Salvador:

> Here they wanted ID in order for me to get ID from here. I spent about a *month* trying to get my paperwork, running from here to there, waiting in lines, not understanding what they're telling me, buying things that I don't need. I get to the window, "No, this is not want you need. You need to go back and you need to wait in line. And you need to do this again." Every now and then I would find someone who spoke English to help me out a little. But it was a very long process to get your *cédula* [national identification card].

Legally abandoned as "undocumented" Salvadorans, deportees were vulnerable to legal actions and social discrimination. A staff person at a migrant shelter described these difficulties: "First, they don't get jobs easily. Second, they can be detained by the PNC [Policía Nacional Civil/National Civil Police] as undocumented. And there has been a problem in that the authorities don't want to give [them] cédulas. In some cases, we have been told that they have to conduct an identity trial, bring witnesses to say, 'He was born here; he left at a certain age.'" For these reasons, another immigrant advocate pointed out, it was necessary to help retornados "find a way to resolve the problem of legality in the country." Revealingly, one advocate commented that a goal of his work with deportees is "to help them to feel that they have a country."

Although many deportees are welcomed by their relatives in El Salvador, others either lack relatives or are rejected by relatives, community members, and Salvadoran society at large. According to NGO members who worked on immigration issues, deportees who had failed to send remittances to family members might find these relatives reluctant to provide them with financial support. An NGO member explained, "Suppose that the family provided financial support so that he could go, but when he was in the United States, he didn't help them. When he is deported he goes to the family. But the family tells him, 'Now that you come in bad conditions you look for us, but when you were in the United States earning dollars, you didn't help.'" Changes in migrants' behavior, such as wearing baggy clothing, getting tattoos, and speaking in ways that were not considered polite could also provoke rejection, as an immigrant advocate recounted: "The things that they say strike people as appropriate or as inappropriate. So that is a conflict because the other person is perceived as violent. And maybe that's not it, but rather it's a sense of how one says things." These views were echoed by King and Puppet, who complained that because of their style of dress, which they said contrasted with the "preppy" style popular in El Salvador, they were regarded with suspicion by others.

In addition to lacking documents and family support, deportees may find themselves at a complete loss economically and socially. As one immigrant advocate put it, "It's like a child who doesn't have any idea what the country is like, how it works." This advocate described the experiences of a relative who had been deported:

> A brother of mine was deported from Los Angeles one year and nine months ago. He has been here for almost two years, and he isn't working. So, of course, he feels like a burden. And, of course, if the parents weren't giving him assistance, he would be a person who would be completely abandoned. He is a dependent person despite being thirty-two years old. That is an age when one should be planning one's future, and, sadly, he is losing his future.

Even deportees who were able to find work sometimes found Salvadoran wages—minimum wage was about $140 per month at the time of my research (Ministerio de Economía, Gobierno de El Salvador 2005)[13]—and standards of living difficult to accept. Puppet, for instance, was shocked by the poverty that he experienced when he was first deported:

> I get to this place where I'm supposed to live, you know? And it's *ugly*! It's ugly, like, no place in L.A. looks like that, you know? It's like a big giant shack with like tools everywhere, and it's ugly, you know, and dirty, you know. I think, "Oh, man! I'm not going to live here, man! I can't!" This is like below my standards, you know? Even like being poor in L.A. beats that, you know?

Retornados who had not spent years in the United States before being deported also faced economic difficulties. A staff member at a migrant shelter told of one such case:

> This was a young man who was twenty-eight years old, but he said that he felt like he was forty. I asked him if he had been to his house yet, and he said, "What house?" He didn't feel like going there. He said that one and a half months ago he had sold his mother's land and four cows in order to get the money to come. He hadn't told his family that he was back. "They think I am there," he said. "How am I going to tell them? What will they think if they see me return empty-handed? I have five kids."

In short, deportation can be alienating, humiliating, and economically devastating.

To prevent them from being completely abandoned, a program called Bienvenidos a Casa (Welcome Home) provided deportees with information about El Salvador, bus fare, temporary shelter, medical assistance, referrals, job counseling, and other basic services. Bienvenidos a Casa was conceptualized through the Conferencia Regional de Migración (Regional Conference on Migration, also known as Proceso Puebla), a regional governmental effort to coordinate migration and migration policies in North and Central America. It grew out of concern about the effects of deportations on receiving countries and on migrants themselves (see Mahler 2000b). The program was initiated in 1999 with institutional support from the Salvadoran government, funding from the U.S. government, and technical assistance from governmental and nongovernmental entities in San Salvador, and was administered by Catholic Relief Services, an NGO. A U.S. official in El Salvador explained why the United States was funding this program:

> It's essential to reintegrate returnees, regardless of the reason that they are returning. It is in the interests of the receiving country too. Otherwise, they will just turn around and go back again, and they will face enormous risks on the way. There are lots of dangers in traveling to the United States illegally. This is a very important issue, particularly for returnees who left El Salvador at a young age and their rootedness in El Salvador is attenuated.

To counter such attenuation, Bienvenidos a Casa presented arriving retornados with a brochure entitled, "General Information about Your Country." Significantly, the brochure's final section, "Important Information," features sketches of a border crosser and a prison, and warns retornados of the legal consequences of returning to the United States after deportation.

Despite the assistance that they received, and despite deportation's supposed purpose of merely placing individuals within their country of legal citizenship, some retornados experienced deportation as akin to incarceration. King argued that his prior experience adapting to prison life had helped him learn how to adapt to life in El Salvador. Puppet and Greg both wondered why, when they were deported, the judge had not specified the length of time that they had to stay away, as one would when announcing a prison sentence. Greg observed: "[The judge] said, 'You're deported.'" He didn't say for ten years, or three months, or anything like that." Puppet remarked, "You can't just say, 'You're expelled for life. You're deported for life.' I mean, I hope not!" According to a staff member of Homies Unidos, a gang violence prevention NGO with offices in San Salvador and Los Angeles, El Salvador seemed like a prison to deported gang members because they were separated from family members, they encountered hostility, and they were so stigmatized that they could not walk around "without people harassing you, not without thinking that at any minute somebody can kill you." When Puppet first arrived in El Salvador, he feared that he would be killed, and in fact he almost drowned on the beach:

> I thought it was like the beaches over there [in the United States], you know. Kind of like calm. This beach that I went to was sort of like, on a little cliff, and the currents were like really strong, and the riptide was strong, and you know, I confided in my ability to swim, and I went out real far, and I couldn't come back in. So I was drowning for about half an hour. I was about a block and a half in the ocean, just floating. And I was like, "Damn, it's my second day here, man, and I'm gonna die." You know? . . . And I was like, "Damn! I was born here and damn, I just came back to die."

Puppet's account of nearly drowning is remarkably like Greg's description of the way that he experienced deportation: "It's like asking someone, taking you two miles out in the ocean and saying, 'Swim back.' It's very, very defeating."

Although they were physically removed to El Salvador and were forbidden to return to the United States, there is a sense in which some deportees did not fully arrive at their destination. Alienated from El Salvador, they remained apart. For example, when Puppet was first deported, he felt like a tourist:

> I go in the malls looking around and just seeing everything. I mean, 'cause it's all new to me, you know? I'm here thinking I'm a big shot who can walk around 'cause I speak English, and I think nobody else does, and you know? . . . I didn't attach to this country till like just a few years ago. I've been here almost four years, and, you could say I was kind of lost, you know?

Although he eventually came to feel that he belonged, King also tried to live in El Salvador without actually being there:

> I was *lost*, man! I was like if I was busted again, if I was in *jail*! Because I was like, I knew a place that, I knew how it was, and I knew I could be there [in the United States], and I knew I had family, and people I know there. I

wouldn't face the facts, you know, reality, that I was here, you know what I mean?

Some deportees re-created their U.S. lives within El Salvador and thus, in a sense, brought something of the United States with them when they were deported. Puppet explained:

> I stay like in a little tightly knit circle of people just like me that were sent here and that were waiting for another opportunity, but didn't get it. So, I have my little circle of friends. I've met some like people from here, born in the States but [living] here because their parents work here. So all my friends speak English. I speak English at home. I mean, I haven't, like, really lost what I you know learned and what became of me in L.A., you know? I brought L.A. back with me, you know? My backyard has, like, you know some artistic graffiti, spray paint, and I have an occasional barbecue with friends—stuff that you would do in L.A. that's not too common here, you know?

Other deportees found that, whether they liked it or not, they could not escape the United States by going to El Salvador. One interviewee had this experience. After attempting to fight his immigration case, he signed deportation papers, thinking that it would be an opportunity to relive some of his childhood memories:

> I was anxious. I was anxious to smell the air. I was anxious to go see that curve and the railroad tracks and the bridge that I remembered. I wanted to see the scene from that cliff on the back of where we lived that had the view of the mountains. I wanted to go. When I got off there, I was like, riding in the back of a truck going towards this address that I had in this envelope. I was just enjoying the view and everything green and nice and beautiful. You can't ride in a pickup truck standing up in back, here [in the United States]. And all of a sudden I saw a big rock coming up out of the mountain. And it had some writing on it—it said, "MS-13." It had my gang name on it, and I said, "I can't get away from them." Because I wasn't thinking of all that. I wanted to know El Salvador. I didn't want to know about gangs. I knew about gangs already. I didn't want to be involved. I didn't want problems. And then it's just right there, hitting you, slapping you in the face.[14]

Of course, many deportees did not stay in El Salvador. Immigrant advocates who worked with deportees in El Salvador estimated that 40–60 percent of deportees returned to the United States, albeit illegally.[15]

When deportees brought something of the United States to El Salvador, their country of origin received a "return" on their emigration. Whether this return was positive or negative was the subject of some debate.

Return

Deportation entails particular sorts of accountings. U.S. immigration authorities record the numbers of aliens expelled from the United States, the administrative reasons for removal, and whether they were criminals or noncriminals. These figures enable authorities to demonstrate that they are doing their job and are part of the "return" that U.S. taxpayers get for funding border control. At the same time, authorities in the countries for which deportees are destined fear the societal effects of mass deportations. U.S. officials must therefore remove as many "undesirable" or inadmissible aliens as possible without overwhelming any single country. In the case of El Salvador, the United States attempted to be accommodating by arranging for deportees to arrive by day rather than at night, notifying Salvadoran authorities of impending arrivals, providing initial funding for the Bienvenidos a Casa program, and suspending deportations during national emergencies, such as the aftermath of Hurricane Mitch in 1998 or the 2001 Salvadoran earthquakes. Countries that receive deportees also "account for" return. In El Salvador, for example, many assumed that returnees had committed crimes and were to blame for gang violence within El Salvador. In an effort to transform such images, community groups that worked with deportees conducted their own accounting. These groups sought to convince the Salvadoran public that deportees had valuable skills, and that their return benefited rather than harmed El Salvador.

The belief that deportees were criminals was widespread in El Salvador. News headlines such as "L.A.'s Deportees Send Murder Rate Soaring in El Salvador" (Jones 2000) and the U.S. policy of returning deportees in shackles supported this view. Hector, who had hoped to become reacquainted with El Salvador after being deported, recounted:

> There had been [an] article written in [a] magazine called *La Gente* that said they were going to be deporting six hundred people a month, most of them from prison. This magazine had said that "the 600 are coming. "Allí viene los seis cientos. The worst of the worst. Assassins, murderers, rapists, thieves, gang members. They're here. And they have masks on." [They had drawn a cage hanging out of an airplane on the front cover of the magazine with] all

these men with long hair, mohawks, or with earrings, or with tattoos [say-ing] "MS" [or] "18," and some with hoods on. Everybody was saying I was the first of the six hundred. So that really put a different outlook to every-thing that I had in mind about knowing El Salvador.

An immigrant advocate reported that as recently as 1999, when a group of deportees arrived at the airport, the shops lowered their curtains and put out security barriers. A U.S. official in San Salvador said that due to the problem of absorbing "hard-core criminals" who are "very violent people," U.S. immigration authorities could not deport too many criminals at one time. This statement implies that only limited numbers of deportees can be "absorbed" with ease. An immigrant advocate echoed this concern about absorption, focusing not on the alleged criminality of deportees but rather on the already high rates of poverty and unemployment in El Salvador. This advocate noted that deportations, particularly on a massive scale, would mean a loss of remittances for the country. Employers, advocates pointed out, hesitated to hire deportees who might have criminal pasts. Puppet confirmed that deported gang members were subject to social dis-crimination. He related, "People look down on me like I'm a piece of trash you know, 'cause of my tattoos, 'cause of the way I dress, you know?"

The Bienvenidos a Casa program responded to these concerns, though accounts of the nature of this response differed. Some officials saw the pro-gram as a means of monitoring deportees. A U.S. official who was inter-viewed in San Salvador said that the purpose of the Bienvenidos a Casa program was to keep track of criminals by constructing a profile of depor-tees. The need to keep track of criminals was also mentioned by a Salvado-ran official, who pointed out that Salvadoran police met deportees at the airport and created a record of their presence. In contrast, other officials and Bienvenidos a Casa staff stressed that the program was a means of pro-viding deportees with immediate assistance, helping them with "social reinsertion" (*reinserción social*), and challenging public stereotypes of de-portees. A staff member explained:

> The spirit of the program fundamentally is telling them, "You are not alone, you have opportunities to continue working. We are here to open spaces." The program does not offer them work, it does not tell them they are coming to a paradise, no. "Let's work together. Let's build a country together."

Some who worked with this program criticized U.S. practices that crimi-nalized deportees. One advocate, for example, wondered whether it was legal for the United States to shackle deportees or for Salvadoran police to meet retornados at the airport.

To counter the widespread stigmatization of deportees as dangerous criminals, Bienvenidos a Casa staff conducted an accounting of their own. When returnees arrived at the airport, staff held an orientation and interviewed returnees about their needs and their prior experiences. These interviews enabled staff to determine the particular assistance—bus fare, temporary shelter, medical referrals—needed by individual retornados, and also made it possible to construct a statistical profile of returnees. A report prepared in July 2001, for example, contained tables and pie charts describing returnees' age, years of schooling in El Salvador, years of schooling in the United States, English-language skills, work experience, place of origin, length of residence in the United States, gender, and criminal record.[16] During interviews, advocates pointed out that the label "criminal" was misleading, as it included minor offenses and acts—such as consuming drugs or driving while intoxicated—that were not illegal in El Salvador. According to statistics gathered by the program, only 13.45 percent of returnees had been convicted of crimes that were considered serious offenses according to Salvadoran law, and some 45.38 percent were deported simply for immigration violations (Bienvenidos a Casa 2001).[17] By emphasizing returnees' origins in El Salvador, work experience, and cultural and linguistic skills, and by recalculating their criminality, advocates sought to redefine retornados as people who could benefit El Salvador. A staff member explained that a significant success of the program was "that the public recognizes that the returnee is not antisocial but, rather, is someone who had an incident in the United States such as could happen to anyone here, but that, because of their immigration situation, it caused them to return." Pointing out that Salvadoran émigrés provide tremendous financial support to El Salvador, this advocate suggested that it was unfair for Salvadoran society to reject émigrés if they were deported.

The long-term assistance provided by Bienvenidos a Casa revealed staff members' assessments of differences between the United States and El Salvador. To aid in social reinsertion, Bienvenidos a Casa staff developed vocational and job placement programs. These programs provided returnees with tuition and transportation to training programs (for example in electricity or computers), counseling regarding employers' expectations, and access to particular employers. During an interview, a staff member described the challenges of acquainting returnees with technologies used in El Salvador while encouraging them not to lose the abilities that they developed in the United States:

The job that they did there was, let's say, building a cement wall, and here the walls are almost all brick. That [person] has had important elements, such as new knowledge, treatment of material, a good level of production. We should take advantage of this.

[However, to work in El Salvador, returnees have to change certain attitudes.] If a worker who has had a mask, who has had gloves, who has had all of the labor-safety rules that the North American laws require comes here . . . businesspeople [tell us], "How am I going to give to one worker, who comes from there and who has had a ton of things there, here, how am I going to give to him and all the rest?" [Also], there are people who are very strong, very sure of themselves, [who] come, speak, react, demand their rights. Those are elements that often make it difficult for employers.

The staff member explained that while the program could not tell returnees not to demand safety equipment or rights, it did seek to make them aware of the atmosphere in which they were operating. Advocating for immigrants, in this particular case, meant teaching them how to meet employers' expectations.

The tourist industry was considered a particularly promising career path for returnees, many of whom, like Puppet, may have felt like tourists themselves. A program to train returnees to be tour guides was developed. A Bienvenidos a Casa staff member described this program:

The training touches on different topics. For example, it covers the history of El Salvador, beaches, volcanoes, lakes, mountains, and birds of El Salvador— all of the cultural-historical part. [It includes] first aid, group orientation, how to provide service to tourists. They are actually brought to the places, so that they practice being tour guides.

Ironically, retornados, former U.S. residents who had been exiled, were being trained to introduce tourists to a country that they themselves may not have regarded as fully their own.

Deportees' ability to "bring back the United States" was also considered a valuable resource by Salvadoran youth who admired U.S. culture and, particularly, gang lifestyle. A Homies Unidos staff member in Los Angeles told me, "When you get there you're looked at as an icon, and a god. 'Here he comes, he is from L.A.!' And people are just waiting to jump you into their gang because you're from L.A. and you're the real deal." Puppet had had this experience:

There's a lot of people that look up to us, or me, you know, because I have this knowledge of another country that they've never been to, and that they only see on MTV. And I've *lived* it, you know? I'm kind of like looked upon as—I wouldn't say a celebrity—but like a cool guy, you could say.

Homies Unidos members disputed the contention that deportees were to blame for gang violence in El Salvador (see also chapter 6). A staff member in Los Angeles argued that the civil war was responsible for the violence of Salvadoran society: "The conditions are there. It's a very violent society. It has to be manifested in some way. The fact of the matter is that we [Salvadorans] love American anything. And the gang style is not that different." Homies Unidos members in El Salvador also blamed the news media for promoting fear of crime. Mario Nolasco pointed out that when the January and February 2001 earthquakes occurred, news about crime dropped, and people began to wonder what had happened to the gang problem.

Regardless of whether they had valuable skills, retornados were forbidden to return to the United States. Individuals who had been ordered deported or who had been deported and then had returned had to live in hiding, even if they were not, in other respects, different from those around them. Marta Córdova, a Salvadoran woman in her fifties who lived in Los Angeles and who had a pending application for legal permanent residency, told me of such a situation. She immigrated to the United States in the late 1980s when violence in El Salvador intensified, leaving behind several children, including a son who was seventeen at the time of our interview in 2001. Earlier that year, she had arranged for her son to join her in the United States, though he lacked a visa, but he was caught at the U.S.-Mexico border. After being given a court date, he was released. Pointing proudly to diplomas that were displayed prominently on her living room wall, Marta told me that her son was studious and well behaved, that he had had no criminal problems, and that he had no involvement with drugs or gangs. Her son had nonetheless been afraid to attend his court hearing and had been ordered deported in absentia. Marta left no stone unturned in seeking a legal remedy for her son, but she was advised that nothing could be done. Sick with worry, Marta developed health problems. "If they take him away from me, it will send me to my tomb!" she told me. For security reasons, Marta said, her son slept in different houses each night. He wanted to get a car and to travel to other parts of the United States, but Marta feared that if he did so, he was more likely to be apprehended. Marta herself hoped to change addresses, so that it would be more difficult for U.S. immigration authorities to find her, even though, as a NACARA applicant, she was almost certain to be awarded legal permanent residency. Marta's son, who was a source of great pride to her, was also a deportable alien and a fugitive.

The deported and the deportable expose the limitations of policies that extend legal and societal recognition to émigrés. Out of place, and therefore not fully present, these individuals fall between countries, belonging to both and neither simultaneously.

Being Elsewhere

Removal literally takes people out of the ranks of the socially legitimate, erasing their presence, breaking off their connections, and placing them "elsewhere." Retornados are excluded in many senses: they are banished from U.S. territory, "exiled" to a land of birth that they may not actually know, prevented from living with U.S. relatives, relegated to lives that are in many ways unfeasible, and, if they do reenter the United States illegally, forced to live as members of what could be a permanent underclass comprised of individuals who may never be able to legalize their presence. It is true that retornados came to the United States without authorization, violated the conditions of their visas, or were convicted of crimes that made them deportable. It is also true that some individuals may thrive despite deportation, using their "return" as an opportunity to turn over a new leaf, extricate themselves from unhealthy relationships and activities, and resume lives in El Salvador. It is further true that, for some, deportation may be a temporary setback before they once again return clandestinely to the United States, where they may not have had legal status prior to being deported in any case. Nonetheless, removal exposes the deep rift between official versions of reality, according to which citizenship, national membership, and territorial presence correspond, and the versions lived by emigrants, who maintain ties to multiple nations, move whether or not they are granted permission to do so, and live in territories where they lack legal status. Sometimes, as is described in the next two chapters, official policies take unofficial realities into account, granting unauthorized residents legal recognition or reaching out to distant citizens. Even when this occurs, however, retornados are often left by the wayside. As a Homies Unidos staff member in Los Angeles observed:

> You're nothing when you leave your country. You have to get out of there, and work so hard to finally try to make something out of yourself, so that

you can consider that you made something, and contribute, and keep the country afloat, for them to do something about your situation here that they should have done to begin with. In your country, so you didn't have to leave. And now, the reason why they do it is because you're sending money. Isn't that crazy? It's amazing. And then, when your kids are deported, then you're not "hermano lejano" ["distant brother," a term used to honor Salvadoran migrants] no more.

As this staff member suggests, retornados expose the limitations of inclusive policies adopted toward Salvadorans in the United States.

CHAPTER 2

La Ley NACARA (Nicaraguan Adjustment and Central American Relief Act)

> The juridical order does not originally present itself simply as sanctioning a transgressive fact but instead constitutes itself through the repetition of the same act without any sanction, that is, as an exceptional case. This is not a punishment of this first act, but rather represents its inclusion in the juridical order.
>
> Giorgio Agamben, *Homo Sacer: Sovereign Power and Bare Life*

Law assumes multiple forms. Alongside official versions of law exist unofficial, often transgressive versions that are the way things work in practice. For example, in the United States, all are supposed to be equal before the law, but in practice laws are applied differently to different groups (Barbalet 1988; Flores and Benmayor 1997; Frohmann 1997; Nelson 1984; Sapiro 1984).[1] Law is, of course, designed to combat that which deviates from officially sanctioned behavior. The U.S. Border Patrol struggles against the unauthorized immigration "system" of coyotes and illicit entrants, the police attempt to destroy the illegal drug economy, authorities try to disrupt and prohibit youth gangs. Law is nonetheless complicit in and dependent on the very realities that it combats. Stiffening border enforcement and criminalizing drugs make both alien-smuggling and the drug trade more profitable (Andreas 2000), while police sometimes tolerate or reward snitches who engage in illegal behavior (Marx 1981). Prohibited realities thus generate alternative (and unofficial) legalities in which distinctions between the "legitimate" world of law and the "illegitimate" world of the criminal are weak or inoperative. Thus, in certain neighborhoods dealing drugs may be one of the few viable occupations (Hagedorn

1991), and in certain countries immigrating to the United States without authorization may be one of the few ways of supporting one's family. Once the distinction between legitimate and illegitimate activities is blurred or erased, the execution of the law may itself appear illegitimate and even criminal. To some, for instance, the fees that the U.S. immigration authorities receive from immigrants are morally undifferentiated from payments made to coyotes (Hagan 1994). There are moments, in fact, when authorities acknowledge and redefine the very acts that the law prohibits.

Over time, the relationship between official and unofficial legalities constitutes the path of law—the legal, the right way, as distinct, perhaps, from other paths, such as the criminal. The path of law is not only a route but a boundary that separates the permissible from the impermissible. Retracing the path of law uncovers law's embeddedness, the degree to which particular legal distinctions carve out categories of persons or activities that then become the basis for further distinctions or modifications. Those who implement the law must stay true to this path in that they can tweak but not completely redefine legal categories and practices. At the same time, in that law and illegality form two sides of one surface, the prohibited can cause the path of law to deviate. The path of law can be redrawn so that activities and persons that were once in the domain of the illegal are now (and therefore always were) on the road to legality. As paths are redrawn, law itself moves into the (former) domain of the prohibited. There may therefore be a place for law *within* the illegal and vice versa. Law may perform the very acts that it prohibits, creating a "zone of indistinction" (Agamben 1998, 6) between law and illegality. Within this zone of indistinction, the prohibited becomes, in fact, the path of law, and law itself can take on pathological characteristics.

In this chapter I examine the paths that led to and emerged from the Nicaraguan Adjustment and Central American Relief Act. During the 1980s, when Salvadorans and Guatemalans were being massacred, bombed, abducted, assassinated, and tortured, U.S. immigration officials seemingly allowed cold war ideology to influence asylum adjudications. Generally speaking, Nicaraguans, who fled the leftist Sandinista government, were welcomed, and Salvadorans and Guatemalans, who fled right-wing regimes, were not.[2] To challenge such distinctions, refugee service organizations sued the INS commissioner and the U.S. attorney general. In the early 1990s, a settlement agreement and the award of TPS acknowledged that, while they (for the most part) had immigrated without authorization, Salvadorans and Guatemalans needed refuge. Although they were merely granted temporary status, migrants' years of living and working in the United States eventually created grounds for arguing that these Salvadorans and Guatemalans deserved permanent residency. After NACARA was approved in 1997, the Clinton administration developed regulations that ensured that the vast majority of Salvadoran and Guatemalan NACARA applicants would obtain permanent status. Of course, there were important *limitations* to this outcome. For instance, the settlement agreement carved out a particular class, benefits were only extended to members of that class, cold war ideology influenced the nature of these benefits, and the U.S. government retained the authority to rebut NACARA claims. Further, even migrants who are defined as deserving can experience the sort of abductions described in chapter 1. Nonetheless, the policy-making process that produced NACARA reveals how law sometimes acknowledges the very realities that it prohibits.

The Prohibited

During the 1980s, Salvadoran and Guatemalan migrants were prohibited on multiple grounds. Those who immigrated without authorization or who stayed beyond the expiration dates of their visas became, like other undocumented immigrants, illegal aliens, subject to detention and deportation if apprehended. Although Salvadorans and Guatemalans were not specifically targeted in INS enforcement practices, U.S. authorities considered immigration from El Salvador to be a problem. As Assistant Secretary of State Elliott Abrams stated during a 1984 congressional hearing, "El Salvador . . . is a country with a history of large-scale illegal immigration to the United States" (House of Representatives 1984, 67). Salvadorans and Guatemalans were also prohibited on political grounds. As the U.S. government was providing military and economic support to the governments of El Salvador and Guatemala in their wars against guerrilla insurgents, granting safe haven to nationals of these countries would have tacitly admitted that a U.S. ally was committing human rights violations. The State Department, which was required to weigh in on asylum cases, routinely advised INS district directors to deny Salvadoran and Guatemalan asylum cases. These recommendations were generally followed. During the early 1980s, asylum applications filed by Salvadorans and Guatemalans were denied at rates of 97 percent and 99 percent, respectively (U.S. Committee for Refugees 1986). An immigration attorney who began his practice in the late 1970s recalled:

In 1980, 1981 . . . we started to file asylum applications [for Salvadorans, and] we started to see that they were being denied. Even though the cases were stronger than anything I had ever seen from any country. . . . In El Salvador at that point in time the government was, you know, on a terror campaign, and in Guatemala too. They would go and wipe out a village and then cut off people's heads and then put them on stakes so that people would see them and be terrorized.

Through prohibiting presence and denying asylum, official legal categories were made visible. When they criticized illegal immigration, U.S. officials drew sharp distinctions between authorized and unauthorized residents. Unlike legal residents who were entitled to be in the United States, illegal aliens were deemed infiltrators to be identified and rooted out. INS executive associate commissioner Doris Meissner warned a House subcommittee that "Salvadorans, along with all other illegal aliens, are able to manage to sink roots, and . . . time is the greatest enemy of the Government in terms of its ability to effectively enforce departure and an orderly immigration system" (House of Representatives 1984, 103). This comment suggests that the presence of illegal aliens is illegitimate, and that any "roots" that such immigrants develop threaten the rule of law itself. Similarly, U.S. authorities insisted that if Salvadorans and Guatemalans were denied asylum, this was because they did not deserve it. At a hearing on a proposal to grant temporary safe haven to Salvadorans, for instance, a member of Congress commented that when people are deported, "the determinations are made on an individual basis that they are economic migrants" (House of Representatives 1984, 27). Similarly, Abrams remarked, "When we are talking about EVD [extended voluntary departure] for the group which is not eligible for asylum, we are discussing generally whether people who emigrate from El Salvador to the United States illegally should be permitted to reside here" (House of Representatives 1984, 67). According to these remarks, economic migrants were distinct from political refugees and could not be permitted to remain in the United States. Presumably, law could clearly distinguish legitimate and illegitimate reasons for immigrating.[3]

As prohibited beings, Salvadoran and Guatemalan migrants had to travel clandestinely, live an "underground" existence, and generally avoid being detected by U.S. authorities. Although documentation requirements were less stringent in the early 1980s (e.g., undocumented immigrants could get drivers licenses, and work permits were not created until 1986), it was still a hardship to be undocumented (Mahler 1995). Individuals could be asked for identity documents during a variety of transactions, such as when applying for a job, college admission, or housing. The undocumented were often economically marginalized, working in low-paying, insecure positions such as domestic employment, the garment industry, construction, and agriculture. Undocumented workers were vulnerable to being reported to immigration officials by disgruntled neighbors, demanding employers, or suspicious acquaintances. Those who were apprehended by immigration authorities were pressured to sign deportation papers. Immigration agents reportedly forced detainees to stand in the hot Arizona sun all day, threatened detainees, told detainees that if they applied for asylum, information from their applications would be sent to Salvadoran authorities, moved detainees to detention centers where little legal assistance was available, and failed to inform Central Americans of their right to seek political asylum (see *Orantes-Hernandez v. Meese* 1988). Migrants who *were* able to file for political asylum faced skeptical officials who routinely denied their cases. Asylum interviews were conducted rapidly, without privacy, by officials who had little knowledge of asylum (*Mendez v. Reno* 1993). When persecution victims' asylum claims were denied, their experiences were also denied. Both they, and the reality of their persecution, were prohibited.

Although official versions of law made it appear that Salvadorans and Guatemalans were illegal and undeserving residents, alternative accounts suggested that "official law" was off the mark.[4] During the 1980s, a solidarity movement made up of religious groups, political activists, and legal advocates sought to establish that Salvadorans and Guatemalans deserved refugee status (Coutin 1993; C. Smith 1996). Members of this solidarity movement accused the U.S. government of violating the 1980 Refugee Act, international law, and basic principles of legal fairness. An attorney who was part of the class counsel in a lawsuit filed on behalf of Salvadoran and Guatemalan asylum seekers characterized 1980s asylum practices as "a whole system that was premised on the use of discriminatory and illegal criteria in the adjudication of claims." Similarly, another attorney said that his organization had joined in this lawsuit out of a concern about "whether the government is complying with the law." Religious activists who declared their congregations "sanctuaries" for Salvadoran and Guatemalan refugees and who helped these migrants cross the U.S.-Mexico border argued that such actions enforced laws that the U.S. government was violating (Coutin 1995). When they accused the U.S. government of judging asylum cases on the basis of nationality rather than justice, applying law in

a discriminatory fashion, and deporting refugees to the site of their persecution, solidarity workers and legal advocates suggested that U.S. immigration authorities, rather than Salvadoran and Guatemalan migrants, were
committing illegal acts.

As it officially prohibited Salvadorans and Guatemalans but welcomed
Nicaraguans, Cubans, and Eastern Europeans, immigration law became, in
the view of some, pathological, a system that sent an undetermined number of
individuals to their deaths (see also Rosenblum 2000). Remarks made by an
attorney involved in a lawsuit on behalf of Salvadoran and Guatemalan asylum seekers conveyed the view that 1980s asylum practices were pathological:

> Not only were we supporting these human rights abusers in El Salvador, then
> we were in a way perpetuating a further terror on that same population in
> the United States by depriving them of their rights under the law—and try-
> ing to send them back to the very human rights violators that the United
> States government was supporting. And so that whole systematic violation of
> the law and of human rights was just so profoundly offensive.

Complicit in perpetrating human rights abuses, the law itself became, in
the eyes of some, criminal. The nonapplication or misapplication of U.S.
asylum law fostered efforts to obtain special protections for Salvadorans
and Guatemalans.

Distinction

During the late 1980s and early 1990s, advocates were able to create new legal forms that, without invalidating official law, made Salvadorans and
Guatemalans eligible for temporary legal status in the United States. Arguing that immigration officials had failed to recognize Salvadorans' and
Guatemalans' legitimate claims for political asylum, advocates sued the
U.S. government on behalf of these asylum seekers, proposed legislation
that would grant safe haven to these migrants, and sought administrative
action that would forestall their deportations. These strategies, all of which
were ultimately successful, constituted Salvadoran and Guatemalan immigrants as unique groups, whose reasons for migrating, dates of entry, treatment by U.S. officials, and eligibility for particular remedies *distinguished*
them from other migrants. Defining Salvadorans and Guatemalans as distinct groups was accomplished through legal "exceptions" that left such categories as illegal immigrant, political refugee, and legal immigrant intact,

but that created other statuses for Salvadorans and Guatemalans. The exceptional nature of these other statuses placed Salvadorans and Guatemalans in an ambiguous position: they were granted temporary authorization to remain in the United States, but, as this authorization would evaporate if Salvadorans and Guatemalans were once again subjected to the versions of law that constituted them as economic immigrants, these migrants remained legally vulnerable. These elaborations of legal exception nonetheless became part of the path of official law.

Efforts to secure legal protection for Salvadoran and Guatemalan refugees began during the early 1980s, as the extent of human rights violations in El Salvador and Guatemala became clear and as asylum procedures in the United States were being formulated and litigated. The Refugee Act of 1980 had just established that, in contrast to prior U.S. refugee law that limited refugee status to individuals from Communist countries and the Middle East, persecuted aliens who reached U.S. territory could petition for asylum, regardless of country of origin (Kennedy 1981).[5] This neutral adjudication standard was tested almost immediately, with the arrival of large numbers of Cubans, who were paroled into the United States, and Haitians, who were generally denied asylum (see Churgin 1996; *Haitian Refugee Center v. Smith* 1982; and Kennedy 1981). Lawyers' committees and immigrant-rights centers began to proliferate in major U.S. cities such as Washington, D.C., San Francisco, Los Angeles, Chicago, and Boston. These centers connected attorneys who were willing to represent asylum seekers on a pro bono basis with Salvadorans and Guatemalans who were in deportation proceedings. A San Francisco attorney who coordinated this work recalled that "our whole expectation was [that] we were going to represent people and string their cases along as far as we could, hoping that the war would end, or we'd win temporary protected status." Despite these legal networks, many Central Americans were unrepresented. Another attorney commented: "The reality was that there were still lots of people who were being deported. They didn't have access to lawyers, they didn't know what the heck was going on, they were still getting coerced with [incorrect] information [about their legal rights] at the borders."

In addition to representing individual asylum seekers, legal advocates filed class-action suits designed to force the INS to change its policies. *Orantes-Hernandez v. Meese*, which was decided in 1988, prohibited U.S. immigration officials from coercing Salvadorans into agreeing to depart the United States, required officials to inform Salvadorans of their right to apply for asylum, and prohibited the INS from transferring detainees to detention centers that were geographically distant from detainees' attorneys.

The so-called Young Male Case (*Sanchez-Trujillo v. INS* 1986) sought to establish that young Salvadoran men who were at risk of being forcibly recruited by the Salvadoran military deserved political asylum (see Compton 1987; *Sanchez-Trujillo v. INS* 1986).[6] Although it was unsuccessful, this suit is indicative of the growing significance of Central American refugee issues to immigration and human rights networks. As an advocate who I interviewed in 2001 commented, "Most of us have spent practically all of our careers on this."

Legal advocates and other activists also sought legislation, known as Moakley-DeConcini (after its sponsors, Joe Moakley and Dennis DeConcini), that would grant extended voluntary departure status to Salvadorans. EVD, a discretionary status awarded by the executive branch, grants recipients temporary permission to remain in the United States due to an emergency situation in their homeland. EVD had previously been granted to migrants from Ethiopia, Uganda, Iran, Nicaragua, Poland, and Afghanistan (Churgin 1996). The Reagan administration opposed the Moakley-DeConcini legislation on numerous grounds. Administration officials argued that the asylum system was working, that most Salvadorans had come to the United States in search of jobs rather than safety, that a grant of EVD would serve as a magnet to additional illegal Salvadoran migrants, that countries of resettlement were available in the region, and that the United States could not take in the world's poor. As Elliott Abrams put it, "Maybe not Canadians, or something, but, you know, basically, everybody in the world would be better off in the United States" (House of Representatives 1984, 110). Proponents of Moakley-DeConcini, in contrast, contended that the asylum system was not able to recognize victims of generalized violence; EVD would be available only to those already in the United States and not to future migrants; the United States had greater resources than other countries of resettlement; Salvadorans were seeking safety, not jobs—that, in fact, many Salvadoran professionals experienced downward mobility after migrating; and that no one had proposed that the United States take in the world's poor.[7] During the 1980s, repeated attempts to pass Moakley-DeConcini, including an effort to attach it to the 1986 Immigration Reform and Control Act (IRCA), failed.

While the Moakley-DeConcini bill languished in the U.S. Congress, advocates devised a new class-action suit on behalf of Central American asylum seekers. In 1985, the U.S. government filed criminal charges against U.S. religious activists who had declared their congregations "sanctuaries" for Salvadoran and Guatemalan refugees (Coutin 1993, 1995).[8] In response, advocates decided to sue U.S. authorities in civil court. An attorney who was involved in conceptualizing what came to be known as *American Baptist Churches v. Thornburgh* (or simply ABC) described the origins of this case:

> ABC in particular was actually conceived of initially as more responsive to the sanctuary prosecutions than it was to the discriminatory treatment of Salvadoran and Guatemalans. When the government started prosecuting church people for assisting Salvadorans and Guatemalans, networks of people were talking about how to respond to that and not just always to be put in a defensive position, but to try to do some affirmative litigation to try to stop the prosecutions.
>
> Our central argument was [that] Salvadorans were refugees, it was just that the U.S. wasn't recognizing them as refugees. But the U.S. was in violation of both its international and national legal obligations, and, consequently, they shouldn't be prosecuting people who were just doing what they were supposed to be doing, which is protecting people from *refoulement* [return] to torture and persecution.
>
> And so we decided to do litigation that would focus both on trying to enjoin the sanctuary prosecutions and trying to stop a discriminatory treatment of the refugees.

The ABC lawsuit, which was filed in 1985, originally had three components: (1) it sought to bar future prosecutions of sanctuary workers, (2) it sought to prohibit additional deportations of Salvadorans and Guatemalans, and (3) it charged that the asylum process was biased against Salvadorans and Guatemalans. The first two of these claims were dismissed on the grounds that U.S. immigration law had changed since the sanctuary prosecutions occurred and that, as U.S. asylum laws were not self-executing, the courts could not grant blanket safe haven to Salvadorans (*American Baptist Churches v. Meese*, 1987, 1989). Litigation on the third claim nevertheless went forward.

As attorneys in the ABC case prepared for discovery proceedings, the U.S. government, which had fought the case for almost five years, suddenly offered to settle in 1990 (Blum 1991). A member of the ABC class counsel recounted how this occurred:

> I remember one day getting a call from someone who—it's actually funny, because you get a call from X person, he's a lawyer. And I said to [my staff person], "Stall, I'll be with him in a minute," and did a few things, and got on the phone and it was real staticky. And I asked, "Where are you calling from?" "I'm in an airplane." It wasn't [INS general counsel] Bill Cook. It was

an aide. "Give Bill Cook a call. There might be some talk you two might want to have regarding settlement."

Several factors may have been responsible for this reversal. First, efforts to reform the asylum unit were already under way. As ABC attorney Patty Blum (1991, 356) relates, "The INS Commissioner Gene McNary and other INS officials addressed the Annual Convention of the American Immigration Lawyers Association (AILA), promoting the regulations as an attempt to create a new, fairer asylum system. The trial in this case would have put the INS in the awkward position of defending . . . old procedures which it had effectively renounced." Second, the discovery process was likely to be both financially burdensome and politically embarrassing. An immigration official told me that it was his understanding that "plaintiff located a videotape that had been used in training. . . . And the speaker was somebody from the State Department. And, in essence, what the person was saying was 'Be as generous as you can in granting asylum to Nicaraguans but you really need to look very, very carefully at asylum from Salvadorans, Guatemalans, and don't just be throwing asylum around in those cases.' " Third, this case was connected to a social movement. An attorney involved in the litigation recalled, "Every time we went to court, the courtroom was filled with people from the sanctuary movement. And they would do prayers out front beforehand and be there with their habits and collars and everything in court and it was a very powerful statement." Fourth, the political situation in Central America had changed. Following the 1989 Salvadoran final offensive by the FMLN, which demonstrated the near impossibility of resolving the conflict militarily, efforts to broker a peace agreement intensified.[9] In this changed scenario, denying asylum to Central Americans may no longer have been as important to U.S. interests. Nonetheless, the decision to settle offended some immigration officials. One official related, "After the settlement had taken place, there was feeling in INS that the section of the Justice Department which had settled the case had gone too far—that they should not have agreed to a settlement."

While settlement negotiations were underway, advocates succeeded in overcoming opposition to legislation granting temporary status to Salvadorans. An immigrant-rights advocate who was involved in this legislative process recounted his version of how this was accomplished:

Here's the anecdote: So the 1990 Immigration Act, which was a big deal, beyond Central Americans, is literally being held up by Jesse Helms. He has a hold on the bill. One senator can prevent consideration. But Jesse Helms is holding up final Senate consideration of this immigration bill, which includes TPS. I draft a letter from [Salvadoran] President [Napoleón] Duarte to the U.S. Senate, which the [Salvadoran] ambassador urges Duarte to send. Duarte does. My wife literally—this is a twenty-four-hour deal or [the legislation is] dead—delivers it right into the hands of Jesse Helms. And Helms says, "Alright, if President Duarte wants this to happen, I'll let it happen." So all of these kind[s] of connections created this opportunity at the moment.

Another immigrant-rights advocate provided an account of how Senator Alan Simpson dropped his opposition to granting Salvadorans temporary legal status:

I was in the room when Senator Simpson agreed to the Immigration Act of 1990. Moakley's staffer had been to El Salvador. Jim McGovern. He's a congressman now himself. And he was there [in 1989] around the time that the Jesuits were killed, and for him, it was very personal. He knew [assassinated Jesuit] Segundo Montes. And Moakley was pushing it toward conference. It also helped that Moakley was the chairman of the Rules Committee. And, Simpson wanted the immigration act to pass. Moakley promised that he would not support an amnesty for the Salvadorans who were getting temporary protected status. And then Simpson agreed to support the bill. I was there when he said it. And then we went out into the hall, and there were cheers!

The 1990 Immigration Act, which was signed by President George Bush,[10] created "temporary protected status" and declared that Salvadorans who had been in the United States prior to September 19, 1991, could receive eighteen months of this status.

The ABC settlement agreement took the passage of TPS into account and was painstakingly crafted. An attorney for the ABC class described the process:

Then we got involved in this long, extremely protracted and complicated negotiation process on the settlement agreement. And that played out over a long period of time at an unbelievable level of detail and involving the State Department, the INS, the Executive Office for Immigration Review, which was the immigration court—BIA [Board of Immigration Appeals]. We really tried to anticipate the issues that would come up, and to deal with all these different aspects of implementation, and avoid opportunities for the government to basically undermine the settlement by some weird interpretive thing that they could adopt later. . . . And the government's interest, obviously, was in trying to have the people covered by this be a closed set.

That set, as another attorney recounted, was defined fairly broadly:

The INS first would only agree to settling on cases that had been denied, and only by the INS. Their position was "immigration judges are immigration judges. They are impartial. So we are not going to touch their decisions." And it took us a long fight to say, "No, the judges have been just as complicit in these denials as the INS officials themselves. And we're not going to give up the cases before the immigration judges." And then the next major push was those who never applied. And their initial thing was, "On what basis do you claim any right to, that those people should get relief?" And we said, "Well, people weren't applying because they knew they had no chance. It was suicide to go and file the application once it became clear that you were going to deny 99 [or] 97 percent of it. Those who were inhibited from applying because they knew there was a huge likelihood that those applications would be denied." So getting those in, included also, was a very big step.

Ultimately, the settlement agreement established that every Salvadoran and Guatemalan who was in the United States prior to 19 September 1990 (in the case of Salvadorans) or 1 October 1990 (in the case of Guatemalans) had the right to apply or reapply for political asylum and have a de novo hearing on their claims. Special rules to ensure fair hearings were established, advocates were given the right to train asylum officials regarding conditions in Central America, and immigration officials agreed to publicize the agreement so that Central Americans would be aware of their rights. Salvadoran TPS applicants were deemed to have registered for the benefits of the settlement agreement, and both Guatemalans and Salvadorans were also permitted to register for benefits directly. This decision had an immediate impact. An immigration official recalled, "I used to work for the immigration judges, and I remember in early '91 we came in one day, and the judges' caseloads had suddenly dropped. Someone had gone through and closed the Salvadoran and Guatemalan cases, from one day to the next, because of the ABC settlement."

Because TPS was temporary, and because the outcomes of ABC asylum cases were not assured, organizations debated whether to encourage Salvadorans and Guatemalans to register for these benefits. An attorney explained that he advised groups:

"Hay que quedarse en el barco grande [You have to stay in the big boat]. You apply for TPS, and when you finish TPS, what happens? Then you apply for ABC." And I'd call people up from the audience and I'd go place by place by place. "If you stay in the big boat, you're going to be okay. If you don't stay on the big boat, see that sign over there?" And I would point to the exit sign. "Then you get the premio de TACA" [the prize of TACA, a Central American airline, that is, a plane ticket back home].

As this attorney notes, the settlement agreement carved out a distinct class of people. Some 240,000 Salvadorans and Guatemalans applied, but when applicants' immediate family members are taken into account, the number of people who benefited from the settlement agreement is actually larger. The magnitude of this class can perhaps be grasped by the following story, told by the official from the Asylum Policy and Review Unit of the Department of Justice who was responsible for manning the single post office box to which ABC class members sent forms of various sorts:

My responsibility was to get all these registration forms entered. We had clerical staff working on them, we had people coming in on weekends working on them, and we had just boxes and boxes of these registration forms all over. When I first got there I could not get into my cubicle because it was completely loaded with boxes, so I took those, piled them up as best I could. I was sitting in my cubicle one day, and all these boxes fell down on top of me.

Although the settlement was crafted to govern asylum applications and interviews, which presumably were to occur after the agreement was finalized, immigration officials did not begin scheduling ABC asylum cases for some six years (see also Mahler 1995). The reasons for this delay are complex. The asylum unit was already facing criticism over its huge backlog in adjudicating asylum cases (Beyer 1994). Because they presented less opportunity for fraud, the ABC cases were a lower priority than either newly received applications or already pending cases. As an asylum official commented, "The truth, the very fact that you've got a potential 250,000 [ABC asylum] cases that are on the backlog of the backlog. 'You don't have to worry about them right now,' I think, in essence, that doesn't help but facilitate keeping current [with new asylum receipts] and even being able to begin to dig into your backlog of non-ABC cases." This official added that the complexity of the settlement agreement, with requirements for particular sorts of notices to be sent to applicants, also made it difficult to launch the interviews. Furthermore, an ABC attorney suggested, there was speculation that an alternative program would make it unnecessary to adjudicate ABC cases: "There was general agreement—these cases would basically stay on hold and eventually people would qualify for some sort of suspension-type relief. And there was neither a push by the INS, nor of course class counsel, to expedite asylum adjudications." An asylum official echoed this belief, relating that "around here it was said with jocularity, but with a sense of 'boy, wouldn't it be nice,' and that was 'amnesty.' 'Amnesty.' " He added, "Well, there is the standard joke around here that ABC is going to give employment to generations yet."

Although ABC asylum interviews were delayed, both Central American activists and the Bush administration faced the more immediate question of what to do when TPS expired after the allotted eighteen months, a question that was complicated by the fact that peace accords were signed in El Salvador in 1992. Central American groups lobbied heavily for an extension of TPS, and new groups and coalitions—such as the Association of Salvadorans of Los Angeles (ASOSAL) and the Salvadoran American National Network (SANN)—grew out of this effort. Bush administration officials were less than enthusiastic about granting an extension. At the same time, they believed that deporting large numbers of Salvadorans could destabilize postwar El Salvador. An official who served in the Department of Justice (DOJ) during the first Bush administration provided an account of how this dilemma was resolved. I quote my notes from this interview:

> When TPS was about to expire, INS and the State Department had decided not to renew it, because to do so they would have had to certify that it was unsafe to return, and it wasn't. The staff member [that I interviewed] had decided to go along with this. Then, the chief of staff for the attorney general called to say that Bush had promised [Salvadoran president] Cristiani that he would renew TPS, so please do it. The staff member thought about it, then he called back to ask if there was another mechanism through which it could occur, and that's when he invented DED [deferred enforced departure]. DED was invented because it was an executive action. It didn't require renewing the certification that it was unsafe to return to El Salvador.

Salvadoran TPS recipients were permitted to register for DED, which was in turn extended until January 31, 1996, the deadline that immigration officials eventually set for Salvadoran ABC class members to file for political asylum under the terms of the settlement agreement. Yet another "different" status had been created for Salvadorans. The rationale for this status had shifted, however, from migrants' need for safe haven to El Salvador's need for remittances and stability.

ABC, TPS, and DED, which had been crafted to address the exceptional situation of Salvadoran and Guatemalan refugees, became part of the path of law. New statuses were created, a class of migrants eligible for these statuses was carved out, and new procedures and guidelines were developed. In a stunning but incomplete reversal, Salvadorans and Guatemalans who had formerly been prohibited as illegal aliens were redefined as individuals who had fled emergency conditions and were thus eligible for temporary legal status. This redefinition was brought about by emphasizing the legal contradictions that prohibiting Salvadorans and Guatemalans had entailed. Thus, the ABC lawsuit claimed that the asylum process was discriminating against Salvadorans and Guatemalans in violation of their right to due process, and proponents of EVD argued, among other things, that the asylum process was not evaluating individual cases appropriately, therefore making a blanket grant of status necessary. The argument that, in denying Salvadorans' and Guatemalans' asylum claims, official law had become pathological was not formally accepted, as neither the ABC settlement agreement nor the TPS legislation admitted any error on the part of U.S. officials. Nonetheless, the strength and persistence of the Central American solidarity movement, shifting political circumstances in Central America, institutional changes in the asylum process in the United States, ongoing renegotiations of U.S. immigration policy, and the Salvadoran government's own request that Salvadorans be permitted to remain in the United States eventually gave credence to the previously officially denied claim than Salvadorans and Guatemalans were fleeing emergency conditions and could not safely return to their homelands. Salvadorans and Guatemalans were not, however, granted political asylum or another permanent status in the United States. They therefore remained vulnerable to being redefined as illegal aliens who did not deserve political asylum (Menjívar 2006). This vulnerability increased during the 1990s, as anti-immigrant sentiment grew in the United States and as peace agreements were implemented or developed in both El Salvador and Guatemala. Salvadorans' and Guatemalans' claim that, unlike other migrants, they could not safely return to their countries of origin became more difficult to sustain.

Indistinction

Although the beneficiaries of the ABC settlement had been constituted as a distinct class, these migrants were also undifferentiated from other immigrants in at least two senses. First, as the amount of time that they had lived in the United States increased and the likelihood of winning political asylum decreased, ABC class members began to argue that their lives were in many ways identical to those of permanently legal residents. This argument suggested that they were de facto residents, and that law, which defined them merely as DED recipients and as asylum applicants, did not accurately reflect social reality. As these migrants appealed to their need to live and work in the United States, the very argument—that they were economic immigrants—that previously had been used to *discredit* them became a basis for their claims. Second, their lack of permanent legal status made ABC class members vulnerable to measures that targeted illegal aliens. If their claims were denied, these migrants would face detention and deportation. In this sense, ABC class members were not unlike undocumented immigrants.

During the early to mid-1990s, these migrants' similarity to both permanent residents and to illegal aliens was exploited by immigrant rights advocates and opponents. When interviews on the merits of ABC class members' asylum claims were pending, immigrant advocates and administration officials began to explore a possible blanket grant of legal permanent residency to ABC class members. Seemingly, some immigration officials believed that it would eventually be possible to grant ABC class members suspension of deportation, a status awarded to aliens who could prove seven years of continuous presence, good moral character, and that deportation would be an extreme hardship. This effort, however, encountered opposition. A member of the ABC class counsel recounted, "For a while it looked promising, and then I think it just foundered on all the political dynamics in Washington and all that sort of thing. They said ABC was this big new amnesty, and it was pre-'96, before Clinton was going to be up for reelection and all the anti-immigrant stuff." In contrast, one of the immigration officials in charge of the ABC caseload attributed the difficulty in granting this request to law rather than politics, saying simply that "the plaintiffs' counsel was pushing the INS to consider the ABC class members' cases in a different way. And we just couldn't do it, because of the limitations of the law."

As efforts to obtain a blanket grant of permanent residency for ABC class members foundered, anti-immigrant sentiment in the United States grew, resulting in legislation that dramatically changed the legal context in which ABC class members' cases would be adjudicated. IIRIRA and AEDPA, both of which were approved in 1996, made many common legalization strategies impossible to pursue. For instance, immigration attorneys sometimes sought to delay adjudications or appeal cases until their clients accumulated the seven years of continuous presence that would make them eligible for suspension of deportation. In the meantime, as individuals with pending cases, their clients would be able to remain in the United States with work authorization. Applying for political asylum had also been, until 1995, a means of obtaining a work permit, as the backlog of asylum cases made it unlikely that individuals' cases would be heard quickly.[11] IIRIRA redefined such practices—each of which had inadvertently benefited the ABC class—as crafty, suspect, and questionable. To do so, IIRIRA created a "stop-time" rule, such that the issuance of a notice to appear in court halts the accumulation of time for immigration purposes. In other words, an individual who had only been in the United States for five years when notified to appear in court could never accumulate more time. Suspension of deportation was replaced by cancellation of removal, which requires proving ten years of continuous presence, good moral character, and that deportation would be an extreme and exceptional hardship on the applicant's U.S. citizen or legal permanent resident spouse, parent, or child. A cap of four thousand was placed on the number of individuals who could be granted suspension or cancellation in a given year. Asylum was also reformed. Individuals were required to apply for asylum within one year of entering the United States, unless they could demonstrate changed circumstances within their country of origin. INS officials then held "credible fear" hearings, and only those migrants who were deemed to have a "credible fear" were scheduled for asylum interviews. Other individuals were placed in expedited removal hearings. Judicial review of immigration adjudications was also curtailed. In short, tactics through which individuals had attempted to define themselves as deserving were made unviable, and temporary residents (e.g., those with pending cases) were defined as not particularly different from illegal immigrants who deserved deportation.

These provisions of IIRIRA were devastating for ABC class members, many of whom had planned to apply for suspension if their asylum cases were denied (Wasem 1997). As few had applied for suspension as yet, it was unlikely that they could argue that their cases had been in process before suspension had been eliminated. Even if they *were* permitted to apply for suspension, the four thousand cap made this an unlikely remedy for the 240,000–plus ABC class members. Furthermore, orders to show cause (earlier versions of notices to appear) were issued to Salvadorans in 1992, at the end of the eighteen–month TPS period, but they were never mailed. Would these be interpreted as stopping TPS recipients' accumulation of time?

Those class members who could not prove ten years of continuous presence or who lacked a legal permanent resident or U.S. citizen spouse, parent, or child would not be eligible for cancellation. Even those who could prove ten years and who had such a relative faced the burden of meeting a higher hardship standard. Class members' asylum cases, which may have been strong when they first immigrated, were less likely to be granted as the events that had led class members to flee receded in time and as political changes occurred in both El Salvador and Guatemala.

In April 1997, in this changed legal context, immigration officials began to interview ABC class members on their asylum claims. As Central American nations braced for what they feared would be mass deportations, Central American advocates and community groups in the United States sought to counter the effects of IIRIRA on ABC class members. Could law be made to recognize the claims of a group that had initially been prohibited and that had now been deeply stigmatized once again?

Deviation

The presence of the prohibited can, under certain circumstances, cause the path of law to deviate. ABC class members were ambiguously positioned. They were a distinct class, but they also resembled both permanent legal residents and illegal aliens. They were thus simultaneously on the path of law—they had pending asylum applications, they had, for the most part, also received TPS and DED—and in the domain of illegality—they were, in essence, unauthorized residents awaiting the adjudication of asylum petitions.[12] Although they were ambiguously positioned, ABC class members' presence within the United States had been documented, they had been given alien numbers, they had immigration files, and they had a history of alliances with powerful advocates. Whether initially prohibited or not, ABC class members insisted that their presence required a reckoning, an acknowledgment of their years of residence, their U.S.-born children, their social, economic, and familial ties to U.S. communities, and the violence that had forced them from their homelands. To conduct this reckoning would mean acknowledging claims—that these migrants were refugees all along, and that living in the United States for prolonged periods is a means of building legal equities—that had been denied or rendered suspect. To acknowledge these claims and to move ABC class members conclusively into the domain of law would require retroactively recognizing prohibited acts (i.e., living and working in the United States) as having been part of "the path of law" all along. Such retroactive recognitions redefine the boundary between legality and illegality.

After IIRIRA made it appear that many ABC class members would eventually be ordered deported, Central American advocates sought to establish that ABC class members were long-term residents whose legal status, though temporary, made them much more like permanent residents than like recent entrants petitioning for the right to stay. At first, this effort seemed doomed to failure. A Los Angeles–based advocate recalled that shortly after NACARA passed, she and a colleague met with Washington, D.C., attorneys who, she said had been "aware of these issues for their entire careers and who were very sympathetic" but who advised them that Congress would not approve a remedy for the ABC class. Administration officials were not, however, uninterested in creating such a remedy (Rosenblum 2000). For example, an immigration official recalled being distressed at how IIRIRA affected the ABC class. She commented, "Everyone in the world assumed that they would be able to apply for suspension and that they would get to stay." U.S. officials were also concerned about how deportations, or at a minimum the revocation of work authorization, would affect Central American nations. A Democratic staffer commented that deportations would be a strain on the economic and political situations there, and that those who were returning would be an instant rebellion force. When Clinton traveled to Central America in May 1997, he told the Central American presidents that it would be problematic to return Central Americans who had lengthy ties to the United States and who supported their countries financially through remittances to countries where their presence could be destabilizing. Clinton remarked, "These Central American countries are in a rather special category. After all, the United States Government was heavily involved with a lot of these countries during the time of all this upheaval" (Clinton 1997, 571).

Advocacy on behalf of Central Americans, combined with support from some U.S. and Salvadoran government quarters, gave rise to legislative remedies for the ABC class. Following Clinton's visit to Central America, immigration officials drafted legislation that restored the suspension eligibility of ABC class members and participants in the Nicaraguan Review Program (see note 2), and that exempted these migrants from the four thousand annual cap. In a bipartisan effort, this legislation was introduced by Senators Bob Graham (Democrat) and Connie Mack (Republican) of Florida. As an immigration measure, this legislation faced difficulty. Some, such as Senator Lamar Smith, a staunch proponent of restrictive immigration measures, apparently regarded it as another amnesty (Wasem 1997). Others, who regarded the Nicaraguan Contras as "freedom fighters" and the Salvadorans and Guatemalans as illegitimate economic immigrants, were only interested in creating a remedy for the Nicaraguans. An advocate provided an account of how this opposition was overcome:

> [House Speaker Newt] Gingrich was basically proimmigrant. . . . Republican Latino congressmen [Lincoln] Diaz-Balart and [Ileana] Ros-Lehtinen from Florida pick up the banner for Nicaraguans who were based in Florida, the Nicaraguans basically being more anticommunist—they fled the Sandinistas. And we forge this three-way coalition, Salvadorans and Guatemalans and Nicaraguans. . . . We're being resisted tooth and nail by Lamar Smith. And it's bottled up. But we get ahold of a big-time Texas Republican fundraiser who had raised money for the Contras. And she and a coterie of her Texas wealthy Republicans who helped the Contras want to help the Nicaraguans here. Well, [we said], you can't help the Nicaraguans without the Salvadorans and Guatemalans, and vice versa.

Salvadorans, Guatemalans, and Nicaraguans (with the support of Cuban activists) joined forces to lobby for this legislation. The Salvadoran government hired Rick Swartz, a political consultant in Washington, D.C., who specialized in "left-right coalitions" and immigration advocacy. Central American activists organized vigils, fasts, and rallies, and former Contra supporters held joint press conferences with advocates who had participated in the Central American solidarity movement.

Using cold war ideology to secure support from legislators who were lukewarm on immigration matters gave rise to a disparity within the legislation that was approved by Congress. Nicaraguans who were in the United States prior to 1995 were given the right to automatically adjust their status to that of legal permanent residents, whereas Salvadorans and Guatemalans who had received TPS or had applied for asylum prior to 1 April 1990, and who were in the country on the requisite dates were given the right to apply for suspension of deportation, a lengthier, more complex, and less certain process. Knowing that this disparity would offend Salvadoran and Guatemalan supporters, the White House considered how to respond. A Clinton administration official related:

> There was a debate over whether or not the president should veto NACARA. And the decision was not to threaten to veto. The president didn't approve of Republicans giving more to the Nicaraguans and the Cubans. But it wouldn't

be a good idea to throw the baby out with the bath water. So the president signed NACARA and he sent a letter to Speaker Gingrich disparaging the unequal treatment. . . . Moreover, NACARA was attached to the D.C. appropriations bill. There had been a budget fight that year, and if he vetoed the bill, then what were the chances of getting something else with a better remedy? The president felt that it was best to sign the bill, and that the disparity could be resolved administratively.

NACARA, which was originally termed the Victims of Communism Relief Act, became law. Salvadorans, Guatemalans, and Nicaraguans had been exempted from the more restrictive immigration measures adopted in 1996, but the discrimination that had given rise to the ABC lawsuit in the first place also shaped the differential treatment that was created by NACARA.

The disparity within NACARA was galling to Salvadoran and Guatemalan activists and officials. For example, a high-level Salvadoran official in the United States described NACARA as "a liquidation of the accounts (*cuentas*) of the cold war."

> George Bush *told* the Nicaraguans to come. He promised to give them residency. If you check the *Congressional Record*, you will find a congressman said that the Nicaraguans should be included because they were freedom fighters and the Salvadorans should be excluded because they were communists. Just because the Salvadorans left a country whose government was being supported by the United States, that makes them communists? What a vast oversimplification of reality. Every Nicaraguan immigrant was a freedom fighter? Every single Salvadoran was a communist? When these immigrants came during the *same* period, for the same reasons?

Calls to rectify the disparity took two forms. First, advocates proposed parity legislation, which extended NACARA benefits to Hondurans and Haitians, moved the eligibility date to 1995 rather than 1991, and granted all the same remedy—adjustment of status. Second, there was considerable pressure to create parity administratively, by interpreting the law in ways that would equalize the treatment of Salvadoran, Guatemalan, and Nicaraguan NACARA beneficiaries. During a 1999 trip to Central America, President Clinton promised Central American leaders that he would minimize disparity in treatment.[13] A Department of Justice official recalled that when Clinton returned, "he gave us our marching orders. These were to be as equitable as possible in reconciling the disparity but to be consistent with the law."

Ongoing advocacy on behalf of Salvadoran and Guatemalan NACARA beneficiaries influenced the next phase of lawmaking: the crafting of the regulations that would implement this law. During the comment period that followed the promulgation of the proposed rule, advocates submitted thousands of recommendations. An attorney who helped to coordinate this effort described the process:

> There was a massive outpouring of comments. They said they'd never re-
> ceived so many. They were looking at thousands! We had comments that
> were signed by refugees. I'd never seen that happen before. I mean, they
> didn't write them, of course. But they were in English and Spanish, and they
> signed them, and then we organized mailings. I think we got hundreds and
> hundreds of comments by the refugees themselves.

The officials responsible for writing the regulations faced a variety of pressures. Central American advocates, Salvadoran and Guatemalan officials, the National Security Council, and the White House were pushing for interpretations that would minimize disparity. U.S. officials were concerned, among other things, about the negative effects that an interruption of remittances could have on El Salvador and Guatemala. Hurricane Mitch, which hit Central America in 1998, created added pressure to assist Salvadoran and Guatemalan NACARA beneficiaries. Proponents of more restrictive immigration measures opposed liberal interpretations of NACARA. There were internal debates within the Department of Justice and the Immigration and Naturalization Service over how to interpret NACARA. Finally, through-out all of these pressures, the regulations had to be "true to the statute." As one of the regulations' authors commented, "How do you do what is the right thing to do and at the same time be consistent with what is legal according to the statute? How do you interpret a statute? Members of Congress come to you and say, 'Well, this is what we meant when we passed this.' But the statute doesn't *say* that, so what do you do?"

Through a process that one participant described as "torturous," involving meetings and exchanges of drafts between asylum officials, the INS Office of General Counsel, the Executive Office for Immigration Review, the Office of Immigration Litigation, White House officials, and legislative analysts, regulations that created unprecedented solutions to a series of issues were crafted. One debate concerned who should adjudicate NACARA claims. To date, only immigration judges had heard suspension claims. However, most registered ABC class members had asylum petitions pending with the asylum unit of the INS. ABC class members were more likely to win suspension than asylum, but the only way for them to come before an immigration judge was first to be interviewed by an asylum official on the merits of their asylum claims. Such a cumbersome process could produce lengthy delays. Advocates therefore asked the INS to streamline the NACARA process by granting asylum officers the authority to adjudicate applicants' suspension claims. Immigration judges reportedly opposed this move, arguing that only they had the authority and expertise to adjudicate suspension claims. Others worried that streamlining the process would be unfair, as certain NACARA beneficiaries (e.g., individuals who had applied for TPS but not political asylum) would only go before an immigration judge, whereas others (e.g., registered class members with a pending asylum application) would first have their claims assessed by the asylum unit and then, if they lost, by an immigration judge. The latter would have "two bites at the apple." Despite these concerns, the attorney general took the unprecedented step of granting asylum officials the authority to adjudicate NACARA claims. One of the regulations' authors explained, "We [the asylum unit] had the files, and asylum had to do the interviews anyway. Most would lose their asylum cases but be granted NACARA. It was a time-saver to do them together. Moreover, the issues in the asylum claim and in the suspension claim were interconnected." To reduce fraud, this benefit was only extended to the "known universe" of NACARA applicants (and their family members), with asylum claims pending at the asylum unit, and not to other NACARA beneficiaries. Procedurally, the asylum unit's possession of these files gave them jurisdictional authority over these migrants.

A second debate concerned the enumeration of hardship factors. Advocates urged the INS to specify ways that the ABC class met the hardship criteria. Immigration judges, on the other hand, reportedly stressed the importance of adjudicating NACARA claims according to established case law. One individual involved in negotiating the regulations summarized this issue:

> Should the hardship factors come from the case law that has been developed around suspension cases, or from the particular situation of ABC class members? The NGO community wanted the hardship factors to be defined by the particular situation of ABC class members. And the view that prevailed was that the hardship factors were defined by the relevant case law.

The regulations nonetheless took the unprecedented step of *specifying* these hardship criteria. Case law was codified through the NACARA regulations. The rationale for codification was stated in the regulations as follows:

Because of the breadth of the case law governing the "extreme hardship" standard, the Department has concluded that a regulatory compilation of the relevant factors and standards identified within this body of law would provide a more uniform and focused source for evaluating extreme hardship claims (Department of Justice 1998, 64903).

Finally, a third debate focused on whether the INS could grant a blanket finding of hardship to ABC class members. In their comments on the NACARA legislation and on the first published version of the NACARA regulations (i.e., the proposed rule), advocates urged the INS to find that the ABC class had met the extreme hardship standard according to suspension law. Such a finding would virtually guarantee a grant in almost all NACARA cases (except, for instance, those in which the applicant had become statutorily ineligible, e.g., due to criminal convictions) and could make individual interviews of NACARA applicants unnecessary, thus greatly speeding adjudication. The Department of Justice balked, arguing that case-by-case adjudications were required and that to grant a blanket finding of hardship would go beyond the authority of the statute. Gradually, however, the idea of granting *certain* NACARA beneficiaries— primarily, the ABC class—a *rebuttable* presumption of hardship emerged. An official recounted:

> These [ABC class members] were *people we knew*, people who had strong equities. They had lived here a long time, they had kids, they were working— they had had working authorization. We felt that most officers could adjudicate without the presumption. But the advocacy community really wanted it. So we looked at it, and we decided we could do it. The presumption of hardship shifts the burden from the applicant to the INS. (emphasis added)

Granting NACARA applicants a presumption of hardship was legally complex, as an official explained: "The analytical hurdle was that the advocates wanted a blanket determination of hardship, but the case law on suspension always says that these are 'case by case' adjudications. It wasn't until we stepped back and said, 'Wait a minute. Can we look at this a different way?' that we were able to devise the presumption of hardship." The necessary precedent derived from the presumption that individuals who have suffered past persecution have a well-founded fear of future persecution (*Matter of Chen* 1989). Once individuals prove past persecution, the burden of proving or disproving a well-founded fear of future persecution shifts from the applicant to the government. Unlike past persecution-based asylum cases, however, the presumption of hardship was being extended to a group of people before information about their personal histories was in evidence. What made this legally justifiable, officials related, was their determination that ABC class members were known to share particular characteristics. An asylum official explained:

> With the ABC class, there were several things that they had in common. One was why they were here. They came during a period of violence and civil war. And even though peace accords were signed in 1992, the U.S. government felt that there were reasons to allow them to stay here in 1993, so they were granted DED. And in the situation of the Guatemalans, they didn't have DED, but peace accords weren't signed until 1996. There were difficult conditions in their country for a long time. Second, they were protected. They didn't have to fear that they were going to be deported. That allowed them to become more established, to set down more roots in the community. And they had employment authorization, which meant that they could work.

The interim rule, published on May 21, 1999, stated that "*ABC* class members . . . will be presumed to satisfy the requirements for extreme hardship" (U.S. Department of Justice 1999, 27866).

The NACARA hardship criteria, like suspension law more generally, acknowledged the realities of unauthorized immigrants' lives (see also Coutin 2001b). Living and working in the United States, accumulating time in the country due to delays in adjudication, and treating work permits as permission to remain in the United States became, de facto, grounds for legalization. During the 1980s, Salvadorans and Guatemalans had been denounced as economic immigrants, yet through ABC, TPS, and DED they had become "people we knew," a group that was considered deserving. Their temporary documentation was deemed, retroactively, to have placed them squarely on the path of law rather than among illegal aliens with insecure status. The fact that they had "met the filing deadlines" (Department of Justice 1998, 64898) defined them as a delimited and "known" group within INS procedures. Without conceding any wrongdoing by the INS, the regulations did explicitly recognize the conditions that brought Salvadorans and Guatemalans to the United States:

> These individuals fled circumstances of civil war and political violence in their homelands during the 1980s, and some applied for asylum in the United States. In 1985, advocates for Guatemalan and Salvadoran refugees,

church groups, and refugees themselves brought suit against the United States Government for allegedly discriminatory treatment of Guatemalan and Salvadoran asylum applicants. The Department settled the litigation in 1990, following significant developments in its asylum and refugee law and procedures, including the creation of a professionally trained asylum officer corps and Congress's grant of TPS to Salvadorans. (Department of Justice 1999, 27865)

NACARA, TPS, DED, and ABC came to be deeply significant to Central Americans, solidarity workers, immigration and refugee rights advocates, and the officials who were involved in these cases. One official who helped draft the NACARA regulations told me that on the day that the regulations came out, she saw a news story about how people were celebrating, and tears came to her eyes. "I'm proud of what I've done," she concluded.

The Path of Law

The statutes, regulations, agreements, and executive actions designed to address the "exceptional" case of Salvadoran and Guatemalan asylum seekers became part of established law. By linking unprecedented legal developments to prior statutes, cases, categories, and procedures, NACARA was embedded in law, even as it gave rise to new possibilities. This process was not without ironies. The ABC case might not have been filed if the U.S. government had not prosecuted sanctuary workers; NACARA would probably not have been proposed if it were not for IIRIRA; and the NACARA regulations might not have granted applicants a presumption of hardship if it were not for the disparity between Nicaraguans, Guatemalans, and Salvadorans. Perhaps the greatest irony of all is that through NACARA, Salvadorans and Guatemalans, who had previously been undeserving economic migrants, turned out to be deserving "protocitizens" who had "fled circumstances of civil war and political violence." Through this redefinition, NACARA took alternative legalities (including sanctuary workers' claim that Salvadorans and Guatemalans deserved legal protection) into account, even as NACARA was always limited by "the scope of law." The ability to legalize the illicit suggests that there is something lawful within illegality, and that the illegal can exist within law. That is, the essential legality and deservingness that law eventually acknowledged was part of Central American asylum seekers when they were still being denounced as illegal immigrants. Moreover, other groups can also take advantage of such indistinctions.

Commenting with some pride on Salvadorans' pioneering legal role, one Salvadoran activist pointed out, "I remember Lamar Smith from Texas saying, 'This is an absolute mistake. The minute that you give anything to anyone, everybody else will want the same.' They had it absolutely correct. The minute you establish a precedent, given the judicial and political history in this country, it's pretty hard to say no to anyone demanding equal treatment." Despite such recognition, the illicitness of their original entries made these immigrants vulnerable to shifts in the law. The figure of the deportee haunts assessments of deservingness.

The Salvadorans who benefited from NACARA were people whose entries and exits had particular meanings within their country of origin. Initially regarded as probable subversives, these migrants were eventually hailed as "anonymous heroes" by Salvadoran authorities. As the United States debated how to respond to Salvadoran and Guatemalan migrants, El Salvador became increasingly dependent on the remittances that its emigrants sent to family members in El Salvador. The continued presence of this "absent population" was increasingly important to Salvadoran authorities. As they claimed and began to advocate on behalf of Salvadoran émigrés, Salvadoran authorities implied that unauthorized migration, an officially prohibited act, was not to be morally condemned. This is a complicated position for a state—which by nature must affirm boundaries, territories, and the significance of citizenship—to adopt.

CHAPTER 3

Atención a la Comunidad en el Exterior (Attention to Salvadorans Living Abroad)

Our compatriots in El Salvador say, "Emigrant brothers, distant brothers, you are a very important piece of the economy of the country. You are national heroes. But be there, stay there. Send dollars, but don't come."

Salvadoran businessman in Los Angeles

We realize that we are the country that expels the most people, that has the highest proportion of people living abroad, one-fourth of the population. You have to accept that your identity has changed, and if you don't want to accept it, it's enough to go to any small town in order to realize that today, country folk are going around on bicycles wearing Nike tennis shoes with flashing lights, and a Florida Marlins baseball cap.

Salvadoran journalist in San Salvador

El Salvador's recent relationship with its dispersed citizens has taken the form of transnational nationalism, claiming emigrants as part of the nation, and indeed an effort to promote Salvadoran identity among emigrants. When peace accords were signed in 1992, Salvadoran national authorities (who, since 1989, have been from the conservative Alianza Republicana Nacionalista/Nationalist Republican Alliance, or ARENA) began to reevaluate their relationship with the Salvadoran emigrant population. During the civil war, attempts to eradicate those who were deemed to pose a subversive threat had led many to flee the country; yet outside of El Salvador these migrants gained access to valuable resources, such as jobs and foreign currency. As sources of international assistance dried up and migrant remittances continued to grow, officials sought to maximize emigrants' economic potential. With anti-immigrant sentiment and policy on the rise in the United States, Salvadoran officials participated in efforts to secure Salvadorans' rights to remain there. In the waning days before Salvadorans' opportunity to file ABC asylum applications expired, officials (from the very government of claimed persecution) urged eligible migrants to apply (Mahler 2000a), and when 1996 immigration reform threatened ABC class members' abilities to stay in the United States, the Salvadoran government advocated the passage of NACARA. After NACARA was approved in 1997, Salvadoran authorities distributed a pamphlet about NACARA, created legal services departments at consulates, and pressured U.S. officials for additional immigration relief. Officials also promoted the 2001 postearthquake TPS and registration for subsequent extensions. In addition to legal advocacy, Salvadoran officials created the General Directorate of Attention to the Community Living Abroad (Dirección General de Atención a la Comunidad en el Exterior, DGACE), required all government ministries to report on their efforts in relation to Salvadorans in the exterior, developed a website with more than five hundred pages of information for and about Salvadorans in the exterior, devised a competition to award matching funds to support hometown associations' development projects, and, in 2004, created a ministry post devoted to the community in the exterior. A formerly "suspect" population was reconstituted as an "ally."

Salvadoran officials' attention to emigrant citizens is not unique. For example, El Salvador's programs are modeled after those of Mexico; the former Haitian president declared Haitians in the United States to be a department of Haiti; and other Central American nations have created forums, boards, or councils to attend to immigration issues (Mahler 2000a). What is, perhaps, unique to the Salvadoran case is the speedy transition to reclaiming citizens who were earlier pushed out of the country by political violence and economic difficulties. Indeed, migrants are now hailed by Salvadoran officials as compatriots who extend Salvadoranness throughout the world. These migrants' position is nonetheless somewhat ambiguous. Even as migrants are claimed as, in certain respects, the epitome of Salvadoranness, the term "the community *in the exterior*" positions migrants as outsiders.[1] Through migrants' externality, the nation-state is also both reinforced and reconceptualized. It is reinforced in that attention to Salvadorans *abroad* makes reference to national boundaries. It is reconceptualized in that locating a piece of the "interior" (i.e., a citizen) beyond national boundaries blurs distinctions between outside and inside. Thus, just as U.S. law's inability to completely exclude the undocumented allows formerly prohibited practices to retroactively become grounds for legalization, so too can citizens' departures create a basis for incorporation and national reconfiguration. The form that such incorporation should take is, however, a matter of some contention.

Civil War

During the Salvadoran civil war, government authorities treated citizens who supported or who were suspected of supporting the Salvadoran guerrilla forces as individuals who, by engaging in subversive activities, had abrogated the contract between citizens and the state. Such individuals were, in essence, *excluded* from the citizenry, not directly, through expulsion and denaturalization, but indirectly, through political violence that often led suspect individuals to leave the country. After leaving, these supposed enemies, ironically, became a source of national financial support through the remittances they sent to family members in El Salvador. Exteriorization therefore also entailed interiorization, that is, situating Salvadoran émigrés as key components of the national community, albeit in the exterior.

During the civil war, the Salvadoran state, with the support of the United States, defined guerrillas and their supporters as agents of international Communism. This stance depicted the Salvadoran civil war as an instance of foreign aggression against a sovereign nation rather than as an indigenous conflict rooted in competing social, political, and economic interests. As early as 1966, Salvadoran colonel Manuel Alfonso Rodríguez, who eventually became chief of staff of the Salvadoran armed forces, wrote an article based on the "premise that 'subversive' guerrillas are by definition Communist, and Communist guerrillas are by definition proxies of foreign powers" (McClintock 1985, 212). These ideas were echoed many years later by the Salvadoran provisional president, Álvaro Alfredo Magaña. Following a 1981 meeting with U.S. president Ronald Reagan, Magaña argued:

> [Social inequalities within El Salvador] provided the opportunity for extra-hemispheric interests, most particularly those of the Soviet Union and her satellites working through two Latin American countries to make us victims of their expansionistic policy. . . . This external aggression has destroyed villages, forcing hundreds of thousands of humble Salvadorans to abandon

their homes. . . . El Salvador fights not only for the survival of its own democratic system; we also defend western democracy. (Reagan 1981, 883–84)

According to this argument, guerrillas and their supporters had betrayed
the nation of El Salvador.

The contention that the Salvadoran civil war was a battle between Western democracy and international Communism was key to securing economic and military assistance from the United States (Quan 2005).[2] The
Reagan administration insisted that if the guerrillas gained power in El Salvador, then Communism could spread throughout the region, thus threatening the security of the United States. According to a 1983 National
Security Council document, "We [the United States] are committed to defeating the Marxist-Leninists in Central America. We believe that should
we fail to do so on the current battlefields of El Salvador and Nicaragua, we
shall have to face them in Mexico and on the [Panama] canal where the
stakes will be much higher" (quoted in Byrne 1996, 95).[3] In fact, Reagan
defined El Salvador as *almost* part of U.S. territory. In a 1983 speech to the
National Association of Manufacturers, Reagan (1983, 372–73) stated, "El
Salvador, for example, is nearer to Texas than Texas is to Massachusetts. . . .
The Caribbean Sea and Central America constitute this nation's fourth border." During the 1980s, the U.S. government sent $6 billion in military and
other aid to El Salvador (Schwarz 1991). In 1988, U.S. economic assistance
made up "between 25 percent and 33 percent of the funds the U.S. and Salvadoran governments spent in El Salvador" (Byrne 1996, 143; see also
Quan 2005 and Schwarz 1991). Opponents of such assistance complained
that the United States was supporting a government that violated its citizens' human rights, and that the U.S. government could become embroiled
in a Vietnam-like conflict. In response, the Reagan administration argued
that the human rights situation in El Salvador was improving; that reform
could be more effectively accomplished through engagement than through
withdrawal; that assistance was limited to funds, equipment, and advisers;
and that compelling national interests were at stake.[4]

In contrast to Salvadoran and U.S. authorities, guerrilla forces, known as
the Frente Farabundo Martí de la Liberación Nacional (Farabundo Martí National Liberation Front) or FMLN, emphasized the indigenous nature of the
conflict, calling it a "people's war" (Gordon 1989; Montgomery 1995). The
FMLN was founded in 1980 and was made up of five organizations: the FPL
(Fuerzas Populares de Liberación/Popular Forces of Liberation), the ERP
(Ejército Revolucionario del Pueblo/Revolutionary Army of the People), the

FARN (Fuerzas Armadas de Resistencia Nacional/Armed Forces of National Resistance), the PCS (Partido Comunista de El Salvador/Communist Party of El Salvador), and the PRTC (Partido Revolucionario de los Trabajadores Centroamericanos/Revolutionary Party of Central American Workers) (Byrne 1996; Montgomery 1995). Each of these groups was linked to particular mass organizations and, while their internal philosophies differed, was generally leftist in orientation. These groups sought to challenge gross disparities in the distribution of wealth and a lack of access to political power. They resorted to armed revolution following a military coup in 1979 and increased repression of political dissidents. According to Byrne:

> As 1980 drew to a close, the space for negotiation and compromise appeared nonexistent and a full-scale war imminent. The country's military leaders and their elite landowning allies had rejected any meaningful changes through peaceful, democratic methods in the distribution of wealth and income and in access to political power. This intransigence helped ensure that when movements for change developed and were repressed, the option of counterviolence appeared to many Salvadorans as the only, or at least the most viable, method of bringing about needed reforms. (Byrne 1996, 68)

Guerrilla groups saw themselves as fighting on behalf of the masses, and FMLN leaders assumed that if the right conditions presented themselves, civilians would rise up in a popular insurrection.[5] Guerrilla leaders alleged that the Salvadoran government, rather than the guerrilla forces, was alienated from the Salvadoran people and that it was being supported by foreign interests, particularly the United States.

In this polarized situation, the Salvadoran military defined anyone who directly or indirectly supported or could be presumed to support the guerrillas as an "enemy" to be destroyed or neutralized. As Barry, Vergara, and Castro (1988, 84) note:

> National security doctrine assumes an astute, underhanded enemy who can disguise his or her ideas and infiltrate every aspect of society; included are individuals and organizations that endorse social change and eventually anyone who does not support the repressive policies required by the dictates of the doctrine. Effectively combating this amorphous enemy requires drawing lines of battle in every area of national life where the enemy might operate— the economy, diplomacy, unions, and religious organizations, all potential components of the rearguard.

Civilians who lived in areas of guerrilla control were considered to be col-
laborators and were driven out through bombing campaigns (Binford
1996; Montgomery 1995).[6] Such operations were referred to as "sweeps,
'cleansing' campaigns, or 'cleanups'" (McClintock 1985, 307), implying
that guerrillas and their supporters were "dirt" that made the nation im-
pure. Children were killed so that they "did not grow up to avenge their
parents" (McClintock 1985, 307). Such tactics were designed to deprive
guerrilla forces of civilian support, as Byrne (1996, 130) explains: "Applying Mao Zedong's maxim that guerrillas are like fish swimming in a sea that
consists of its civilian base of support, the Salvadoran armed forces and
their U.S. advisers adopted a strategy of 'draining the sea.'" The targets of
repression were widespread, as the armed forces "equate[d] the government's critics with the enemy, repressing trade unionists, campesino leaders, opposition politicians, and student protesters with the same or more
force than they use[d] on the real insurgents" (Schwarz 1991, 25).[7] Widespread surveillance of the population, through roadblocks, searches, and
undercover informants, treated all as suspect.

In addition to "draining the sea" through violence, the Salvadoran government sought to turn civilians against the guerrillas ideologically.[8] Byrne
(1996, 131) recounts:

> Psychological operations, directed toward the population at large or targeted
> groups, presented the government and armed forces as the legitimate author-
> ity, supported by the vast majority of the people, and dedicated to demo-
> cratic ideals, human rights, and reconstruction. The FMLN was portrayed as
> an isolated terrorist group, linked to external forces of subversion, and dedi-
> cated only to acts of destruction that hurt the civilian population.

According to Benítez (1990, 88), between 1984 and 1988 there was a campaign to convince the military to "change its attitude . . . toward the civilian population—to no longer conceive of all inhabitants of zones under the
control or influence of the FMLN as their sympathizers." Efforts to
strengthen civilian-military ties included economic development projects,
gifts of food and goods, and speeches. Civil defense patrols, made up of
civilians, were also formed in order to encourage civilians to identify with
the existing order.[9] In the face of continued human rights violations, these
efforts were of limited effectiveness. As Schwarz (1991, 55) notes, "Civic
action's emphasis on pep talks and charity assumes that the rural populace
is either ignorant of political issues or that its loyalty can somehow be purchased."

The tactics used to enforce exclusionary definitions of membership resulted in a massive dislocation of the Salvadoran population. By 1984, "within El Salvador there were 468,000 displaced people (9.75 percent of the population), 244,000 in Mexico and elsewhere in Central America, and 500,000 more in the United States, for a total of more than 1.2 million displaced and refugees (25 percent of the population)" (Byrne 1996, 115). By the time that peace accords were signed in 1992, Salvadoran community groups in the United States estimated that there were one million Salvadorans in the United States alone.[10] Many of these migrants entered without authorization and were regarded by U.S. authorities as economic immigrants, subject to deportation if apprehended.

Among the Salvadorans who came to the United States during the civil war were political exiles who launched a campaign in solidarity with popular organizations in El Salvador.[11] Not surprisingly, the relationship between solidarity activists and Salvadoran authorities was adversarial. Activists held demonstrations at consulates and publicly denounced Salvadoran authorities. A northern California activist recalled:

> The eighties was a decade, obviously, of confrontation, and we were—I can't deny it—very identified with an anti–Salvadoran government politics. There was a huge political difference in the sense that we were struggling to be recognized as political refugees. The Salvadoran government continually denied that our departure was due to our situation of war, to the political situation, but rather [said] that it was the economic situation.

Similarly, a Washington, D.C. activist recounted: "In the 1980s, when we were going around asking for TPS, they looked at us like that was subversive work and against them." Salvadoran officials also acknowledged that refugee-rights groups and the Salvadoran government had had an adversarial relationship in the past. At a public speech to community groups in 2002, a high-level Salvadoran official stated:

> I believe that you all remember, and of course particularly the members of El Rescate [a refugee service organization founded during the 1980s, and in whose Los Angeles offices this speech was occurring], that if we return to the decade of the 1980s, there was practically a total and absolute divorce between an institution like El Rescate and the government of the Republic of El Salvador. Despite everyone being Salvadoran, there was a distancing, an adversity, that created positions almost of enmity. And if, at certain moments, some met others, that almost became entrenched of opposition to what the

government of the republic was doing at that time. I refer not only to El
Rescate but to all of the proemigrant organizations that developed during the
decade of the 1980s, and primarily here in Los Angeles.

Salvadoran activists, in fact, feared that even though they were in the
United States, they or their family members could suffer reprisals for their
participation in solidarity work. Activists also contended that government
suspicion was directed not only at them but at Salvadoran emigrants in
general. According to an NGO member who had been involved in solidarity work in the United States during the 1980s, "During the war, the government had a stereotype that the Salvadorans who had left the country
were people who sympathized with the Left and who had probably participated in some things with the Left. And therefore these people were identified as their enemies. So, there was an attitude of rejection toward these
people."

In 1987, for the first time (to my knowledge) Salvadoran officials sought
to prevent the deportation of Salvadorans living in the United States (see
also Rosenblum 2000). The 1986 Immigration Reform and Control Act
imposed sanctions on employers who hired undocumented immigrants,
thus leading some to conclude that these migrants would be unable to find
work and would have to return home.[12] In April 1987, Salvadoran president Duarte wrote to U.S. president Reagan asking him to grant EVD to
Salvadorans. As grounds for this request, Duarte cited " 'a severe economic
crisis' because of seven years of civil war and the [1986] earthquake that left
300,000 people homeless" (*San Francisco Chronicle* 1987a, 11). Duarte
wrote that a large-scale influx of Salvadoran émigrés "would reduce drasti-
cally the amount of money received by poor Salvadoran people in remittances from relatives who are now working in the United States. . . . My
government estimates that the total value of remittances is some place between $350 million to $600 million annually, and is thus larger than the
United States government's assistance to El Salvador" (*San Francisco Chronicle* 1987a, 11). Duarte also argued that returning exiles could contribute to
political instability in El Salvador (Fagen 1988).

The U.S. response to Duarte's request was mixed. The State Department
initially responded favorably, despite its long-standing opposition to Salvadoran activists' requests that Salvadorans be granted refuge and despite
its continued claim that Salvadorans could safely return home (*San Francisco Chronicle* 1987a, 11). The U.S. attorney general and some members of
the solidarity movement opposed Duarte's request, for different reasons.
The U.S. Department of Justice did not want to interpret immigration laws

"in a way that could result in a flood of millions of other economic refugees" (*San Francisco Chronicle* 1987b, 16), whereas activists in San Francisco feared that granting EVD on economic grounds would draw attention away from human rights abuses being committed in El Salvador (Garcia 1987). In the end, the U.S. government simply ignored Duarte's request (*San Francisco Chronicle* 1987b).

In 1990, the U.S. government changed its stance on both the Salvadoran civil war and the legal status of Salvadoran immigrants. In November 1989, the FMLN launched a "final offensive" designed to demonstrate its military strength and provoke a popular uprising. During the final offensive, six Jesuits at the Universidad Centroamericana were dragged from their rooms and murdered by members of a division of the Salvadoran armed forces. International condemnation of the Jesuits' murder was swift, and U.S. Congressman Joe Moakley, a longtime proponent of granting temporary refuge to Salvadoran immigrants, became involved in investigating the circumstances of this crime. Although no popular uprising occurred, the final offensive made it clear that the Salvadoran armed forces could not defeat the FMLN in the short term. With the collapse of the Soviet Union under way, the geopolitical significance of El Salvador to the United States decreased, and U.S. authorities became more willing to pursue a negotiated settlement to the conflict. At the same time, as previously discussed, the Department of Justice, which was revising its asylum proceedings, offered to settle the ABC lawsuit out of court, and the U.S. Congress passed the 1990 Immigration Act, which awarded Salvadorans eighteen months of TPS.

The 1992 peace accords were designed to create conditions in which all government institutions and former combatants would respect citizens' civil and human rights (Córdova Macías 1993). The guerrillas agreed to lay down their arms and were permitted to become a political party. The Salvadoran armed forces were to be purged of those responsible for human rights violations and were to act only against other nations, not Salvadoran citizens. Security forces (the National Guard and the Treasury Police) that had violated citizens' rights were abolished and were replaced by the PNC, 20 percent of whom were to be former guerrilla combatants. A Procuraduría de Derechos Humanos (PDH or Human Rights Ombudsry) was established to monitor the observance of human rights in the future. A truth commission was charged with investigating and reporting on human rights violations that occurred during the civil war. A national reconstruction plan was to be devised through consultation between government institutions, FMLN leaders, NGOs, and citizens (Popkin 2000; Sollis 1993).

The 1992 peace accords permitted a new consensus on the significance of expatriate Salvadorans to emerge.

Reconstruction

In the years following the civil war, Salvadoran migrants, the nation of El Salvador, and the relationship between migrants and their country of origin underwent reconstruction. The peace accords put an end to large-scale political violence and presumably made it possible for most Salvadoran émigrés who were in the United States to return safely to El Salvador. Some did return, and there were important repatriations of villages that had been displaced by the war (Edwards and Siebentritt 1991; Janzen 1994; Landolt 2003; Moss 1995). Many, however, chose to wait. The war had been devastating for the Salvadoran economy, which now had to absorb the former guerrilla fighters as well as decommissioned soldiers and members of the security forces. It was unclear whether the peace would last. Those who had been directly threatened or persecuted worried that their lives were still in danger. Some feared returning to sites of traumatic events. Migrants had also established lives in the United States, where many had children, jobs, and homes. Relatives in El Salvador described the continued difficulties in their home communities, and often needed financial assistance from Salvadorans living outside the country. Furthermore, migrants continued to leave El Salvador even after the peace accords were reached. According to a New York–based Salvadoran activist, "Actually, the large exodus of Salvadorans took place after the signing of the peace accords, when they saw the country impoverished, full of crime, traumas, and all the problems of the region."

In El Salvador, the years immediately following the civil war were devoted to implementing the peace accords. A former staff member of the PDH recalled, "Immediately after the peace accords, people didn't know what was going to happen. They didn't know whether the armed conflict could arise again, or whether they were entering a period of stability." Through a consultative process, the Salvadoran government developed the National Reconstruction Plan designed to reintegrate ex-combatants and severely affected civilians, improve conditions in the areas most affected by the war, rebuild damaged infrastructure, and involve all sectors in reconstruction (Sollis 1993, but note his criticisms of this plan's implementation). The Commission on the Truth for El Salvador, which was mandated by the peace accords, accepted denunciations of human rights abuses and produced a report that analyzed the violence and recommended reforms (Commission on the Truth for El Salvador 1993; Hayner 2001; Kaye 1997). The Salvadoran armed forces immediately denounced this report, and, within a week of the report's issuance, Salvadoran legislators approved an "amnesty" for those responsible for "political crimes" during the civil war (Kaye 1997). In 1992, the PDH was established in order to monitor the ongoing human rights situation (Montgomery 1995). In 1994, the FMLN, ARENA, and other political parties competed in the first postwar presidential election. During a runoff, the ARENA candidate, Armando Calderón Sol, defeated Rubén Zamora, the candidate supported by the Democratic Convergence and the FMLN (Byrne 1996; Montgomery 1995).

In the immediate postwar period, Salvadoran community groups in the United States sought both to secure legal status for Salvadoran immigrants and to support the process of reconstruction in El Salvador—initiatives that activists considered interconnected. Legal efforts focused on extending TPS beyond the eighteen-month expiration date. Activists argued that the situation in El Salvador was still unstable, that the potential for human rights violations and reprisals still existed, that the large-scale return of émigrés could destabilize the country, that émigrés should have been granted refugee status (which would have been permanent) all along, and that émigrés could provide greater assistance by working in the United States and sending money to relatives in El Salvador than by returning. As part of the TPS-extension efforts, Central American groups in the United States sent delegations to El Salvador, urging political leaders to make this issue a priority. A San Francisco–based activist who participated in one of the first such delegations recalled:

> With the end of the war . . . we were working at a national level on a campaign to extend TPS. And that's how we began to travel to El Salvador. We began the first efforts to develop a consciousness in Salvadoran society of the importance of the migration theme. I can say with great certainty that the work of Salvadoran organizations in the United States toward El Salvador contributed greatly to the migration theme being important at a general level, at the level of the communications media, at the level of society in general.

In the mid-1990s, Salvadoran officials' advocacy on behalf of migrants increased. In 1994, a monument to migrants was built in San Salvador "as a public recognition of the compatriots that with their support from abroad maintain the economy of the country" (Ábrego 2004). The monument, originally titled *Hermano Lejano* (Distant Brother), featured two large arches and was located in San Salvador along the highway from the airport. Presumably, returning (or visiting) migrants would be greeted by this monument as they entered the capital. In the mid-1990s, Ana Cristina Sol, the former Salvadoran ambassador to the United States, began to prioritize working with Salvadoran hometown associations in addition to more traditional diplomatic work (Calderón Sol 2002). Current embassy staff recalled that ex-ambassador Sol made frequent visits to Salvadoran communities in the Washington, D.C., area and opened an office dedicated to assisting hometown associations with fund-raising and donations to communities in El Salvador. In 1995, as the January 31, 1996, deadline for applying for asylum under the terms of the ABC settlement agreement approached, Salvadoran consular officials were quoted in the Spanish language press urging eligible Salvadorans to apply. Significantly, the very government that ABC class members were claiming had either violated or failed to protect their human rights was *advocating* that they seek asylum (see also Mahler 2000a).

In 1996, when IIRIRA dramatically changed U.S. immigration laws, the already growing interest in immigration issues exploded in El Salvador. Interviewees attributed this intensified concern to a variety of factors. One member of a proimmigrant NGO in El Salvador recalled that immigration reform in the United States "created an enormous fear that there would be massive deportation." A Salvadoran economic official stated that remittances emerged as an important economic alternative as, following the cessation of armed conflict, foreign assistance began to dry up. The shift from defining Salvadoran emigrants as refugees to defining them as immigrants also facilitated collaboration between immigrant rights advocates and Salvadoran authorities. A member of a proimmigrant Salvadoran NGO remarked in 2000, "The theme of migrants is . . . not conflictual, not polemic, it is accessible to discuss with any party in El Salvador. That is, you can sit down with ARENA as much as with the FMLN, and there is no problem bringing up the theme." Similarly, another advocate remarked, "The end of the war contributed to developing certain *acercamientos* [rapprochements] with the government in terms of identifying a theme independently of how they saw and how we saw the reasons for our departures."

As concern about the effects of IIRIRA grew, the scale and number of promigrant initiatives by Salvadoran officials and NGOs escalated dramatically (see also Rosenblum 2000). In 1997, as President Clinton prepared for a summit meeting with the Central American presidents, U.S.-based Central American community groups urged political leaders to advocate

Fig. 2. *Hermano Lejano* monument. Photograph by author.

immigration relief for Central Americans with pending immigration cases. Using language not unlike that adopted by the solidarity movement during the 1980s, Calderón Sol described his meeting with Clinton: "I spoke to President Clinton seriously and in the name of all of Central America, which had been torn apart in a war in which the United States had participated actively. Now it was time to alleviate the needs (*penurias*) of our fellow citizens, who for the most part emigrated because of the very same war" (2002, 111).[13] Clinton promised to try to ameliorate the effects of IIRIRA on Central Americans, and, according to interviewees in the Department of Justice, within two days the DOJ had drafted legislation restoring suspension rights to members of the ABC class and the Nicaraguan Review Program. My interviews with congressional staff members and U.S. officials indicated that the Salvadoran government played a strong role in advocating for the passage of NACARA. A Clinton White House aide stressed that "there was constant communication with the Salvadoran ambassador, and the Salvadoran foreign minister was in town"; while a Republican staffer commented that "the Salvadoran government has been key in getting immigration legislation passed—or in influencing executive actions." When NACARA was approved, the Salvadoran government promoted it by publishing and distributing a pamphlet describing the application process. Moreover, when Hurricane Mitch hit Central American in 1998, Salvadoran officials pressed for immigration relief, and U.S. officials pointed to the NACARA regulations, which granted ABC class members a presumption of hardship, as a partial response.[14]

In addition to pushing for the passage of NACARA, Salvadoran officials and community groups took other steps to prioritize immigration issues. In 1996 and 1997, Maria Victoria de Áviles, the human rights ombudsperson in El Salvador, took up the cause of migrants' rights, traveling to the United States to meet with Central American community groups in Los Angeles and San Francisco, and founding the Mesa Permanente sobre Migrantes y Población Desarraigada (Permanent Board on Migrants and Uprooted Population). Through these actions, a Salvadoran government human rights institution that grew out of the civil war directed its attention at the United States as a potential abuser of the rights of Salvadorans living abroad. A Salvadoran NGO member who was involved in this board recalled, "At that time, the priority was Salvadorans at risk of being deported from the United States. Much of the work of the ombudswoman at that time was visiting the United States [to meet] with congresspeople, senators, officials from different states there, to intercede and see what possibilities there were for applying the law [IIRIRA] in a less drastic fashion than had been announced." In 1997, at the ombudswoman's initiative, the Legislative Assembly of El Salvador declared the first week of September to be Semana del Migrante (Immigrant Week), an event that has been observed ever since. The Mesa Permanente developed into the Foro del Migrante (Migrant Forum), composed of twenty-seven groups, including government agencies (particularly from the Ministries of Foreign Affairs and the Interior), NGOs, and church groups.

The development of the Mesa Permanente and then of the Foro del Migrante marked a shift in the institutional focus of migration work in El Salvador. Previously, church groups, human rights organizations, the OIM (Organización Internacional para las Migraciones/International Organization for Migration), and UNHCR (United Nations High Commission for Refugees/Alto Comisionado de las Naciones Unidas por los Refugiados) had focused on the needs of refugees and displaced persons. The UNHCR eventually closed its El Salvador office on the grounds that there were no longer refugees or displaced persons there. According to a participant in the Foro del Migrante, UNHCR officials assumed that their work would be taken up, as needed, by the Procuraduría and by civil society. Cáritas (Catholic Charities) became the ongoing representative of theUNHCR in El Salvador. At the same time, in 1996 El Salvador joined other Latin American nations in forming the Regional Conference on Migration, also known as Proceso Puebla. Through Proceso Puebla, government officials from member countries meet annually (and remain in contact between meetings) to develop regional approaches to migration, such as mechanisms designed to prevent trafficking and to ensure migrants' safety. NGO members participate as observers (Cubías and Monzón 2005; Mahler 2000a). A Foro del Migrante member remarked concerning the initiation of this process:

In the case of El Salvador, there was a consensus that "refugees" and "displaced persons" were no longer the principal problem of El Salvador. Rather, one of the principal problems was in our country transit toward the United States. And also that we have one-fourth [of the population of El Salvador] there in the United States. And the flow of deportations that was already arriving, and the violation of rights.

One result of El Salvador's participation in Proceso Puebla was the Bienvenidos a Casa program.

Proimmigrant initiatives by Salvadoran officials gave rise to unprecedented collaboration between the Salvadoran government and U.S.-based Salvadoran community groups. Remarking on the fact that a Los

Angeles–based community organization had allowed Salvadoran consular officials to open a passport-renewal office on its premises, a Salvadoran activist who had been a guerrilla fighter during the civil war commented, "From the eighties and nineties, one never saw that [type of thing]. And it used to be said that the organizations, the community institutions were the consulates of the people because they responded more to the needs of the community. But today, from the nineties to the present, we are now changing this view—since the peace accords." Mistrust nonetheless remained. Some activists suggested that Salvadoran officials' work with Salvadorans in the United States could serve the interests of ARENA, particularly if Salvadorans living abroad were given the right to vote. Others criticized the "hermano lejano" imagery. A Salvadoran NGO member who had lived in the United States during the 1980s and early 1990s commented, "It's like saying, 'you over there are abandoned.' . . . So it's a name with which the Salvadoran community does not identify, a complete rejection."[15]

A revised vision of the role that Salvadorans in the exterior could play in the life of El Salvador was developed through a broad consultation with Salvadorans living within and outside of the country. During his presidency, Calderón Sol created the Comisión Nacional de Desarrollo (National Development Commission), which in 1998 sponsored a series of consultations with Salvadoran academics, professionals, and scientists on specific themes. The results of this consultation were published in a 432–page report, which was presented as an expression of the nation itself: "There could not be a bad or good, regular or deficient plan, but only the Plan of the Nation" (Comisión Nacional de Desarrollo 1999, iii). Two of the themes—"Sociedad sin fronteras" ("Society without Borders") and "Los salvadoreños y salvadoreñas en el exterior" ("Salvadoran Men and Women Living Abroad") spoke specifically to the relationship between emigrants and El Salvador. The plan's authors (who included Salvadorans living abroad) emphasized the need to "overcome the stereotype that identifies us [Salvadorans in the exterior] solely as 'money machines' " (333) and stressed the idea that Salvadorans living abroad had much more than money to offer El Salvador. Statements such as "the Salvadoran emigrant professional, trained in the exterior, can . . . share his advanced or specialized knowledge" (343) depict the "exterior" as a place where Salvadorans progress and acquire new capabilities. The emphasis on Salvadoran émigrés' desire to contribute to national development promotes a sort of transnational nationalism (see also Baker-Cristales 2004). That is, the nation is deemed to transcend borders, but is still a key source of identity and object of devotion. For example, the authors assert that "living outside of our national borders (*fronteras patrias*) does not make us foreigners, that is to say, it is a reality that tends to strengthen our national identity" (336). Urging the Salvadoran state "to take the Salvadoran community in the exterior into account as a key partner (*socio*)" (351), the plan's authors argue that emigrants can promote national development by sharing their expertise, purchasing Salvadoran products, investing in Salvadoran businesses, and engaging in tourism. All of these initiatives, they suggest, require action on the part of the state.

This revised vision of the relationship between Salvadoran émigrés and El Salvador was consistent with new strategies to make El Salvador more competitive in the global market. According to literature from the Banco Interamericano de Desarrollo (BID), such programs promote high-quality goods and services, modernize infrastructure, integrate regions, support innovation, strengthen networks, identify particular national and regional advantages, and rely on public-private collaboration (BID 2001, 2002a, 2002b, 2003). In 1996, through loans from the World Bank, BID, and other international financial institutions, El Salvador launched the Programa Nacional de Competetividad El Salvador 2021 (National El Salvador Competitiveness Program 2021). An official who worked in this program explained: "Over the course of twenty years, if we follow this prescription, this formula, we will create bases such that El Salvador can create its own development. . . . One has to work in many sectors—improve the business climate, make structural adjustments, work on themes such as consumer protection, improve record keeping, work on quality and productivity." Salvadorans living abroad were identified as a competitive advantage, as one official explained, "because few countries, with the exception of Mexico, that logically, due to its territorial border, has this advantage and has thirty million Mexicans in the United States. Well, El Salvador has one-fourth of its population living in the United States, and strategically located on both coasts." To develop this competitive advantage, Salvadoran officials launched a "clusters" program designed to link Salvadoran businesspeople in a particular region of the United States with businesspeople in El Salvador. These clusters could then facilitate investment in Salvadoran businesses and create a new "ethnic market" for the export of Salvadoran goods, in the words of Calderón Sol (2002, 115). Revisions to Salvadoran law permitted any Salvadoran who had lived outside of El Salvador for at least one year to enjoy the legal advantages afforded to Salvadoran investors.[16] Further, a special "hermano lejano" credit line helped expatriate Salvadorans purchase real estate.

The cultivation of émigrés' Salvadoran identity was key to the success of such programs, as a Salvadoran official noted: "Really, what we are selling to the Salvadoran who lives in the United States is nostalgia." In addition to business exchanges, officials hoped to promote the transfer of expertise from Salvadoran émigrés to Salvadorans in El Salvador. As one official remarked, "By now, we have a second and even a third generation of Salvadorans born there, who are already professionals or technicians, but who still feel and think like Salvadorans, and they want to support their country. And they can show us how to do things better."

Such revised thinking about the significance of the Salvadoran emigrant community laid the basis for institutional change in the 2000s.

Emigrant Citizenship

Government and other initiatives designed to more fully recognize Salvadoran émigrés' involvement in Salvadoran life reclaimed emigrant citizens as kin ("hermanos"), connected to El Salvador by birth, blood, culture, and love of country. The minister of foreign affairs characterized Salvadorans living abroad as people who "long to remember their customs, see images of their people, transmit their culture to the children that have been born to them in the United States, in short, they want to remain connected to El Salvador" (Brizuela de Ávila 2003). The notion that such connections could be solidified through, among other things, service to and sacrifice for country was linked to the efforts to increase El Salvador's competitiveness in the global market. Emigrants' potential as a market for Salvadoran exports, investors in Salvadoran businesses, and sources of expertise would only be realized if Salvadoran emigrants continued to identify closely with El Salvador.

As they sought to strengthen their ties to Salvadorans living abroad, government officials reconceptualized the Salvadoran populace as transnational, a reconceptualization that was accompanied by institutional changes. During the 1999–2004 term of Salvadoran president Francisco Flores, Vice President Carlos Quintanilla Schmidt took responsibility for ensuring that all government ministries in some way addressed the needs of Salvadoran émigrés. At a public speech in Los Angeles in 2002, the vice president described these changes:

> A few months into our administration, I called a meeting of . . . the ministers of education, health, agriculture, tourism, culture, [and so forth]. I told them, "Every one of you can think of some project that you can develop in

favor of the communities of Salvadorans who live abroad." And some of them said to me, "Look, but if we don't have any relationship with the Salvadorans who live abroad?" I told them, "Well, look for one."

To facilitate these projects, in October 1999 the DGACE was founded within the Ministry of Foreign Affairs. Modeled after similar programs in Mexico, the DGACE was designed to support and coordinate the work of the other government ministries. According to the director of this new office:

> We identified three great needs: One, economic, in relation to businesses. It is possible to develop business opportunities, investments, publicity, and products by working with the community in the exterior. Two, culture and education. . . . Our goal was to create cultural encounters, to identify the talents of Salvadorans in the exterior. Three, community affairs. There are many associations of Salvadorans who work with their hometowns. . . . But we needed to work with them. There was a lack of information and coordination within their work. And follow-up was needed. It would be good to put these associations in touch with state institutions.

The DGACE's activities emphasized the transnational nature of Salvadoran society. For example, to meet the needs of Salvadorans living abroad, the DGACE developed an extensive website featuring guides (e.g., to U.S. immigration programs, to securing tax-exempt status for goods being imported into El Salvador as donations), explanations of the DGACE's mission, an online magazine, descriptions of Salvadoran emigrant communities throughout the world, a virtual stand of Salvadoran products, a database of Salvadoran emigrants with particular areas of expertise, and announcements about hometown associations' activities. Interestingly, one document—a table enumerating distribution of the Salvadorans in various parts of the world—was almost the inversion of U.S. immigration authorities' tables of the sources of immigration to the United States. Both of these tables divide the world into regions. The Salvadoran table enumerates the Salvadoran population in particular cities, countries, and regions, including North America, Central America and the Caribbean, South America, Europe, Asia, Africa, and Oceania. In some cases, tiny numbers of emigrants— for instance, 316 in the Palestinian Authority, 80 in Israel, 19 in Jordan, and 4 in Egypt—permit entire regions to appear.[17] The Salvadoran table seems to emphasize the global nature of the Salvadoran population. In contrast, the U.S. table lists the numbers of immigrants *to* the United States from countries and world regions, and thus seems to indicate that people "from everywhere" have immigrated to the United States.[18] Together, these tables suggest that the United States and El Salvador are nations of emigrants.

In addition to the DGACE and government ministries, other government offices had responsibilities to Salvadorans living abroad. Within the Ministry of Foreign Affairs, the Dirección de Servicio a la Comunidad (Directorate of Service to the Community) provided such services as helping locate documents, including police records or birth certificates. The Unidad Social (Social Unit) participated in regional government conferences on immigration and addressed the needs of migrants in transit. The Bienvenidos a Casa program, which received support from the Salvadoran government as well as from NGOs, provided assistance to Salvadoran deportees. And of course, the Salvadoran consulates and embassies attended to Salvadorans in the exterior by providing traditional consular services, assisting community associations with donations and projects, and publicizing information about U.S. immigration programs (particularly TPS and NACARA). One embassy official described her work as "diplomacia a pie" (diplomacy on foot). "Other embassy staff may spend their time at receptions with a glass of wine in their hands, but we [Salvadoran embassy staff] are at festivals, with *horchata* [a Salvadoran beverage] in one hand and a *pupusa* [a thick tortilla commonly filled with cheese or beans] in the other."

Salvadoran officials also sought to maximize the productivity of emigrants' donations to El Salvador. In 2002, officials launched a program called Unidos por la Solidaridad (United in Solidarity). This program sponsored regular competitions through which Salvadoran hometown associations could seek national and municipal matching funds for development projects in their communities of origin. According to a video that was played in Los Angeles when an agreement between local winners of this competition and the Salvadoran government was signed, "the government has been developing programs that facilitate the participation of communities, small and large businesses, churches, communities, and other entities with the goal of combating poverty together. We only had not yet involved you, Salvadoran brothers who live in the exterior." As projects are designed and carried out by hometown associations, this matching fund program is consistent with projects that privatize social welfare activities, promote enterprise, and rely on practical expertise. As O'Malley (2000, 479–80) notes, within "current discourses of neo-liberal business enterprise . . . expertises appear as grounded . . . in the practical forms of indigenous governance that are imagined by these writers as the hallmark of the entrepreneur. . . . Government should not interfere with these autonomous 'indigenous governances' for it cannot achieve its ends without their operation." Such emphasis on "practical knowledge" and "indigenous governance" may also appeal to those who, whether or not they favor neoliberal economic policies, seek to empower grassroots organizations. Interviews with NGO members in Los Angeles and El Salvador indicated that there was widespread support for the idea that the government should contribute to hometown associations' development projects.

Institutional change and economic initiatives were also linked to continued governmental efforts to secure what the 2004–9 Salvadoran president, Elías Antonio ("Tony") Saca González, referred to as "estabilidad migratoria" (migratory stability) for Salvadorans living abroad.[19] Officials characterized legal status as central to émigrés' well-being and therefore an important government priority, and as central to the continued flow of remittances. After NACARA was approved, Salvadoran officials pressured the Clinton administration to minimize disparity in the treatment of Central Americans. Following the January and February 2001 Salvadoran earthquakes, Salvadoran officials (at the instigation of community groups, some activists argued) sought and obtained a new TPS for Salvadorans. Through pamphlets, festivals, a hotline, and legal advice at the Salvadoran consulates, officials promoted NACARA, TPS, and, when TPS was extended beyond its initial expiration date, reregistration for TPS. With pride, an embassy official told me, "It's no accident that there are three hundred thousand Salvadorans registered for TPS and that when the time came for them to reapply, three hundred thousand Salvadorans reapplied." In addition to supporting NACARA and TPS, embassy officials told me, the Salvadoran government was promoting both an ongoing legalization or guest worker program and the Central American Security Act (CASA), another version of parity legislation.

Some insight into the importance that Salvadoran officials' placed on TPS, as well as into at least some U.S. officials' rationales for granting temporary status, is provided by controversies that arose during the 2004 Salvadoran presidential campaign. Tony Saca, the ARENA candidate, pledged that he would make extending TPS—which was then scheduled to expire in March 2005—a high priority if elected (Weiner 2004). Certain U.S. officials stated publicly that if Saca's opponent, FMLN candidate and former guerrilla commander Shafik Handal, were elected, then the U.S. government should reconsider the immigration programs that permitted Salvadorans to obtain work authorization and thus to send remittances to family members.

Speaking on the floor of the U.S. House of Representatives, Congressman Tom Tancredo (R-CO) said:

> Under an FMLN Presidency, the United States government would have no reliable counterpart to satisfy legitimate national security concerns. . . . Therefore, if the FMLN takes control of the government in El Salvador, it may be necessary for the United States authorities to examine closely and possibly apply special controls to the flow of $2 billion in remittances from the United States to El Salvador. (*Congressional Record* 2004, E389).

Salvadoran community organizations, as well as other U.S. officials, quickly denounced these comments and argued that remitting was a private matter, controlled by the individuals involved, and not a product of U.S. policy (Soriano 2004). This debate, which some consider a key factor in ARENA's victory (Boudreaux 2004), is nonetheless an indication of the geopolitical significance of El Salvador to the United States, the continued influence of cold war politics in immigration matters, and the importance of the Salvadoran emigrant community to El Salvador. In July 2004, only one month after assuming office, President Saca traveled to Washington, D.C., to request an extension of TPS.[20]

Increased governmental collaboration with Salvadoran émigrés and emigrant organizations was accompanied by shifts in rhetoric regarding the civil war and the causes of emigration. State officials sought to put the war in the past, and thus improve the public image of El Salvador.[21] During a public speech at a Central American community organization in Los Angeles in 2002, a high-level Salvadoran official characterized the 1980s as "part of a memory. And it is part of a history that, while it is a sad history, is what should make us not look toward the past but rather look toward the story of the future that we have in front of us." Instead of emphasizing the divisiveness of the war, officials such as this speaker depicted the war as a source of commonality: "We suffered through the war as every one of you suffered through it." Consistent with this changed rhetoric, activists who were involved in the solidarity movement and officials affiliated with the ARENA party now attribute emigration to both political and economic motives. For example, during a 2001 interview, one Salvadoran activist commented: "At the beginning of the '80s, many people abandoned their country simply due to the catastrophic situation [which was] as much economic as political. . . . Everyone was in danger or at risk of becoming one more victim of the war. . . . Many left simply due to fear that something would happen to them, or others also left to look for better work opportunities." Similarly,

during a public speech in San Salvador in 2001, a high-level Salvadoran official attributed emigration to "the search for better opportunities to grow
and progress, . . . the danger that many of us felt due to the circumstances
of the war, . . . [and] the adventurous spirit of Salvadorans." Citing a group
made up at least in part of Salvadorans who had been active in the solidarity movement, one Salvadoran official took pride in the degree to which
Salvadorans in the United States had formed organizations: "It is interesting that even though Salvadorans have only been in the United States for a
short time, there are already networks at the national level. There are high
levels of organization. Maybe this is due to the war."

Increased attention to Salvadorans living abroad was also linked to reassessments of Salvadoran identity. Officials, NGO members, scholars, and
others frequently characterized Salvadorans living abroad as "more Salvadoran" than Salvadorans living in El Salvador. For example, at a conference in San Salvador, Salvadoran vice president Quintanilla Schmidt
remarked that "we can probably say that . . . those who have had to leave feel
much more united to this land that saw their birth than those of us who live
in it." At the same conference, a Salvadoran scholar commented, "In foreign
lands, that is when the Salvadoran most feels the need to identify himself,
and that is where he dreams of his country. In most cases, distance makes
identity stronger." These comments echo Edward Everett Hale's famous
story of the "Man without a Country," who, forbidden to set foot on U.S.
soil, surrounded himself with American flags and other patriotic symbols
(Hale 1917). The notion that Salvadoran emigrants have the strongest cultural identities is also reminiscent of the idea that naturalized U.S. citizens,
who cannot take citizenship for granted, are the "real" Americans
(Coutin 2003). In the case of both Salvadoran émigrés and naturalized
Americans, these assertions of authenticity may consciously or uncon-
sciously counter the notion that these citizens' grounds for belonging are
questionable. The claim that Salvadorans living abroad feel more Salvadoran may also be linked to fears that Salvadoran society is being destroyed by
transculturation and the desire to emigrate. One Salvadoran NGO member
commented, "Salvadorans who live here [in El Salvador] try to seem more
like people [who live] or they want to live like in the United States." The notion that émigrés have the strongest cultural identities may be proscriptive
as well as descriptive. That is, without negating the intense nostalgia, longing, patriotism, and sense of connection that many émigrés feel, it also
seems clear that many people are telling them that they are *supposed* to feel
this way (Baker-Cristales 2004).

Reassessments of cultural identity also redefine spaces and presence.

Interviewees repeatedly stressed that territory no longer fully bounded the nation of El Salvador. As Salvadoran vice president Quintanilla Schmidt told a group of U.S. academics in 2002, "El Salvador is no longer only El Salvador with the six and one-half million inhabitants who live in Central America. Today, El Salvador is wherever there is a Salvadoran." Similarly, an economic official told me that she had come to envision El Salvador more as a nation than as a country: "Our borders are no longer sufficient for us. . . . We are one nation no matter where we are." This concept of nationhood relies on kinship, as shown by the comment of a Salvadoran attorney interviewed in El Salvador: "I am proud of Salvadoran workers and their families who are abroad. Not necessarily because they are practically maintaining the economy of this country . . . but rather because they are part of our blood. Because they are part of our history. Because they are part of our cultural identity." Such references to blood, identity, and brotherhood domesticate the expatriate population and thus the spaces that they occupy. Like offspring, émigrés are depicted as being linked to their parent nation through ties of love, kinship, and sacrifice. Émigrés have unofficially become Departamento 15—the fifteenth department of El Salvador— which is now the name of a regular section of the Salvadoran newspaper *La Prensa Gráfica* (see http://www.laprensagrafica.com/dpt15/). Despite being geographically distant, émigrés are hailed as present in El Salvador. Speaking via a video shown at the signing ceremony awarding matching funds to Los Angeles–based hometown associations, a Salvadoran official stated, "Although it's true that there are many miles of distance between the United States and El Salvador, it is also true that your presence is felt. I, personally, have felt your presence through the projects that you realize." In a 2000 speech, Salvadoran vice president Quintanilla Schmidt argued that the Flores administration had "opened the door so that you can enter your country. . . . When we began the administration of President Flores, Salvadorans were only seen as synonymous with dollars. . . . Today, you are respected and recognized in El Salvador." One of the first acts of the 2004–9 Saca administration was to create a vice ministry of Attention to "Hermanos en el Exterior" (Viceministerio de Relaciones Exteriores para los Salvadoreños en el Exterior). Notably, these emigrants are now referred to as "hermanos cercanos" (nearby brothers) instead of as "hermanos lejanos."[22] These comments suggest that emigrants can return to El Salvador through social involvement and recognition, even when they do not move back to El Salvador.

Despite the widespread emphasis on émigrés' strong cultural identity, some interviewees suggested that, in the exterior, Salvadorans' identities were threatened. A Salvadoran journalist pointed out that the émigré dream of returning to El Salvador was a bit utopian: "Utopian in the sense that when the time comes to put their feet on the ground, they say, 'Why am I going to go back to El Salvador? So that they kill me, they kidnap me, they assault me, to live in poverty again, when here I have a house and a car?' " Other interviewees pointed out that the circumstances under which Salvadorans left the country could create a feeling of alienation. One Salvadoran official who worked with Salvadorans in the United States commented, "Even though he [a Salvadoran] may long for his country, he also feels a certain rejection toward the country or the government because he thinks that 'if I had to leave here it was not because I wanted to but rather because I could not be in El Salvador. Whether for political reasons, because they were going to kill me, or because in my town there was nothing to do and I was dying of hunger.' " The second and third generation of migrants was believed to be particularly at risk of losing their identities. A San Francisco–based activist observed, "There are many in our community who . . . feel like they are from here, like from the United States, especially the young community, all those children who came when they were less than ten years old, who speak almost perfect English, who really remember little of the war. They know absolutely nothing about what El Salvador is. If they go there, they will be strangers." To inculcate Salvadoran roots, officials were exploring the idea of creating culture camps through which emigrant youth could tour the country, learn about Salvadoran history, study Spanish, and visit archaeological sites. Community organizations were also developing exchanges or retreats that would bring Salvadoran youth to El Salvador.

The recognition of Salvadoran émigrés as members of the Salvadoran nation has not yet led to full political enfranchisement. To vote in Salvadoran elections, citizens must be physically present in El Salvador. Although emigrants can vote if they return to El Salvador for an election and if their documents are in order, there is no procedure that would allow them to submit ballots from the United States or elsewhere in the world. Arguments in favor of permitting Salvadorans to vote abroad focus on constitutional rights, the economic contributions that Salvadorans are making to El Salvador, and democratization. As one Los Angeles–based Salvadoran activist pointed out, "The constitution of El Salvador gives the right to vote to all Salvadorans. . . . It doesn't say 'only the Salvadorans who live in El Salvador.' " Similarly, a member of a Salvadoran NGO that advocates for voting rights noted the contradiction between expecting assistance from emigrants but not granting them such rights. Finally, some argued that, by living in the United States or elsewhere, émigrés had acquired democratic experience that would enable them to demand accountability and transparency from Salvadoran politicians. Those who opposed voting abroad stressed that reforming the internal voting system was a higher priority, that those who lived outside of the country should not be setting policies that primarily affected those who lived in the country, and that it was very complicated to determine who would be able to vote, how, and for which offices. Not all Salvadorans living abroad wanted voting rights. One activist, whose organization promotes civic involvement in the United States, commented, "The people who have the most right to decide the destiny of [the people in El Salvador] are those who are there. We [Salvadorans in the United States] are already here, and we should worry more about incorporating ourselves into the political system of this country. And through our political empowerment, contributing to internal changes in El Salvador." It seems, however, that voting in the exterior may eventually come about, as Salvadoran officials have begun to issue the Documento Unico de Identidad (DUI or Unique Identity Document) in the United States, a step that would probably be necessary if voting rights were to be extended to those living abroad. The debate over voting rights nevertheless provides some indication of the current limitations on the degree to which Salvadorans in the exterior are part of political life of El Salvador.

Transnational Nationalism

Salvadorans who, during the civil war, were deliberately or otherwise pushed out of El Salvador by political violence and economic problems have come to have tremendous significance to El Salvador. During the 1980s, emigrants were seen as a somewhat suspect population that included individuals who had ties to the guerrillas and who therefore served international Marxism rather than national interests. By the 1990s and 2000s, emigrants had been redefined as heroes who sacrificed for the nation of El Salvador. Institutional changes within the Salvadoran state and terms such as "hermanos cercanos" recognized émigrés as de facto residents, despite their geographic distance. De facto residence in El Salvador is the counterpart of de facto "citizenship" in the United States. Significantly, de facto residency has been construed as domestic or quasi familial, based on blood, culture, and sacrifice, rather than on complete political enfranchisement. Recognizing de facto residence has changed the significance of territory. During the 1980s, suspect populations were excluded from areas of guerrilla control and, in some cases, from the national territory itself. Now, through attention to the community in the exterior and through the idea that "El Salvador is wherever there is a Salvadoran," "territory" is extended to émigrés. Territorial "extension," however, is limited by the fact that it is precisely émigrés' location *in the exterior* that makes them so valuable for El Salvador. Because they are outside of the country, émigrés can transfer goods, remittances, and know-how to El Salvador. In contrast to the 1980s, when the "international" (as in "international Marxism") was seen as potentially dangerous, during the 2000s access to the international and the global is considered key to El Salvador's economic future. Given new development thinking that privileges microenterprises, even international financial institutions have become interested in the role émigrés (as part of business "clusters") can play in enhancing El Salvador's competitiveness. Despite this interest in the transnational and the global, the success of these economic programs depends in part on promoting émigrés' identity as Salvadorans. And one way that the Salvadoran state has reclaimed Salvadoran citizens has been by advocating for their right to be temporary or permanent legal residents of the United States.

Becoming an emigrant citizen often requires making an arduous journey to the United States. Thus, although the relationships that are being forged between emigrants and the Salvadoran state in many ways defy traditional notions of state, territory, and citizenship, when Salvadorans attempt to migrate without authorization, these categories become all too real.

CHAPTER 4

En el Camino (En Route)

If they say it's a crime for us to travel to the United States without papers, then why don't they give us papers?

Question posed by an adolescent girl following a panel presentation
on immigration in Santiago de María, El Salvador, in 2004

Salvadorans who migrate to the United States without authorization
must erase their departure, journey, and presence, even as they leave, travel,
and, with luck, arrive. Such erasures plunge emigrants into a clandestine
realm that is nevertheless a visible (and even acknowledged or necessary)
dimension of social reality. Of course, many Salvadorans—an average of
twenty-seven thousand annually between 2000 and 2005 (U.S. Department
of Homeland Security, Office of Immigration Statistics 2006)—migrate to
the United States *legally*, and this number is likely to grow as more Salvadorans acquire legal permanent residency, and thus the ability to petition for
family members. A Salvadoran official interviewed for this book nonetheless estimated that as recently as 2001, 70 percent of those who emigrated
did so without authorization. Unauthorized migrants become clandestine
in that they hire alien-smugglers and travel outside of authorized paths, for
instance, through undeveloped deserts and mountains, alongside rather
than on roadways, in boats instead of by land, and on top of rather than
within trains. Some use false identity documents, which enable them to
pass through border checkpoints, but as someone other than themselves.
Portions of emigrants' journeys may be mundane, for instance, traveling by
bus from El Salvador to Guatemala, or flying to Mexico City. Their unauthorized status—or their intended destination—nonetheless makes them
vulnerable to authorities, who can detain them, demand bribes, or commit

abuses. The routes that emigrants traverse are *known*, to some degree. Authorities, smugglers, thieves, and certain vendors know where emigrants congregate, and in fact such sites are produced through both the prohibitions that make certain migrants' travel illegal and the desires (e.g., employers' desires for cheap labor) that incite their movements. The *fact* of unauthorized movement is acknowledged through international financial reports that calculate the remittances that emigrants, whether authorized or not, send to family members; through policies that permit certain authorized residents to legalize; and through state recognition of diasporic citizenries. Despite the ways that unauthorized movement has become key to certain economic and political processes, the erasures that illegal migration entails are potentially violent in nature. Human yet a good to be smuggled, illegal yet juridical persons, clandestine yet present, migrants are sometimes literally *dismembered*, their legs detached by trains, their lives separated from those of their relatives, their identity removed from their selves.

The erasure of presence makes the trajectory of unauthorized migrants' movements unclear. Their departures are sometimes furtive or mysterious, and may be disguised by relatives who remain behind as nothing more than temporary absences. While they are en route, migrants disappear. Anxious relatives may have to simply wait for news; authorities who encounter migrants may not be able to identify them accurately; and migrants may remove themselves from locations where they would be most visible. Their destinations are made unclear by policies that forbid their arrival. It is not clear whether they will reach the United States (in the case at hand), be deported to El Salvador, remain in Mexico or Guatemala for a lengthy period, or even die while on their journey. If unauthorized migrants successfully cross the U.S.-Mexico border, they still remain, in certain senses, outside of the United States. As "Intérlopers," unauthorized migrants are not allowed to "complete" their journeys by acquiring U.S. identity documents, securing work authorization, and being recognized as members of the U.S. polity for the indefinite future. For instance, the brief reversal in 2003 of California's policy, adopted in 1993, of denying driver's licenses to undocumented immigrants provoked considerable outcry and became a factor in the 2003 recall of Governor Gray Davis (see Cable News Network 2003). The clandestine sphere in which unauthorized migrants are located *removes* these migrants from the ground on which movements can occur. (Indeed, they are deemed to be "underground.") Thus, although unauthorized migrants traverse many miles, undergo painful separations from family members, and live outside of their countries of origin for years, there is also a sense in which they are doing something *other than* departing, traveling, and arriving; in short, *other than* (officially) migrating.

One of the things that lends a certain fixity to unauthorized migrants, despite their considerable movement through geographic space, is the law. Unauthorized migrants travel without the cover of a temporary legal personae in their intended destination. Legally, therefore, they remain in their countries of origin, even as they physically depart from their national territory. Though they are en route to rather than from the United States, unauthorized migrants are not unlike the deportees described in chapter 1. Legality is erased from unauthorized migrants' bodies, creating "illegal aliens," beings who *displace* legal space within the jurisdictions that they are presumed to "invade."[1] Law thus puts boundaries around unauthorized migrants' bodies, enabling them to simultaneously embody both law (juridical personhood) and illegality. Migrants can live in this multidimensional state indefinitely, legally absent but physically and socially present, clandestine yet "there," foreign yet incorporated, prohibited yet perhaps increasingly acknowledged. Like the dismemberment that some migrants experience when traveling, this state of legal irresolution violates persons, preventing them from being "made whole" and subjecting them to particular rejections and denials, including legal disenfranchisement in their countries of origin. Legal "resolution"—for example, deportation—can also be violent, of course. Perhaps the way to overcome this violence is not through resolution at all, but rather through making it clear that *nations*, as well as emigrants, are "en route" along the very paths that the undocumented travel. Such expanded understandings of *irresolution* could potentially transform prohibited paths that are currently marked by concealment, crime, and death.

Multidimensionality

Because unauthorized migration is illegal, those who attempt to enter a country where they lack legal status become clandestine. Unauthorized migrants must extract themselves from their homes and families, hide from authorities, expose themselves to crime and the elements, and commit prohibited acts. While doing so, they may be able to pose as authorized travelers, tourists, people who have business in a particular area, or even legal residents who are not really travelers at all. At other moments, though, unauthorized migrants may be positioned as fugitives who cannot hide the illicit nature of their journey and who therefore must simply evade authorities.

When migrants act by appearing *not* to act, or by attempting to erase their actions, they enter a hidden dimension of social reality. They travel alongside those who are recognized as legitimate, or they even travel legally, hiding their true destinations. Their presence transforms the places through which they travel, making territories "countries of transit," train yards gathering places for the unauthorized, and canyons places of unmarked death. When they enter such clandestine places, the unauthorized become, in a sense, stateless or extrastatal, lacking recourse to either their country of citizenship or presence. Yet, the clandestine, though real, is also not always particularly clandestine. Potential illegalities are presupposed by the laws that prohibit illegal entry, the officials who enforce borders, and the entities that profit from illegal migration. Legality and illegality are intertwined, but locating the prohibited in clandestine spaces obscures such interconnections and thus allows the "aboveboard" to assume its unremarked status as the dominant account of social reality.[2]

My understanding of the clandestine spaces occupied by the unauthorized is based largely on interviews with immigrant-rights advocates and with NACARA applicants whom I met through NGOs in Los Angeles and San Salvador. Interviews with advocates usually took place at advocates' offices, while interviews with NACARA applicants and other migrants associated with NGOs occurred at a place of their choosing, such as a restaurant or their homes. NACARA applicants were interviewed in Los Angeles, advocates in both Los Angeles and San Salvador, depending on the location of their organization. Most of the NACARA applicants interviewed still had pending immigration cases.

According to interviewees, unauthorized migration is preceded by a flurry of illicit and quasi-illicit negotiations. For instance, unauthorized migrants' trips are often financed through a series of loans. Relatives in the United States "send for" migrants by giving them money for their trip, and migrants may also sell property or borrow money locally. Often these loans—which do not occur through official channels—must be repaid after a migrant reaches his or her destination. For example, it took Miguel López Herrera six months working in the garment industry at $4.25 an hour to repay his friend the $750 he had borrowed to migrate. If the trip is unsuccessful, these expenses can be overwhelming. Loans are often used to pay for alien-smuggling, which, though it is illegal, is governed by what might be termed standard business practices. For instance, there are standard fees for particular services (in 2004, I was told, it cost $5,000 to $7,000 to be "guided" from El Salvador to the United States), it is common to offer up to three attempts at entry for the same fee, and it is standard practice for clients to pay half of the fee up front and half on arrival. *Coyotes* (alien-smugglers) acquire their clients through word of mouth, and some even advertise in the newspaper.[3] Such standard practices do not mean that coyotes treat their clients well.[4] On the contrary, coyotes have been known to rape clients (some suggest that this is part of the "price" that coyotes charge), hold clients hostage in hopes of extracting more money from clients' relatives, abandon clients, force clients to carry illicit goods, and otherwise endanger clients' lives. Immigrant-rights activists sometimes caution would-be migrants about coyotes' tactics. An advocate in San Salvador pointed out that "no coyote offers this service, telling them of the risks that it [unauthorized migration] brings." An advocate in Tijuana warned two women whose smuggler had abandoned them in a locked car trunk: "That's a lot of money that you spent, and you should get better service for your money. Don't go with someone who is going to tell you to get in the trunk of a car. Find an easier way." These advocates' use of the term "service" draws attention to the seeming normalcy of the illicit.

Unauthorized migrants may become clandestine while they are still in their country of origin, as an immigrant rights' advocate in San Salvador explained: "From the moment that this guy [a would-be migrant] speaks with the coyote, he is immersed in a world of clandestinity. Why? Because the coyote doesn't go around publicly offering his services. And the guy has to do it in a hidden fashion because one goes, generally, without any documents, right? So they live this problem of clandestinity throughout their travels." Although it is not illegal for a Salvadoran to travel within El Salvador, unauthorized migrants' departures are said to be shrouded in mystery. The immigrant rights' advocate quoted above described a "typical" departure:

> Generally, when the young men leave their communities, they leave in the middle of the night, in the early morning. They disguise what they are doing, they don't tell anyone. Even the very same family, one arrives and asks, "Hey, and where's Pedro?" "Oh, he's working." "When can I speak to him?" "Well, I don't know when he's going to come." At last, they manage [to say], "No, actually Pedro already left for the north." See, the very same family participates in the mystery of the guy's trip.

Despite their mysterious nature, such departures are common. During an August 2000 interview, an editor of *La Prensa Gráfica*, one of the two major newspapers in El Salvador, reported, "We did an investigation here in December, a survey, in which one out of every three Salvadoran people said that they were looking for some way to leave here." The strength of this desire to emigrate belies the danger and illegality of unauthorized migration.

Unauthorized migration locates migrants *outside* of established or authorized routes. Migrants travel across rough terrains rather than on roads, through sewer pipes or underground tunnels, and hidden in compartments that are usually used for cargo. Miguel López Herrera, who left El Salvador in 1990 at age twenty, had many of these experiences. After making his way to Tijuana by bus, he arrived at the U.S.-Mexico border:

> That day, we decided to cross at like one in the morning, taking advantage of the darkness. And well there you go blindly, because you stumble on rocks, in water, on branches, but you can't see. So it is more the desperation of wanting [to be on] the other side that [makes this] not matter, right? So we had to cross like where there were houses, always running.
>
> Once we arrived at the edge of the freeway . . . I think it is San Diego, there we had to be on the edge, where the rainwater passes through. For like three hours. Then a van appeared, right? So into the van went a quantity of people that you can't imagine, thirty, thirty-five people in a minivan, there you had to fit any which way, right? So you get in, that time we got in, and they had taken us to like an abandoned place, like a hillside. There we spent like eight hours waiting for them to decide when it would be good to pass through, because we were going to pass through San Clemente.
>
> And from there we once again got into the van and we crossed through San Clemente, but before we arrived, *la migra* [Immigration] is there. On the freeway, on the 5, where they have lots of equipment, and they are in the middle of the freeway and everything. We were about a mile away, and *la migra* hadn't left. So it was at that moment that you realize that the vehicle that you are going in is stolen. That is, part of the crime of having crossed the border is that you take the risk of traveling in a stolen car. And those who were driving the van among themselves said that if they [Immigration] didn't leave, they would have to leave the van here in the freeway and open the doors, and everyone would have to go wherever they could. But then one thanks God, because we were almost there when suddenly they left and gave us free passage.

Carmen Nieto, who traveled to the United States from Honduras in 1989, when she was in her mid-thirties, had similar experiences. Carmen traveled part of the way with a coyote, but when she ran out of money, continued on her own. She recounted:

The trip was very hard (*duro*). I had no money, and on the way, I owed money to the people who were bringing me. At one point, they suggested that I do the thing that involves women, at a hotel, in order to pay off my debt. But my sister answered, and she sent money, and I was able to pay them and continue.

I was with a group and with a coyote, but when our money ran out, the coyote left us. We were in southern Mexico, in Tecún Umán. Only a cousin and I made it. We took the cargo trains and made our way to the border. We were at the border with Texas. And I have to say that God helped me during my trip, because there, we were picked up by a church, a church that helps migrants. It was in Mexico. And the priest was very helpful. I told them that I wanted to cross the border into the United States. And I met a man who also wanted to cross. He helped me find an inner tube. That is, a life preserver.

And we took the inner tube and we went very early in the morning and crossed the river. [It was not scary] because it was so early in the morning. But what *was* scary was when we crossed the border. There were cars coming this way and that way, and we had to jump to get across the highway. . . . I was afraid that Immigration would catch us. Because when we crossed the river, it was very early in the morning. But by the time we got to the border (*línea*), it was later. We were worried that Immigration would spot us and that we would be caught. After crossing, we caught a taxi. We still had some money left from what my sister had sent. And I think that we took the taxi to a bus station. I can't remember exactly where we went even. But the bus took us all the way to Los Angeles, *gracias a Dios*, and we arrived here. My sister met us.

Unauthorized migrants who obtain false documents *are* able to use established routes, but they cannot travel as themselves. Alicia Montalvo, who came to the United States from El Salvador in 1987 at age nine, traveled under an assumed identity. She recalled that her trip

was easy 'cause I wasn't really thinking about it. I was just doing what my dad [who was traveling with me] told me to do. We traveled by plane from El Salvador to Tijuana. And from Tijuana, we crossed the border. I crossed the border by car because they just gave me a piece of paper to memorize and I memorized it [to be prepared] if they asked me any questions. . . . I guess I was traveling with somebody else's identification. Like somebody else's daughter, or something. And I just had to remember their names, and where

I was born and the town that I lived in, my address, my phone number and stuff.

Crossing the border did not frighten Alicia: "It was just a car ride. Because they told me to pretend like I was sleeping." Alicia did have to leave her father while crossing, however: "I was with total strangers and I didn't know where I was going. I didn't even know if I was ever going to see him." Even migrants who do not obtain false documents sometimes pretend to be Mexican while they are in Mexico. Félix Dubin, who came to the United States from El Salvador in 1989, described his trip as difficult: "One thing was that in Mexico, one's accent and way of speaking are a problem. I would try not to speak in public, but when I went to the store to buy something, I had to speak."

Whether they assume false identities or travel outside of established routes, unauthorized migrants enter a lawless realm, peopled by criminals and potentially abusive authorities. In addition to traveling in a stolen vehicle, Miguel López Herrera had to bribe authorities in Guatemala and, in southern Mexico, he was assaulted and robbed. Carmen Nieto was threatened with forced prostitution. Carlos Pineda, who came to the United States in 1982 when he was eleven, was held hostage while the smugglers attempted to extract more money from his relatives:

> They had us in a house in Texas for about four or five months. They were giving us that thing that "it's not safe to go because you're going to get caught, it's not safe because of this or because of blah blah blah." They were giving us all of this [run]around. I don't know if they were doing it because they wanted to get more money out of us. And calling the family and telling them, "They're here but, you know, it's hard and we need more money or something." They always have some way to get money.

Estela Romero, who emigrated to the United States from El Salvador in 1985, had to bribe Mexican officials, who nonetheless tried to deport her and her companions: "There in the airport in Mexico, they put us in like a cage with bars. And there, they took from us—we had already paid like fifty, sixty, one hundred [dollars], which was typical during that period, and they didn't want us to leave. We had to push the policeman [to escape], and among all of us, we did it. That is, they had already taken, as they call it, the *mordida* [bribe]. The door was half-open, and we said, 'We already paid you. Why are you keeping us? We don't have any more money.'" The disjuncture between their self-images as upstanding people and the actions they had to take to immigrate clandestinely bothered many unauthorized migrants. Luis Portillo, who came to the United States from Mexico with his family at age four and who I met through Citizens and Immigrants for Equal Justice (CIEJ), recalled being shocked to see his parents act like fugitives: "My parents never did anything wrong, and they were running." Similarly, Ricardo Sandoval, who immigrated to the United States in 1989, stressed his reluctance to violate U.S. immigration laws: "We left El Salvador because we *had* to. We respect the law as much as possible, so it was *hard* for us to enter the United States illegally. But there are times when one has to choose between the laws of man and one's life. The situation was so bad there that it was impossible to stay."

One of the most difficult things for many migrants, authorized or not, was being separated from their relatives. Migrants left behind grandparents who had cared for them since birth, elderly parents, newborn children, siblings, and spouses. Dolores Magaña, who left her mother and daughter in El Salvador, recalled, "I felt very depressed about my family. I cried for them. I spent a lot of time crying, because I didn't know how long it would be before I could return." The clandestine nature of unauthorized immigrants' journeys made such separations particularly hard. One Salvadoran immigrant compared the situation of migrants, who have to be separated from their family members, to that of slaves: "I think that it's like living in the times of slavery, which we are no longer living, right? But I think that it's becoming like that. The separation of families." Some migrants disappear while en route to the United States, making such separations permanent. When migrants who throw away their identity documents or travel under an assumed identity suffer fatal accidents, their bodies may not be identified and their relatives may not be informed of their fate. An immigrant-rights advocate in San Salvador described a typical situation: "The relative comes to the office and tells us, 'Look, my son or my daughter left for the United States a year ago, but she didn't arrive in that country, but neither did she return. So I don't know what happened to her. The last time that she called me, she was in Tapachula. From there, I had no more contact with her.' "

Although the route traveled by unauthorized migrants is, at least in part, a clandestine, lawless realm, in which family ties that locate individuals socially are at least temporarily severed and in which identities may be lost or assumed, authorities, criminals, vendors, advocates, and migrants themselves *know* this route. Criminals, including coyotes, prey on unauthorized migrants. Authorities can point out houses and areas where coyotes and migrants congregate. According to Mexican immigration officials, street vendors in Tijuana frequent typical crossing points on the Mexican side of the border, selling migrants food and drinks. Some corrupt authorities collaborate with coyotes, accepting bribes in exchange for allowing migrants to pass (see Marosi 2006). According to an immigrant advocate in El Salvador:

> There are coyotes who have contacts with people [officials] who are in what are called "roadblocks." A roadblock is a group of people who are detaining people. So, there are coyotes who know when a roadblock—in a roadblock there will be a friend, if not a friend, at least someone to whom it will be said, "Here, take these five hundred *quetzales*, let me pass."

Advocates are also familiar with unauthorized routes and, in fact, have established a network of shelters that parallels these routes. Thus, "hidden" migration is simultaneously a visible facet and feature of social landscapes.

Hidden or not, clandestine migrants enjoy only limited government protection. Regional governmental conferences, such as the Proceso Puebla (Regional Conference on Migration), do seek to guarantee the rights of migrants in transit, and particularly to combat alien-smuggling (Cubías and Monzón 2005; Mahler 2000a). Advocates also emphasize the importance of ensuring that migrants know their rights, so that they can report any abuses that they experience to the proper authorities. These measures, though helpful, do not address the source of unauthorized migrants' vulnerability: namely, the fact that certain people are not permitted to cross international borders. Prohibitions on unauthorized movement position these migrants outside of the law, leaving their legal selves, in a sense, in their countries of origin. As one Salvadoran official commented regarding the situation in a town where there had been heavy emigration, "There are ghosts there." The ghostlike absence of emigrants is the counterpart of their physical presence in "foreign" territories, where their legal alienage reconstitutes them as illegal beings. The conversion of citizenship into alienage makes unauthorized migration an "in-body" experience.

The Body's Borders

Unauthorized migrants embody both law and illegality. When they emigrate, unauthorized migrants become illegal beings who create "holes" within national jurisdictions. Nations' borders end at the boundaries of these migrants' bodies. It is true that Salvadorans possess the right to travel freely within other Central American countries, and it is also true that many migrants obtain visas to travel legally within Mexico.[5] Nonetheless, as they travel clandestinely, unauthorized migrants *displace* legal space, transforming the geographic locations they traverse, and moving the national borders that they cross. As illegal beings surrounded by law, migrants are defined simultaneously by the law that prohibits their presence and the illegality that makes them clandestine. As they come to embody their transgression, unauthorized migrants are *dehumanized*. The minimum requirements of survival—air, food, water, protection from the elements—may be denied to them, and their presence may be erased when their bodies are buried in unmarked graves. At the same time, in that they embody both law and illegality, unauthorized migrants may disrupt and extend the bodies of various nations. Thus, unauthorized migrants "enter" national territories where they allegedly do not belong, but, as beings rendered wholly alien, they also extend their own national territories.

Border-enforcement strategies constitute unauthorized migrants as fugitives, the embodiment of illegality. Miguel López Herrera described the connections between borders and illegality:

> In Tijuana, standing on the border is something that you will never forget because you look back—there is Mexico. It looks filthy, ugly, dark. And you look in front, and you see those people like in a movie. Everything well lit. Yes, it's like arriving at the promised land. The moment that you are on the border is the most difficult because that is where you must evade immigration [authorities].

Since 1994, when the United States launched Operation Gatekeeper, evading immigration authorities has become more difficult. The number of Border Patrol agents has more than doubled, military technology, such as infrared motion detectors, has been utilized, and additional fencing— made out of material such as landing mats formerly used in Vietnam and the first Gulf War—has been constructed.[6] As a result of these tactics, unauthorized migrants have moved into less heavily policed mountains and deserts, where increasing numbers have died of thirst, heat exhaustion, or freezing temperatures.[7] Moreover, states themselves are now en route in that they are locating border enforcement activities outside of their own territories. A program called Global Reach, for example, posts U.S. immigration officials in selected countries worldwide (USCIS 2001). A U.S. immigration official in San Salvador described his office's primary mission as assisting local authorities in preventing illegal immigration to the United

States.[8] Immigrant-rights advocates confirmed that these enforcement tactics had made passing through Guatemala and Mexico more difficult. One advocate commented, "It is rumored that U.S. immigration authorities are giving money to Guatemalan immigration authorities so that once people cross from here, the pressure begins. That is, the border is no longer in Rio Bravo. They lowered the border to Mexico, and because they couldn't contain [migration] there, they lowered it to Guatemala."

Unauthorized migrants' accounts of their journeys to the United States emphasize the physicality of border crossings. Javier López, for example, recalled, "I came [close to] dying from running. I spent from eight at night to two in the morning running—without stopping, and running fast, not slowly. Because walking slowly, that is possible. But running? One's mouth gets dry, and one feels that one is going to die." Carlos Pineda, who was smuggled into the United States in a station wagon with fifteen to twenty other people, recounted, "I was hardly breathing. I had somebody else's legs right on top of my nose. I was hardly breathing in there." Nonetheless, he said, the worst part of his journey was "all that running and jumping on the fences in order to get over the side." Estela Romero entered the United States in a cargo freight car, where she hid underneath debris from alfalfa plants. Luis Portillo, who migrated to the United States with his family at age four, said that his most vivid memory was running. Unauthorized migrants also spoke of tripping over rocks, traveling in the dark, withstanding hunger, and fearing that they would be bitten by snakes or animals.

Migrants' accounts of running, not breathing, and being transported like cargo indicate how migrants are made to embody illegality. Like prey, migrants must run. In fact, according to an immigrant rights' advocate in San Diego, U.S. immigration authorities use hollow bullets, originally designed for hunting wild game, against migrants who present a threat. A slang term for migrants—"pollos" or "chickens"—also suggests that these individuals are animal-like (Chávez 2001; Heyman 1995). Migrants are defined by their *mobility*, as "boat people" or "feet people" who lack "roots," are unfixed, and lack clear social locations. It is noteworthy that, in an era in which innovations in communication have been heralded, feet and boats are relatively *primitive* means of transportation. Like cargo, migrants become objects to be smuggled. Disconnected from family members, migrants become more "expendable." As they cross borders without authorization, it is as though the border wraps around them, excerpting them from their social surroundings, and making their very humanity questionable. Speaking of unauthorized migrants who enter El Salvador from neighboring countries, one immigrant-rights advocate found it necessary to point out that "the constitution of El Salvador is being violated, but this doesn't mean that they aren't hungry, that they aren't people. They love as strongly as you do."

As they inhabit incompatible realities, migrants are sometimes literally torn apart. Traveling as humans, but outside established channels, unauthorized migrants risk losing limbs. Migrants who attempt to hop trains are sometimes sucked underneath, where their legs are cut off (Nazario 2002). Mexican immigration authorities claim to have found fingers that were caught in U.S.-Mexico border fences when migrants jumped. The ultimate physical form that exclusion from national territory can take is death. During a meeting with university students who were touring the U.S.-Mexico border, Mexican immigration officials told of finding the bloated bodies of migrants who had died of thirst. These individuals, officials related, sometime placed their identity documents on their chests as they died, so that their relatives would be notified. Other migrants disappear, turned into bodies that lack identification and that are buried in unmarked graves. A Salvadoran activist, whose organization attempts to locate and identify such bodies, complained, "That is the problem, that many of the people who die are buried as unknowns, and . . . the majority of Central Americans do this, throw away their documents, or the very same coyotes ask them to throw away their documents."

Immigration authorities and immigrant-rights activists account for these deaths in different ways. Through regional conferences, U.S., Mexican, and Central American officials develop mechanisms for securing the safety and human rights of migrants in transit. Combating trafficking in humans is central to these mechanisms, even though stiffened border enforcement makes it all the more necessary for would-be migrants to hire coyotes. The American Friends Service Committee's border monitoring project, on the other hand, attributes all migrant deaths, whether caused by criminals, the elements, transit accidents, or immigration authorities themselves, to immigration policies. Through imagery such as memorials listing the names of those who have died along the border, billboards listing the number of dead, and crosses marking anonymous graves, immigrant-rights groups highlight and seek to counter the erasures caused by prohibitions on international movement (see figure 3).[9] Immigrant rights groups have asked states to create "safe and orderly" means of migrating, particularly given that, as one analyst pointed out, many migrants eventually succeed. Some groups have also proposed that, much like the establishment of the European Union, free-trade agreements in North and Central

Fig. 3. Luminarios with names of migrants who died along the U.S.-Mexico border. Advocates lit these during Posada sin Fronteras (Posada without Borders), an annual event held at the Tijuana border. In the background, the fence dividing the United States and Mexico can be seen jutting out into the ocean. Photograph by author.

America should permit citizens to move freely throughout these regions. To date, however, such proposals have not been adopted.

Unauthorized migrants' clandestine status continues even after they enter the United States, positioning them as, in certain respects, "outside" of the territory that they occupy. Their "arrival" in the United States can therefore be delayed indefinitely.

Absent Presence and Illegal Time

There are ways in which unauthorized migrants remain "en route" even after they arrive in the United States. Physically present but legally absent, unauthorized migrants are subjected to practices—the denial of identity documents, work authorization, social services, and admission to certain schools, for example—that *forbid* their presence. Although they may have left El Salvador because, as Estela Romero put it, "there was no future," their lack of legal status in the United States makes it difficult to plan. Legal absence can therefore also be temporal stasis, a sort of timelessness or indefinite uncertainty (Mountz et al. 2002). Legally, it may be difficult for them to *account for* this time, if they need to document their continuous presence within the United States (Coutin 2000). At the same time, as of 1996, law conducts its own accounting, imposing a three-year bar on legal entry for 180 days of illegal presence and a ten-year bar for one year of illegal presence. When they are not "here," unauthorized migrants are positioned "elsewhere," in, for example, El Salvador. This present absence may take the form of nostalgia, a deep longing for relatives, homes, and familiar surroundings (Baker-Cristales 2004). Positioning unauthorized migrants "elsewhere" both sets these migrants apart from the rest of the population and transforms the spaces that they occupy. Unauthorized migrants' absent presence thus both sharpens and blurs distinctions between nations, which, in turn, are set "en route."

After the difficulties of their clandestine journeys, physical arrival in the United States was something of an occasion for many unauthorized migrants. Many, for example, remembered their arrival dates—a "fact" that must also be recorded on many immigration forms. Alejandro Vidales, for example, told me, "I arrived the 19th of January of 1989. I have the date recorded in my mind." Similarly, Félix Dubin remembered on what day of the week he arrived: "One of my early memories is that I arrived on a Thursday, and already, on the following Monday, I was working. And I also started to go to night school so that I could learn English right away. That was wonderful!" Arrival sometimes meant being reunited with relatives. Carlos Pineda, who immigrated at age eleven, was captured by U.S. immigration authorities in Texas, was released on bond, and then traveled to Los Angeles on a Greyhound bus. He recalled his arrival, saying, "Well, I was happy because I didn't know my mom. It was my first time ever seeing my mom, so I was wondering who it was. You know how it is. The gladness kind of gets in you."

For many, however, the relief of arriving was coupled with a fear that made them hide their presence. Félix Dubin, for example, "was afraid to go out in public, I was afraid to talk." When Alicia Montalvo's family moved from one Los Angeles neighborhood to another, her parents were afraid to register Alicia for school. She recounted, "I ended up staying home for six months. And then my transcripts, you can see, it's from elementary, it shows that I went to fifth and sixth grade and then when it was time for me to go to seventh grade, it says, 'Unknown origin. Nothing known. Not known where she was at, or anything.' " Puppet was instructed to hide his arrival from the neighbors: "My sister said, 'Don't go out the door. Don't be peeking out the door.' Because, you know, I imagine, you know, you're living in a place maybe a few months, or even a year, and all of a sudden, there's three kids running around, you know? Fairy godmother didn't bring 'em, you know? And they're five, four years old."

In addition to being fearful, many migrants were deeply depressed over being separated from loved ones and the familiar. Carmen Nieto, who left eight children in Honduras when she emigrated, said, "And when one has first arrived, one's heart within is very sad. You don't know how to find work, you don't know how to locate people, and there is a terrible fear." Sorrow over being separated from family members was exacerbated by the alienness of life in the United States. Soledad Martínez, who, in El Salvador, had worked as a professional, parented four children, and organized social-justice projects through the church, experienced painful moments of help-lessness in the United States: "Once I felt maybe smaller than an ant, because I became disoriented on the bus. And because I couldn't speak the language, I managed to understand nothing more than that the driver said he was going to go back. So I didn't get off the bus, but it was a horrible, horrible experience."

Unauthorized migrants were absented from the United States not only through their efforts to hide from authorities and through their nostalgia for home and family but also through their lack of work authorization (Mahler 1995). Although employers who hire the undocumented are rarely sanctioned (Calavita 1990), lack of work authorization confines migrants to certain occupations and makes it difficult for them to find work at all. In search of a factory job, Estela Romero purchased false documents, which made her feel like a criminal. When she applied for a job at a meat factory, she related:

> The lady told me, "So, you say you have a green card." I said, "Yes." "Oh, wait a minute while I turn on the verification machine and then I'll let you know." Then, I was frightened and I told her, "You know what? I think I forgot that I left it at home." "Okay," she says, "go get it." She knew that I didn't have papers.

Estela Romero eventually found work doing housecleaning, but she had to abandon her plan to become a nurse: "All that remained under the ground, that is to say, buried." Other migrants reported that when they were undoc-umented, they were paid less than minimum wage or than co-workers, were mocked by employers or co-workers, or even not paid at all. As Dolores

Magaña, who had studied law in El Salvador and then became a house cleaner, put it, "I had to . . . get used to what here all of us undocumented come to do here." Downward mobility made Roxanna Ábrego's mother, who went from being a teacher in El Salvador to a house cleaner in the United States, physically ill. As Roxanna related, "She went through a depression at that time because of just adjustment coming from over there and being a self-made woman over there, like owning her own house and taking care of her three kids herself, coming to over here and cleaning other people's houses, when in El Salvador she had somebody to clean her house. Everything affects her physically. And so she was very sick."

As they were positioned "elsewhere" through laws that subjected them to deportation, made it impossible to visit homes and relatives, and denied them work authorization, these unauthorized migrants were also, in certain senses, temporally suspended. Unable to continue their studies or advance their careers, unauthorized migrants were placed in a temporal limbo, even as their desire to be reunited with relatives made them all too aware of the passage of time. Some emigrants are permanently barred from legalizing. Dolores Magaña told me that her daughter had failed to attend a court hearing and had been ordered deported in absentia. Although she had subsequently married a U.S. citizen, Dolores's daughter was unable to legalize. The very condition of being undocumented may also make it difficult for emigrants, who may be paid and buy goods in cash, live with relatives, and attempt to hide their presence, to document the amount of time they have lived in the United States. Carmen Nieto told me of an acquaintance who faced this difficulty: "He had no proof. He works on a street corner [as a day laborer]. And as you know, if one isn't careful and doesn't save papers! And he didn't save anything. He has no rent receipts, he has no check stubs." Undocumented presence can be equivalent to absence (Coutin 2000).

Positioned spatially and temporally outside of the United States, unauthorized migrants are, in a sense, *in* El Salvador, even though they are physically within the United States. Roxanna Ábrego, who immigrated to the United States without authorization but subsequently became a U.S. citizen, felt that part of her remained in El Salvador:

> I kinda know where I stand in the U.S. I don't know where I stand in El Salvador. My home was like an isolated little island of culture, thus different from the culture out here. If I go over there, what was isolated to my home, it's gonna be now part of everybody. [In other words, instead of being unusual and isolated to her home, Roxanna Abrego's culture would be shared

by the general population.] Even though I wasn't there, at the time, I still have so much of El Salvador influencing me. . . . And then, just the fact that my childhood was there, the part of my childhood that grew up in El Salvador. I wanna go see the neighborhood where I grew up for a little bit. There's also family there; it's family I've never met before. So, there's a large part of me that is still there, it's still, you know, living.

Roxanna described El Salvador as "this fabled place. It's enchanted. It's like a fantasy to me." Roxanna's sense that part of her was still in El Salvador was shared by Salvadoran authorities and academics, who reclaimed emigrants as forever present. At a conference in San Salvador in 2000, for example, speakers argued that through migration "the nation of El Salvador surpasses its borders" and that "the second most important city of El Salvador, in number of inhabitants, is that of Los Angeles." Through migrants' presence, "El Salvador" enters U.S. territory. A Salvadoran immigrant-rights advocate gave an example of such territorial reconfiguration:

Today in Hempstead [he probably meant Arlington, Virginia] there are thousands of people from Chirilagua.[10] There was a street called . . . let's suppose that it was called Morgan Street. So, those from Chirilagua came and alongside the "Morgan Street" sign they put "Chirilagua Street." Then came a moment when they took down the Morgan Street sign and they just put up Chirilagua Street. The mayor had to accept that the street was no longer called Morgan Street but was called Chirilagua Street.

The uncertainty of unauthorized migrants' spatial and temporal presence continued as they gained legal status in the United States. Just as a photographic image with low resolution produces a blurry picture, these migrants had difficulty clarifying their legal status, social location, and individual futures. Without legal resolution, unauthorized migrants could not be *fully* present in the United States.

Irresolution

There were key differences between migrants' understandings of their own vulnerability and U.S. officials' accounts of how temporarily legalized migrants were protected by law. Although NACARA cases were approved at rates of 94.5 percent,[11] migrants sometimes interpreted delays as a sign that their cases were going to be denied, or that they were going to be deported. NACARA beneficiaries' understandings of documentation were shaped by their experiences receiving temporary permission to remain in the United States. When they first applied for TPS, political asylum, or the benefits of the settlement agreement, Salvadorans and Guatemalans were issued work permits (employment authorization documents, or EADs), known collo-quially as *permisos*. Although work permits were merely evidence of work authorization, and not of a particular legal status, in practice these docu-ments were used to demonstrate that individuals had the right to be in the United States, at least temporarily (see Coutin 2000). Dolores Magaña, for example, commented that when she received her first work permit, she felt "very happy. I felt more free to walk around, more free to walk in the streets. . . . And also you [I] had a document that established my identity." Work permits, however, had to be renewed annually, making it necessary for migrants to be mindful of expiration dates. Moreover, U.S. immigra-tion authorities were notorious for losing EAD renewal applications, in which case individuals sometimes had to reapply (and pay a new fee). Javier López, who had been waiting seven months for his work permit, worried that there was a "conspiracy on the part of Immigration so that people become illegal and they can deport them." Without work permits, migrants sometimes felt that they were illegal, even though technically, as long as they still had status (albeit temporary), they could not be deported. Javier López, for example, told me, "Right now, I'm illegal, because they didn't send me the new one." Because his new work permit did not arrive on time, Javier also had to forgo a desirable job opportunity.

Although work permits gave migrants some degree of legal protection, the temporary nature of these documents continued to situate their bearers outside of the United States. Katarina Martínez, for example, described the work permit as a sign that she was not wanted: "There are always constant reminders that I'm not supposed to be here. From the legal situation that we're in, always paying somebody to be able to work for ninety months [she meant to say "nine months"] or something, and you have to pay $90, and going to that place [where they renew their work permits.]" Migrants pointed out that U.S. immigration laws could change in ways that benefited or harmed migrants. Estela Romero summarized the risks entailed in ap-plying for a temporary status: "I always thought, apply, in case one day they change the laws and give us the opportunity to stay here. [But applying means] taking a risk and everything. 'Today you don't qualify, and we are going to kick you out.' They have all the information. They have everything. So there's no escape." Similarly, while I was chatting with one interviewee in a MacDonald's restaurant, his brother-in-law pointed out, "In the U.S. law can change retroactively. You could be eating french fries and that could be acceptable, and then one day it could become illegal and you could be placed in deportation proceedings."

Migrants' senses of vulnerability contrasted sharply with official interpretations of the relationship between "roots" and time. According to case law, individuals who have been continuously present in the United States for seven years are likely to have acculturated and set down roots to such a degree that it would be "unduly harsh" to deport them (*Kamheangpatiyooth v. Immigration and Naturalization Service*, 597 F.2d 1253 [1979]). Temporal presence that is authorized through legal documents, such as a work permit, is thought to deepen such roots and was a rationale for granting ABC class members a presumption of hardship. As one of the officials who drafted the NACARA regulations explained:

> [ABC class members] were protected. They didn't have to fear that they were
> going to be deported. That allowed them to become more established, to set
> down more roots in the community. And they had employment authoriza-
> tion, which meant that they could work . . . versus someone who has the
> seven years but who has been living in the United States as an undocumented
> immigrant, working under the table, living with the threat of deportation.

As this official indicates, over time—particularly with the benefit of legal documentation—the barriers between unauthorized immigrants and broader society break down, enabling emigrants to develop community ties. Undocumented time, on the other hand, may not "count." The perceived connection between time and documentation is shown by Miguel López Herrera's comment that "anyone who forgot to renew a *permiso*" would have "lost that year." Some ABC class members had difficulty documenting their temporal presence. One attorney said that in rare cases when ABC class members cannot document their presence, "it's better just to wait until they accrue the more recent years, turn into the tail end of seven years eventually, and then they can apply."

While their cases remained unresolved, NACARA beneficiaries experienced temporal irresolution. Many interviewees stated that they were "pendiente." To be "pendiente" is to be "pending" or "waiting." Carlos Pineda described the uncertainty caused by having a pending NACARA application:

> I'm still wondering. . . . I hope nothing [goes] wrong. I hope it goes the way I
> expected. I have no idea. But I guess it's been over twenty years, and I'm

praying that it goes the right way. At this point until now, I still don't know. I'm kind of blind. My mind kind of flies all over because I don't know what's going to happen. I just gotta wait and see what happens, and I just take it by the day.

Temporal irresolution was accompanied by spatial ambiguity. Long-term residents who had only temporary or provisional legal status were not permitted to be fully present. Katarina Martínez eloquently described the effects of being legally present in a country that she could not remember, and physically present in a country where she lacked permanent legal status:

> And constantly being reminded that I'm neither a resident nor a nonalien. Going to university, looking at the applications, I can't say that I'm a resident, and I can't say that I'm not a resident. And then, I have no memory. Even though I feel out of place [here], at least I have a home, at least I know this world. My family is real. This is where I belong. This is the only place I [have] had to identify with. As long as my family is with me, I have a home. But, other than that, it's like there is nothing. There is nothing here, there is nothing there; it's a strange situation to be in. Because you can't [say,] "Oh, I remember when this"—I don't remember that either. Talking to people, for a minute you have no identity outside of your house. That's what it feels like sometimes. You're just walking around, and you're just, *you're like invisible to everything else. Everybody else is solid but you're not.* (Emphasis added)

While migrants who immigrated at older ages might not feel as alienated from their countries of legal citizenship as did Katarina Martínez, her remarks nonetheless captured something of what it was to be denied a full legal existence in one's country of physical presence (Coutin 2000). Located in multiple spaces, treated ambiguously as "illegal aliens" and as deserving protocitizens, ABC class members and NACARA applicants lacked resolution. They were present, but not completely visible, and visible, but not completely present.

Winning residency is not the only way of achieving a "resolution." In addition, it might be possible to demonstrate that the structures and practices that make some people "irresolute" are themselves of questionable legitimacy. Expanding irresolution in this fashion could reduce the differentiation that situates some in a temporal and spatial elsewhere.

Expanded Irresolution

Unauthorized migrants are not the only ones who are en route. The United States was deeply involved in the civil conflicts that forced Salvadorans and Guatemalans out of their homelands; free-trade agreements have facilitated the movement of capital; and Central American nations, in part through migrants, have acquired a presence beyond their borders. Unlike these other entities, refugees, the poor, and their families have rarely been permitted to cross international borders legally. Forced into clandestine spaces, unauthorized migrants have had to travel outside of established channels, as cargo, as fugitives, and under assumed identities. Separated from their place of legal personhood, unauthorized migrants come to embody both law and illegality and sometimes suffer death, the ultimate exclusion. Their "illegal" status situates unauthorized migrants outside of the territories that they occupy. Temporary legal statuses improve their lot but do not resolve the ambiguity of their presence. Permanent residency promises temporal, legal, and spatial resolution, but leaves the larger systems that criminalize unauthorized migration intact. At the same time, in that legalization causes the path of law to deviate, programs such as NACARA implicitly acknowledge ways that law itself is en route. Laws are not "fixed" in that legal accounts can retroactively acquire meanings that, seemingly, were "there" all along. There is thus a sense in which law travels along the routes forged by unauthorized migrants. As it does so, law renders national jurisdictions irresolute. One example of such irresolution is the role that remittances have come to play within the Salvadoran economy. Produced through unauthorized as well as legal activities and labor, migrant remittances have been deemed to officially count.

CHAPTER 5

Las Remesas (Remittances)

It is we poor who are maintaining this country.

NGO member interviewed in El Salvador

A key reason that Salvadorans migrate to the United States is to earn money to send home to family members.[1] Families may adopt a transnational economic strategy, sending one or more members abroad to improve a household's finances (Andrade-Eekhoff 2003; Gubert 2002; Schiller, Basch, and Szanton Blanc 1995). Individuals who migrate to improve their own economic situation may also have obligations to relatives in their countries of origin (Goldring 2003). Even migrants who do not remit regularly may provide relatives with financial support when emergencies arise (Gubert 2002). In recent years, such transfers have been hailed by international financial institutions as potential sources of development, and have led sending states to create offices and programs for emigrant citizens, receiving states to reevaluate their relationships to migrants, and analysts to debate remittances' social and economic effects. In the case of El Salvador, remittances have been credited with saving the country from economic collapse during the postwar period (J. García 1994, 1997), but they have also been blamed for a variety of social ills, including family breakups, transculturation, dependency, crime, consumerism, and loss of productivity (J. García 1994; Orozco et al. 1997). At a presentation during the September 2004 observance of Immigrant Week in El Salvador, one analyst commented, "This country is addicted to migration and to remittances. And it always needs a larger dose."

Remittances' visibility in El Salvador and elsewhere is made possible by a technical apparatus that traces the paths and qualities of particular transactions. Just as unauthorized immigrants can become legal, so too can unofficial monetary transfers count. Banks, credit unions, currency exchanges, and money transfer services send central banks information about transfers that appear to be migrant remittances. Using this information, central banks report monthly and annual remittance totals as credits in their balance-of-payments statements. International financial institutions, such as the International Monetary Fund (IMF), use central bank information to assess worldwide remittance flows. As they track remittances, such calculations imbue remittances with particular qualities. As Callon (1998, 23) observes, "The most interesting element [of accounting] is to be found in the relationship between what is to be measured and the tools used to measure it. The latter do not merely record a reality independent of themselves; they contribute powerfully to shaping, simply by measuring it, the reality that they measure." For example, remittances are defined as "unrequited transfers," as national income against which no good, service, or payment must be counted and that therefore is pure profit (Pérez-López and Díaz-Briquets 1998). Additionally, remittance income is grouped with donations (for example, from the U.S. Agency for International Development, or USAID) that one government sends to another (IMF 1999). Such accounting practices elevate these informal exchanges between family members to the level of foreign assistance. The fact that some remittances are produced through illicit migration and unauthorized labor is not deemed to lessen their significance within national and international financial accounts.

The technical practices that make remittances visible reposition migrants within national spaces. Through remitting, migrants become an absent presence within their countries of origin. To produce remittances, migrants must leave national territories. Their absences are marked by references to "ghost towns," inhabited only by children and the elderly. Remittances are deemed a mark of membership in and commitment to families, communities, and nations (Libercier and Schneider 1996). Through remittances, migrants become "de facto residents" who contribute to social well-being in their countries of origin but who, by virtue of being outside of the country, lack mechanisms to fully exercise their political rights (Goldring 2003). Their actions nonetheless help to produce the nation, and therefore may be a form of "practical nostalgia" (Battaglia 1995) that looks toward the future as well as to the past. Discourse surrounding remittances also produces a particular *type* of citizen—the "enterprising subject," whose transactions will develop the nation (O'Malley 2000). The emigrant citizen who remits is also, in many cases, the being who is en route, who endures physical, social, and economic deprivation, the being who could be deported. Recognizing migrants for their remittances is therefore a form of *in*clusion through *ex*clusion (Agamben 1998). Remitting and the international financial benefits associated with such transfers are made possible, at least in part, by the violence associated with emigration itself.

The Remittance Phenomenon

As migration from the United States to El Salvador increased during the 1980s, so too did remittances. According to a U.S. embassy report, "Remittances gradually became important during the 1980s, increasing from an estimated USD 74 million in 1980, to USD 232 million in 1985, and around USD 600 million in 1990" (American Embassy San Salvador 1998, 1). By the 1990s, remittances had become key to the Salvadoran economy and were the second most important source, following exports, of foreign exchange (U.S. Department of State 1999), surpassing coffee exports by more than three times in 1993 alone (J. García 1994). Remittance income lessened the impact of structural adjustment programs implemented during the 1990s, creating a picture of financial stability that distinguished El Salvador from neighboring Central American countries (J. García 1994, 1997), and indeed from many "developing" nations around the world (Díaz-Briquets and Pérez-López 1997; Gammeltoft 2002; Orozco et al. 1997). Through remittances, Salvadorans who, during the 1980s, had been driven out of El Salvador by political violence and economic difficulties became, in the 1990s, particularly valuable to their country of origin, leading Salvadoran authorities to seek to maximize the financial benefits of remitting. Remittances also became a factor in U.S. policymaking in El Salvador, as U.S. officials sought to preserve and even increase remittance flows to El Salvador. These shifts were consistent with a broader reassessment of the role that remittances could play in economic development and financial stability. International financial institutions, such as the IMF, World Bank, BID, and the Banco Centroamericano de Integración Económica (BCIE, or Central American Bank for Economic Integration), increasingly saw migrants as economic agents whose practical knowledge and personal financial strategies could redistribute resources to the benefit of communities, nations, and regions.

International excitement about remittances' development potential grew during the late 1980s and early 1990s, as countries experienced economic crises, implemented structural adjustment programs, and sought to improve their balance-of-payments records (Goldring 2003; Itzigsohn 1995; Vargas Uribe et al. 1998). This interest in remittances marks an important shift. As recently as the 1970s, remittances were not considered significant enough to be incorporated into major economic models of migration (Taylor 1999), and only in the mid-1980s did central banks consistently report remittance data to the IMF (Chami et al. 2005). As attention to remittances grew, the IMF encouraged countries to adopt financial reforms that would enable official banking systems to capture a greater portion of remittance flows (Kapur and McHale 2003). Reforms included "allowing the free convertibility of financial flows, permitting migrants to open local convertible currencies bank accounts, removing bureaucratic impediments, maintaining appropriate monetary and exchange rates policies, making accessible safe economic and efficient transfer mechanisms, and providing a safe and secure economic environment" (Díaz-Briquets and Pérez-López 1997, 415). Cumulative estimates of worldwide remittances increased dramatically, from $43 billion in 1980 to $66 billion in 1989 (Díaz-Briquets and Pérez-López 1997) to $71.1. billion in 1991 (McCormick and Wahba 2000) to $100 billion in 2002 (Gameltoft 2002). Although it is not clear whether increases resulted from more money being sent or more transfers being recorded, analysts found these figures remarkable. For example, Díaz-Briquets and Pérez-López (1997, 411) marvel that "this flow is second in size only to the financial transactions associated with crude oil world trade and exceeds global development assistance." Kapur and McHale (2003, 49) point out that remittances are "outstripping foreign aid and ranking as one of the biggest sources of foreign exchange for poor countries," and Gameltoft (2002) found that during the 1990s remittances increased even though foreign aid and private flows of money declined. In a climate that "privilege[s] markets and private investment or private-public partnerships to replace state investment" (Goldring 2003, 3), analysts and international financial institutions have become intrigued with the possibility that migrant remittances might revitalize local communities and national economies (Asch and Reichmann 1994; Durand et al. 1996; El-Sakka and McNabb 1999; Kapur and McHale 2003; Libercier and Schneider 1996).

In El Salvador, public interest in remittances dates to the mid-to-late 1980s. IRCA, which, in 1986, created sanctions for employers that hired undocumented workers, provoked fears that Salvadoran emigrants would return to El Salvador in large numbers (Montes Mozo and García Vasquez 1988). Such fears led Salvadoran president Duarte to ask U.S. authorities to allow Salvadoran émigrés to remain in the United States. Economists concluded that remittances became economically significant in El Salvador after 1984 (Orellana Merlos 1992), and a study of remitting in Latin America observed that El Salvador was distinctive in that it showed the largest increase in remittances over the course of the 1980s (Orozco et al. 1997). Segundo Montes's pathbreaking research on Salvadoran emigrants also drew attention to the social and economic effects of remittances in El Salvador (Montes Mozo and García Vasquez 1988; Montes 1990; Pedersen 2004).[2] In 1990, El Salvador reformed its banking system in an effort to capture a larger portion of remittances (J. García 1994, 1997). Concern over remittances may have helped to secure Salvadoran president Duarte's support for the 1991 Immigration Act's award of TPS to Salvadorans, and, according to Salvadoran officials, after 1992, as foreign aid decreased in the wake of the Salvadoran peace accords, remittances assumed even greater importance. The passage of restrictive immigration measures in the United States in 1996 once again raised fears that remittances would be cut off. "That was when calculations of remittances began," an immigrant-rights advocate in El Salvador recalled. "Once their contribution to the economy was calculated, people realized that if they stopped then there would be a huge problem." By the 2000s, Salvadoran news media regularly reported amounts of remittances that El Salvador received monthly and annually, and during my interviews advocates, officials, and scholars in El Salvador routinely cited these and related statistics.

Although methods of calculating remittances vary, table 5.1, based on data from the Banco Central de Reserva (BCR) in El Salvador, provides some indication of the phenomenal growth of remittances to El Salvador over the past two decades.

TABLE 5.1.
Remittances to El Salvador, 1985–2006 (in millions of U.S. dollars)

1985:	101.7	1996:	1,086.5
1986:	134.3	1997:	1,199.5
1987:	168.2	1998:	1,338.3
1988:	194.2	1999:	1,373.8
1989:	203.5	2000:	1,750.7
1990:	359.5	2001:	1,910.5
1991:	790.1	2002:	1,935.2
1992:	858.3	2003:	2,105.3
1993:	864.1	2004:	2,547.6
1994:	962.5	2005:	2,830.2
1995:	1,061.4	2006:	3,315.7

Source: Banco Central de Reserva data, available at http://www.bcr.gob.sv.

Significantly, despite fears of volatility, remittances to El Salvador increased steadily over this period. The years of greatest reported increase are 1990–1991 (a period when banking reforms were implemented in El Salvador, Salvadorans gained immigration rights in the United States, and the Salvadoran civil war was in its final days), 1998 (when Hurricane Mitch struck El Salvador), 2000 (shortly before dollarization was implemented in El Salvador), 2001 (the year of the two most recent Salvadoran earthquakes), and 2004 (election years in both El Salvador and the United States). As they do not include transfers made through unofficial sources, official figures such as BCR data are generally considered to underestimate remittances, so actual amounts sent may be higher (Orellana Merlos 1992; Libercier and Schneider 1996).

Remittances' macroeconomic impact on El Salvador has been enormous. During the late 1970s, El Salvador suffered from capital flight, factories closed, and the export sector constricted. A drop in the price of coffee (El Salvador's major export), an increase in the cost of petroleum, and a global recession contributed to economic instability. Inflation and the national deficit grew, while exports declined. During this period, foreign donors such as USAID provided funds needed for El Salvador's balance of payments (J. García 1994). In the 1980s, the civil war exacerbated these economic conditions, but gradually migrant remittances began to provide some relief. By the 1990s, the U.S. embassy in San Salvador (1998, 1) reported that "remittances have become vital to supporting macroeconomic stability, offsetting the chronic trade deficit, and keeping the exchange rate stable. . . . Single digit inflation, and ready availability of hard currency for imports of raw and intermediate products are also partly attributable to the abundant supply of remittance dollars" (see also Comisión Económica para América Latina y el Caribe 2000; U.S. Department of State 1999). As El Salvador implemented structural adjustment policies, remittances provided a buffer, maintaining aggregate demand and permitting the country to avoid a recession (J. García 1997). In 2003, as remittances increased, El Salvador's central bank calculated that "remittances cover more than 90 percent of the country's trade deficit and are equivalent to about 60 percent of exports and 35 percent of total imports" (Banco Central de Reserva 2003). During a 2001 interview, a U.S. embassy official compared El Salvador's economy to that of a small oil-exporting economy, commenting, "Remittances are equivalent to the rents that are paid on oil exports. There are many differences between these two types of economies, but their macro finances are similar. It isn't necessary for these countries to borrow, for example. In the case of El Salvador, remittances make up more than 10 percent of the GDP."

Given remittances' economic significance, Salvadoran officials have taken steps to maintain remittance flows, better exploit this source of income, and strengthen migrants' connections to El Salvador. According to a U.S. immigrant-rights advocate with political connections in El Salvador, Segundo Montes's work on remittances in the late 1980s helped to "create this intellectual undercurrent in El Salvador that status in the United States means more pay, more remittances." According to this advocate, concerns over maintaining and even increasing remittance income were key to Salvadoran officials' efforts to secure TPS for Salvadorans in 1991 and 2001 and NACARA in 1997. Speaking anonymously, one Salvadoran official acknowledged, "It's in El Salvador's interests for there to be Salvadorans [living] abroad. Basically, the country is able to live through their remittances. But as a government, you cannot promote this idea." Like other immigrant-sending countries (Díaz-Briquets and Pérez-López 1997; Goldring 2003), El Salvador has developed programs to capitalize on migrant remittances.

As they have become more important to Salvadoran officials, remittances' significance for U.S. policymaking has also grown. U.S. government agencies, such as the State Department (1999) and the U.S. embassy in El Salvador (1998), remark on the role that remittances play in El Salvador's economy. On economic grounds, the U.S. State Department supported Duarte's 1987 request to give Salvadorans permission to remain in the United States (although, due to opposition from the Department of Justice, this request was not granted) (*San Francisco Chronicle* 1987b). Congressional staffers cited remittances as key factors in securing the passage of NACARA in 1997. As one Democratic staffer commented, "The remittances were an important issue. NACARA covers people who put significant amounts of money into Central American economies." The NACARA regulations (and particularly the presumption of hardship), some U.S. officials argued, streamlined the NACARA process and, in the wake of Hurricane Mitch, indirectly provided economic assistance to the region. Finally, in 2001, U.S. officials cited TPS as a means of providing financial support, via remittances, to Salvadoran earthquake victims. During a 2001 interview, a U.S. embassy official commented:

> I was astonished that we went along with the idea of giving TPS to illegal immigrants so that they can continue to provide earthquake relief. . . . It would

be hard to tell someone in Houston that giving legal status to 150,000 illegal immigrants who will then compete with him for jobs is in U.S. interests. But the United States has no particular interest in seeing the Salvadoran labor market be hurt more than it already has been. And it's true that the remittances are a way to get more assistance, from a macroeconomic perspective, into the economy. And it's more efficient this way. The assistance goes straight into people's hands so that they can use it for their own projects, instead of being sent to an NGO.

Interestingly, the remittance phenomenon positions the poor in general and migrants in particular as key agents in local, national, and international development, finances, and policymaking. In the above quote, a U.S. embassy official depicts migrants as particularly efficient providers of earthquake relief. Similarly, Kapur and McHale (2003, 50; see also Orozco et al. 1997) comment, "During economic crises, when developing countries most need the money, it is not powerful wealthy countries or sophisticated financial markets that they can depend on, but rather the millions of otherwise powerless working class emigrants." This notion that the poor, rather than elite experts, are the most efficient and effective agents of development resonates with neoliberal models of enterprise (Hernandez and Coutin 2006). Thus, migrants' individual strategies for personal and familial advancement are deemed to be grounded in practical understandings, and therefore able to accomplish that which eludes economic experts. Through partnerships with migrants—partnerships made all the more necessary by states' reductions in social spending—governments presumably obtain greater returns on their own investments in development. Not all share this sanguine interpretation of the turn to the poor. García (1994, 9–10), for example, writes:

Individual effort to relieve the situation of poverty has been realized at the margin of state actions and in the midst of one of the worst and longest economic crises in the history of the country [of El Salvador]. This converts migrants into the true subjects of recent history and the social group that, paradoxically, upon escaping poverty has facilitated things for dominant groups and for the state, which, on the other hand, has not known how to make productive use of remittances.

Of course, migrants' abilities to be "agents of history" depend on accounting practices that make remittances visible. Without such practices, remittances would not be a phenomenon.

Counting Remittances

The claims that remittances to different nations can be calibrated along a single scale, that remitting can be distinguished from other transactions, and that remittances from around the world can be aggregated to calculate the worldwide "flow" are implicit within the practices that produce national and international financial accounts. Countries' balance-of-payments statements use double-entry bookkeeping methods to record all financial flows into and out of national economies. These methods treat nations as "vessels" in which, at any given moment, particular amounts of value (or indebtedness) are held. In these statements, value is simultaneously differentiated (income from exports has different qualities than does income from international loans) but also rendered equivalent (dollar figures can be attached to each). Financial statements thus have a nested quality: they are produced through a summation of numerous smaller individual or subnational statements; each table in a particular national report produces figures that then appear in other tables in the same report, and these national reports are then incorporated into international financial accounts (see also Maurer 2002). This nested form has a particular aesthetic. Every financial transaction forms part of a larger whole; this whole can be discerned if transactions are properly placed, and the resulting figure should be both complete (all encompassing) and patterned (in that elements produced through lower-level calculations are incorporated into higher tiers). Furthermore, this figure is continually in motion, given that new financial transactions are always occurring. Though invented as a method of making financial processes transparent or visible, such accounting practices are also a "modality of argumentation" (Maurer 2002, 662; 2003). Placing particular transactions within larger financial flows requires identifying the characteristics of transactions, differentiating certain transactions from others, and assessing each transaction's relative contributions to the whole. Thus, when they calculate remittance flows, financial officers simultaneously reveal and assign these transactions' qualities (see also Callon 1998; Callon et al. 2002).

International financial institutions classify remittances as *external transfers*, that is, as money that leaves one economy and enters another (Asch and Reichmann 1994; Barham and Boucher 1998; Gameltoft 2003; Taylor 1999). Remittances have two additional qualities. First, remittances are considered "unrequited," as resulting from "noncommercial considerations, such as family ties or legal obligations, that induce a producer or owner of real resources and financial items to part with them without any return in those same forms" (IMF 1977, 71, quoted in Pérez-Lopez and Díaz-Briquets 1998, 322). In other words, remittances are "nonmarket income transfers" akin to a gift (Chami et al. 2005, 56; Hernandez and Coutin 2006). Second, remittances are considered to be private in nature, and thus contrast with foreign assistance that one government provides to another. The IMF's 1999 Statistical Annex regarding El Salvador, for example, includes a table that lists family remittances in the same column as income from USAID and donations from foreign governments (see table 5.2).

The definition of remittances as private, unrequited transfers makes this income "pure" and therefore particularly valuable to remittance-receiving nations. A central bank official in El Salvador explained:

With *maquila* [foreign assembly plant income], one makes an investment. So, when you calculate the maquila profits, you have to subtract, right? You have to discount all that was invested in creating the conditions to have the maquila, and, with remittances, it's like you don't have to discount anything. We never have to pay anything; it's not like a loan or a sale of goods, in which we receive income but have to give away the good, or a loan in which we receive currency but have to pay it back in the future. [With remittances] there's no payment, it's a pure transfer.

TABLE 5.2.
El Salvador: external transfers (in millions of U.S. dollars)

	1994	1995	1996	1997	Prel. 1998
Net transfers	**1,258.2**	**1,389.5**	**1,254.5**	**1,363.6**	**1,509.4**
Credits	**1,287.7**	**1,394.0**	**1,259.3**	**1,365.9**	**1,517.1**
Private	1,001.8	1,196.8	1,194.9	1,310.5	1,486.0
Family remittances	964.3	1,062.6	1,086.6	1,201.8	1,338.3
U.S. AID (in kind)	5.0	0.0	0.8	0.0	0.0
Other	32.5	134.2	107.5	108.7	147.7
Public	285.9	197.2	64.4	55.4	31.1
U.S. AID[a]	215.0	119.0	36.1	29.9	10.0
Foreign governments	54.2	57.0	22.6	22.5	6.9
Other	16.7	21.2	5.7	3.0	14.2
Debits	**2.5**	**4.5**	**4.8**	**2.3**	**7.7**
Private	0.7	1.7	1.9	2.3	7.6
Public	1.8	2.8	2.9	0.0	0.1

Source: International Monetary Fund's 1999 Statistical Annex regarding El Salvador; data drawn from Central Reserve Bank and IMF staff estimates. Reprinted with permission.
[a]Includes ESF and PL 480, Title II.

Similarly, a Salvadoran businessman described remittances as "fresh money, the true foreign currency, without cost," a Salvadoran professor described remittances as foreign currency that enters the country "clean," while a U.S. embassy official commented that with remittances, "you net 100 percent." Remittances' "purity" therefore takes several forms. Remittances are considered untainted by the market, pure profit, the result of familial and nonlegal ties, originating *as remittances* rather than as the result of something else. They are like the second half of an exchange in which the first half never occurred. In this sense, remittances are unique. In fact, by coining the terms "migradollars" and "migradólares," some scholars imply that remittances resemble a distinct currency (Conway and Cohen 1998; Durand et al. 1996; Massey and Parrado 1994).

In order to calculate remittance income, banking officials have to distinguish remitting from other transactions. During a 2001 interview, a central bank official in El Salvador described how this occurred:

> The normal sources that we have for remittances, the banks and monetary exchanges, are required to report to us all of the operations in foreign currency. They do so daily, and here we receive everything, and we review it, we refine it. It is reviewed document by document, and in some cases, what they report as a remittance isn't. We look at the amount, whether it is a Salvadoran last name or not. And, depending on these characteristics, we can arrive at some quantities based on what they have reported to us as family remittances. And generally, a family remittance is small, five hundred dollars or less.

According to this official, remittance reports are based on something like a sociology of remitting. Officials measure particular transactions against their prototype of a typical remittance—a cash transfer of five hundred dollars or less coming from someone with a Salvadoran surname. These measurements begin at the level of the teller or person working in a monetary exchange and continue in the central bank itself. Regarding questionable transactions, BCR officials sometimes defer to tellers' local knowledge, as this official explained:

> We are in constant communication with the banks. If we have a doubt about a particular transaction, we consult with them. Sometimes they [seeming remitters] are [the banks'] known clients. So, they can tell us, "No, it's that this person is going to use it for . . ." They told them. So, yes, communication with the banks also plays a very important role in being able to refine the statistics.

The scale of this effort is enormous. The official noted, "We go in and look, paper by paper, to review absolutely everything. Not only for remittances, but for all types of transactions. The quantity of boxes that we have is incredible!"

With the dollarization of the Salvadoran economy in 2000, it became more difficult to distinguish remittances from other transactions, as recipients no longer had to convert U.S. dollars into Salvadoran currency before using it. To calculate the amount of remittances, the official related, the BCR began to rely more heavily on surveys and past estimates: "There is a fair amount that comes in as cash. But what has been done is to estimate it based on historical information regarding cash. And they are doing other things, like doing a survey along the border points, so that if, as time passes, historic cash begins to change, we can capture it another way." The official added that to verify her calculations, she compared remittance figures with other estimates:

> There are ways, from a statistical point of view, to go about validating information, that is, there are other matters that are indicators and that tell us, "This has to increase," and if it decreases, well, I can become doubtful. For example, in the case of remittances, in relation to how the United States' [economy] is growing. For example if the United States' [economy] is growing and my remittance is decreasing, I have to doubt my data. Because unless there has been something, for example, actions to detain migrant flows to the United States, massive deportations . . . then that would tell me that I have bad data.

This massive classificatory endeavor simultaneously *measures* and *produces* remittance flows. Currency does change hands, value is transferred from one account to another, and some portion of migrants' income is used to pay for the expenses of relatives in migrants' home countries. Nonetheless, the very methods used to measure remittances imbue these exchanges with particular qualities. In a circular fashion, using particular criteria to distinguish remittances from other transactions predefines remittances as exhibiting these characteristics. Remittances' qualities are both intrinsic and extrinsic, both facets of the original exchange and characteristics revealed through measurement (see Callon et al. 2002). Further, comparing remittances to other sources of foreign currency (e.g., to foreign donations and export income) reveals additional qualities. As Callon et al. (2002, 200) point out, "Qualities which define a good and make it possible to position it in relation to other goods are not established once and for all. They have the strange characteristic of being constituent of the good but nonetheless reconfigurable." The accounting process that quantifies remittance flows and positions these in relation to other expenses and sources of income also reproduces the nested form of national finances. Individual financial transactions become part of banks' and money transfer agencies' reports, which in turn appear in national financial statements, and then in international reports. Ideally, all financial transactions are placed within this system, though, as Asch and Reichmann (1994) note, reporting systems and definitions of remittances have not been standardized from country to country.

Although national financial reports are meant to be comprehensive, alongside official accounts and formal transactions exist informal, and in some cases illicit, exchanges that are not included in these reports. Financial officials are well aware of this problem. As the central bank official who spoke to me in El Salvador acknowledged, "Some escape us if there is someone who comes in with money in their pocket." Unrecordable remittances take two forms. First, remittances in kind rather than in cash are not captured in financial reports (Durand and Massey 1992; Keely and Tran 1989). Second, as noted above, remittances that are delivered by couriers rather than through banks are not officially recorded. In both of these cases, cash is "hidden," either in that it was converted into a good or it is carried in an envelope that is not revealed to a bank or customs official. Some analysts refer to this form of sending remittances as "clandestine" (Keely and Tran 1989; Taylor 1999), while others classify remittances according to the container of transport (e.g., "pocket transfers") (Athukorala 1992; Massey and Parrado 1994). Numerous analysts complain that official data (such as IMF statements) underreport actual remittance flows (e.g., Durand and Massey 1992; J. García 1994; Keely and Tran 1989; Libercier and Schneider 1996; Orellana Merlos 1992), and some have used alternative methods, such as multiplying an average amount of remittances by the total number of immigrants, to estimate remittance income (Durand and Massey 1992). Athukorala (1992, 514) describes hidden cash transfers as "leakages" and notes that "in the existing literature on migrant-worker remittance behaviour, the usual practice has been to treat all informal remittances . . . as foreign exchange leakages from the labour-exporting country."[3]

Both official and alternative methods of calculating remittance flows attempt to approximate a presumably unknowable actual figure, and both analysts and officials agree that it would be best to create mechanisms that encourage the use of official channels and maximize remittances' visibility.

I have come across no study or report recommending informal (and thus unverifiable) modes of transmission. Perhaps this is because, as Callon (1998, 34–35, emphasis added) notes, "money, as an operator of equivalence, cannot be dissociated from its trajectory or at least from a part of it; in other words, from its spaces of circulation. *If the trajectory were not legible, money would lose its quality as money.* Total disorder would settle in since, being able to identify neither issuers nor receivers, agencies would be unable to do accounts, make transfers, impute profits and losses, and so on." Officially, national economies can be complete; unofficially, they have "leakages" in that they cannot encompass the informal and in that they, in certain respects, seep into other economies. Furthermore, money that lacks a "trail," that does not produce receipts and records, cannot be counted and, therefore, much like migrants who travel without authorization, is not really "there."

Informal means of transmission raise questions about the morality of remitting and suggest that, though they are in some respects "pure," such transfers may also be "tainted" by the status of the remitter and the segment of the economy that is fueled by remittances.[4] Orellana Merlos (1992) contended that remittances largely fed the black market in currency, while Montes (1990, 31), writing just before El Salvador's 1990 banking reforms, depicted remitting as being generally associated with illegality: "The phenomenon is predominantly 'illegal' and 'clandestine,' as much in migratory matters as in the sending of remittances, exchange of money and banking affairs." The Salvadoran BCR official quoted above linked informality to the sender's legal status: "If the one who is abroad and is illegal is going to do it [remit], then there are many cases [of] the fear of 'I'm illegal.' So to create a formal link with an institution of another country is something that can expose one at a given moment. The same with sending remittances. There are many [remittances] that enter the economy in cash. We can suppose [those] who are illegal prefer to use informal means, so as not to leave traces." Similarly, a Salvadoran economist explained the connections between illegality and informal exchange:

> You know of people who travel two, three times a month, with as much as $70,000 in cash, which is illegal, because one cannot enter or leave with more than $10,000 in cash. But he who is illegal uses informal channels completely, because he does not want to leave even the slightest [information] about his address anywhere. And because of the family contact. He always asks, "And did you deliver the letter?" "Yes." "And did you see my mother? And how was she?" That is, it's the transfer of news, apart from the money.

Potential connections between remitting and illegality, transparency and informality, and the official and unofficial raise questions about the moral and social consequences of remitting more generally. Some suggest that, far from saving the nation, remittances will bring about El Salvador's downfall.

Salvation and Corruption

Although they are credited with saving the Salvadoran economy, particularly during the postwar period, migrant remittances are also blamed for corrupting El Salvador. Ironically, the very characteristics that make remittances desirable (remittances originate without state expenditures, bring foreign currency into the country, and benefit poor families) are also sources of anxiety (remittances stem from uncontrollable forces, are produced outside of national territory, and are used by average people for their own ends). These anxieties center, among other things, on whether remitting enables people to act as the enterprising subjects of neoliberalism. According to O'Malley (2000, 465) such subjects are to "practice and sustain their autonomy by assembling information, materials and practices together into a personalized strategy that identifies and minimizes their exposure to harm" while also acting as " 'risk takers' . . . who 'reinvent' themselves and their environment." Determining whether remitters and recipients act as such subjects entails deciphering remittances' biographies (Appadurai 1986; Kopytoff 1986). *Do* remittances originate before the moment of remitting (which would imply that they *are* the second half of a prior exchange)? Where do remittances travel after they are received? Do they stay in El Salvador? Return to the United States? Become investments? Fuel consumption? Such determinations are made, in part, on the basis of anecdotal evidence and popular wisdom, forms of expertise that supplement carefully crafted financial reports (Holmes and Marcus 2005, 2006). From such sources, critical accounts that link remitting to exploitation sometimes emerge.

Analysts who worry about remittances' long-term effects suggest that, instead of enabling El Salvador to become financially solvent, remittances have made El Salvador more dependent on forces located outside (and thus beyond the control of) El Salvador. Salvadoran scholar Juan José García (1994, 7; see also Orellana Merlos 1992) writes, "The motor of economic development is no longer in the interior of national activities . . . and has moved abroad due to depending on continually larger amounts of remittances." In contrast to the notion that El Salvador expands through migration, this understanding of dependency focuses on a loss—of population, autonomy, and even a distinctive national identity. García (1994, 26), for example, suggests that migration and remittances "have substantially modified El Salvador, the Salvadoran, and Salvadoranness"; while, at a conference in El Salvador in 2000, another Salvadoran scholar commented that replacing dependency on the United States with dependency on Salvadorans in the United States was not an improvement. Some analysts compare dependency on remittances to drug addiction or to a diseased state (Durand et al. 1996; Taylor 1999), thus suggesting that remittances destroy self-control and create an inappropriate need for substances that are foreign to the national body. Such foreign substances may create vacant spaces within national territory. For instance, an official in the Salvadoran Ministry of Foreign Affairs noted that a large number of those in the economically active sector, such as farmers and mechanics, were leaving. The official commented, "There are places where all that is left are elderly people and children."

The state of dependency that some analysts believe results from remittances is thought to be manifested in the lives of average Salvadoran citizens (Montes 1990). Recipients, it is widely reported, become dependent on remittances and lose the ability to be productive (J. García 1994; Orellana Merlos 1992; but see Zilberg and Lungo 1999). For instance, a staff member of an important FMLN politician related the following:

> The remittance has created a dependency situation. Because [recipients] get money from the U.S. they don't look for a job because it's better to get three hundred dollars from New York than earning fifty dollars in the sugar cane plantation. A rational decision, but this rational decision has taken away [from] most Salvadoran families the incentive to say, "Look, we can do it, we can make it and we don't need any help from outside. We'll work, we'll send our children to school and we'll be a prosperous family."

Similarly, an NGO staff member complained that people "no longer want to work because they are hoping that at the end of the month, they'll receive their check for one hundred [or] two hundred dollars," while a Salvadoran official observed that there is a "parasitism, people just sitting in their hammocks." Such comments may be motivated in part by moral judgments about the source of remittances. As Carruthers and Espeland (1998) note, money that is earned rather than obtained through a handout is considered morally deserved. Such comments also suggest that recipients are passive, that, as another NGO member commented, remittances arrive "without those of us who are in the country having to do anything." Passivity, analysts worry, destroys local and national economies. García (1994, 12), for example, suggests that "many myths regarding Salvadorans' industriousness have been put in doubt due to this new vision of work," while a Salvadoran official commented that, in many parts of the country, workers have been replaced by ghosts (*fantasmas*), the absent presence of Salvadorans who are in the United States.

Dependency on remittances is believed to erode family relationships and thus the broader social fabric. Although remitting itself is sometimes defined as a sign of devotion to family and country (Lianos 1997; Libercier and Schneider 1996), migration can entail lengthy (and often agonizing) separations between family members. Children may resent parents who left them in the care of other relatives, and spouses who are separated sometimes form new relationships with other individuals (Menjívar 2000). According to some analysts, when parents are absent, children may lack discipline and moral values. As a result, according to some, children of migrant parents become more likely to commit crimes or join gangs. For instance, at an ecumenical service during the 2004 Immigrant Week in El Salvador, a religious leader stated that instead of clamping down on gangs through increased criminal penalties, the Salvadoran government should address gang membership's root causes, such as being left behind by migrant parents. Even when children do not turn to crime, analysts suggest, migration can produce a moral hazard problem. Remitters, it is noted, cannot verify how recipients are spending money and recipients cannot assess the financial resources available to remitters (Chami et al. 2005). An interviewee in Los Angeles described one such situation:

> I was paying for the education of my two younger brothers for fourteen years. When I came here, they entered the university. They were in the university for fourteen years and they didn't graduate. . . . When I went to El Salvador after fourteen years—I couldn't leave here [earlier] because I didn't have my papers—I discovered that my younger brothers had a car, had a motorcycle, had homes, had wives, had children, and that it had been years since they went to the university. And, just like that, there are hundreds and thousands of stories of family disintegration, women who come by themselves and in two months find a boyfriend here and break up the home that they had there and leave their children wherever. Or men who come by themselves and do the same thing.

Dependency and the moral hazard problem associated with remitting are believed to encourage recipients to spend remittances on wasteful consumption, rather than on productive endeavors. One NGO member complained, for example, that people who receive remittances spend them on stereos and television sets instead of investments. This interviewee suggested that better education could change such habits. García (1994, 10) argues that such spending patterns have made remittance recipients the key reference group in rural communities, producing a desire for "a lifestyle typical of the middle class in poor and backward contexts." Another NGO member told me of such a situation: "In small towns, there are markets with the latest electrical appliances, there are banks, there are travel agencies. I'd like you to go to Intipucá, for example. You know that the sign at the entrance to Intipucá says, 'Welcome to Intipucá.' In English."[5] (see also Pedersen 2004). A staff member of a Central American community organization in Washington, D.C., worried that remittances produced through great sacrifice on the part of migrants were frittered away in El Salvador: "The two or three hundred dollars that are sent there, sometimes in a matter of days, are gone. And people here [in the U.S.] go about trying to save, and save, and save." At a panel presentation during the 2004 celebration of Immigrant Week in El Salvador, one analyst commented, "El Salvador is becoming one large shopping plaza." Not all agreed that consumption is not productive. One Salvadoran official, for example, told me, "I see people buying things that are productive. For instance, purchasing books to study is a productive use of remittances." Even this official, however, thought that remittances could be made more productive.

Some argue that remittances spent on consumption do not remain within the Salvadoran economy. If consumer goods are primarily imports (particularly from the United States), then remittances return almost immediately to the United States (García 1994; Orozco et al. 1997).[6] Further, some note that, before dollarization, the influx of migrant remittances inflated the value of Salvadoran currency such that Salvadoran products were less competitive internationally (García 1994). Thus, much like unauthorized immigrants, who are positioned outside their country of residence, remittances can have a partial or inconsistent presence in El Salvador. Montes (1990, 19), for example, contended that "remittances . . . for the most part do not even arrive in the country but rather are bank notes that are immediately reexported to the United States or are simply money orders to be cashed here in national currency," while a Salvadoran religious leader speaking during Immigrant Week characterized remittances as simply "traveling through" (*de paseo*). Remittances, like migrants, are en route.

Even if remittances were to remain in El Salvador, many fear that this source of national income is intrinsically unstable. Díaz-Briquets and

Pérez-López (1997, 414–15; see also Orellana Merlos 1992; J. García 1994) point out that "it is also noted [by critics] that countries highly dependent on remittances are at grave risk given that remittances are notorious for their volatility—their volume is highly sensitive to fluctuations in economic conditions and political developments." Given this uncertainty, economic officials in El Salvador have attempted to develop new sources of income (such as tourism) in preparation for remittances' eventual decline. Numerous interviewees recounted anecdotes about friends and relatives who had stopped or would soon stop remitting. For instance, a Salvadoran man who had immigrated to the United States at a young age, completed college there, and then worked in both countries and frequently traveled between the United States and El Salvador told me:

> My family is living in two different worlds. My world, for example, I don't send anybody remittances to El Salvador, but my mother still sends—[she] has been in this country for twenty years. My grandmother is eighty-nine. When my grandmother dies, my mother will stop sending remittances to El Salvador. She might continue sending to the little kids, you know, my cousin to go to school, but we send like a gift.

Similarly, a Salvadoran official suggested that

> There are studies that tell us that the remittance link, as we say, only lasts seven years. That is, remittances will not last forever. The Salvadoran who leaves makes an effort to return, more or less for seven years. Why? Because in those seven years, various things have happened. One, the mother or the grandmother that was left behind dies, or he manages to bring his family, whether legally or illegally, or simply, as happens in many cases, he has forgotten that his children eat, get dressed, and get sick, because he formed a new household [in the United States].

Such analyses suggest that for remitting to continue, new emigration must occur.

In contrast to these pessimistic accounts, other analysts suggest that remittances produce multiplier effects, making remittances' ultimate destination less important than their continued circulation. According to such scholars, remittances "work their way through" economies, indirectly increasing production (Durand et al. 1996; Taylor 1999). As they are transferred from recipient to shop owner to employee to bank to investor and onward, analysts note, remittances generate jobs, support businesses, and fuel investment. Kapur and McHale (2003) refer to this process as "trickle-up economics," while Asch and Reichmann (1994, 14) explain that "even if the family . . . spends all of the remittance on direct consumption of, say, a refrigerator, the refrigerator manufacturer may deposit its revenues with a financial intermediary who will loan the money to an investor." Durand et al. (1996, 428) point out that through multiplier effects, even the most seemingly wasteful forms of consumption, such as beer drinking, "can have positive effects on regional growth." Some suggest that interdependency is a characteristic of the global economy and that there is no reason to single out remitting as particularly problematic. For instance, Taylor et al. (1996, 202) argue that "just as a highly developed North American suburb would be thrown into recession without its commuter workers, labor-exporting countries inevitably are entangled in a web of global economic interdependence. . . . Income sent home by foreign migrants has an effect on the migrant-sending nation that is similar to the effect of commuters' paychecks on suburban downtowns." Numerous analysts stress that remittances play a vital role in providing income, informal credit, and unofficial insurance to impoverished families (Durand et al. 1996; Itzigsohn 1995; Libercier and Schneider 1996; Orellana Merlos 1992; Orozco et al. 1997). Scholars further suggest that expectations of autonomy and productivity are unrealistic. For example, Taylor (1999, 65; see also Keely and Tran 1989) explains:

> A frequently used benchmark is whether migrant sending economies become more or less dependent upon migrant remittances over time; that is, do migrant remittances set in motion self-sustaining growth in migrant sending areas? The use of this criterion in migration studies is peculiar; we do not ask the same question when assessing economic welfare in developed country communities (e.g., American suburbs) whose economic mainstay is supplying labour to outside markets (e.g., urban centers). Nor do we ask whether other kinds of exports enable countries or regions eventually to wean themselves from trade. In an era of increasing market integration, both within and among countries, such questions, indeed, would appear strange.

Debates over whether remittances promote dependency or autonomy, consumption or production, suggest that if policymakers could create the right conditions, remittances' financial benefits could be maximized. Focusing on such technical questions can depoliticize remittances' linkages to poverty (see also Ferguson 1994). To avoid such depoliticization, some analyses explicitly link remittances to exploitation. Segundo Montes's (1990) seminal study of remittances emphasized the financial costs associated with sending a migrant to the United States. More recently, the Mobilidad Humana pastoral project of the Catholic Church produced a dollar-bill-like brochure with the slogan "dolor por dólar" (pain for the dollar). This brochure suggests that regardless of states' accounting procedures, remittances *are* the second half of an exchange, and are therefore far from cost free (see also Hernandez and Coutin 2006). Numerous interviewees stressed that remittances were produced through tremendous sacrifices. A Salvadoran NGO member in Washington, D.C., commented, "The five or six thousand dollars or more that they are sending to the country each year is money that they need here for the education of their children, to buy a house, or to take a vacation and not only to live working, working, working, and working." Further, some argued that remitting ought to garner migrants greater political rights in El Salvador (including the right to vote). To make this point, a Salvadoran businessman quoted the saying "He who pays the mariachi chooses the song," while a member of an NGO located in San Salvador complained that the Salvadoran government and populace were pleased to accept remittances but unwilling to grant voting rights to migrants. Further, some interviewees criticized the Salvadoran government for relying on what they called a "politics of expulsion." To quote a Salvadoran artist living in Los Angeles, "How does it [the government] expel people? [By] not creating jobs. Not creating effective development plans. Being deaf to the crime of transporting the undocumented. Deaf and blind. Not giving educational opportunities to the community; that is the manner of expelling people. Before they were expelled through the war, now through economic necessity."[7]

The lack of consensus regarding remittances' development potential has led some analysts and policymakers to focus on collective remittances (Goldring 2003; Itzigsohn 1995; Lianos 1997). For example, a Salvadoran official in the Ministry of Foreign Affairs told me, "We can't touch the family remittances, because that is what they receive, and we cannot obligate them to put them to a different use. But the collective remittances should be made productive." The controversies surrounding family remittances, however, shape collective remitting as well.

Collective Remittances

Hometown associations are considered one of the most potentially transformative but as yet underdeveloped components of the remittance phenomenon (Fox and Rivera-Salgado 2004). Hometown associations are made up of emigrants who come from the same city or town and who dedicate themselves to raising funds for development projects in their community of origin. Although their work is widely regarded as altruistic, patriotic, and noble, hometown associations are also criticized for paternalism, funding inappropriate projects, promoting dependency, and substituting for services that ought to be provided by governments. Because hometown associations' efforts are directed explicitly toward improving particular municipalities, NGOs, national governments, and international development organizations have sought to improve the quality of these associations' work. Following a neoliberal model, government and international financial institutions are particularly interested in the development potential that could arise through community partnerships in which local knowledge, community resources, state funds, and technical expertise could be directed toward particular projects. Similarly, working out of a community empowerment model, some NGOs seek to direct hometown associations toward productive projects, such as establishing cooperatives, that could promote community autonomy and create employment opportunities. Some hometown associations have responded to such initiatives by seeking greater transparency and accountability and by striving to avoid paternalism and charity in their projects and their relations with home communities. Efforts to maximize the productive potential of collective remittances attest to the limitations of traditional development schemas.

Although their structures vary, Salvadoran hometown associations typically employ social networks in fund-raising activities to support the participants' community of origin.[8] To raise funds, associations sell tickets to picnics, parties, dinners, and other social events and use the profits from ticket sales to finance particular improvement projects in migrants' hometowns. These social events can attract hundreds of people, and also provide opportunities to gather with fellow townspeople, briefly re-create elements of life in the participants' hometown, and acquaint migrant youth with their parents' cultural traditions. For instance, associations often arrange celebrations of their hometown's patron saint day in coordination with festivities occurring in the hometown itself. By selling tickets to events, young women compete to be crowned the association's queen (*reina*), and the winning queen may even travel to El Salvador to participate in traditional festivals there. Associations are usually organized around particular families, and often have formal structures, such as a president, board of directors, treasurer, and so on. Both men and women are involved, though there are sometimes gendered divisions of labor (e.g., women may prepare the food for social gatherings). In Los Angeles, some associations have banded

together to form Comunidades de Ayuda Directa a El Salvador (COMU-
NIDADES), a federation of hometown associations. Although in many
cases participants hold relatively low-income jobs, for instance, as mechanics, housekeepers, printers, or janitors, associations may raise thousands of
dollars annually. These funds are used for such projects as equipping a
medical clinic, providing books and uniforms for schoolchildren, paving
streets, repainting churches, building wells, putting in streetlights, establishing cultural centers, building computer labs, creating sports complexes,
and organizing activities for youth. Frequently, this work is coordinated by
a *comité de enlace* or liaison committee in the participants' hometown.
Some associations also raise money to support participants in Los Angeles.
For instance, members of the Comunidad Salvadoreña (Salvadoran Community) in Los Angeles collected a small monthly fee in order to create a
fund from which participants could take out informal loans when they
needed credit.

According to participants, hometown associations' work is supposed to
evince a purity of motive. For instance, when I asked how much time they
devoted to their hometown association each week, members refused to
measure their time. One interviewee commented, "That which is economic, we have to measure well. But in [relation to] our time, that which is
of service, we do not measure." Interviewees suggested that calculating
their hours of service would imply that they desired compensation, when in
fact "one feels compensated when one sees the project finished." Participants attributed their desire to help their home communities to a sense of
service, patriotism, a knowledge of what it is to be deprived, and a feeling
that, though living in Southern California, they were still part of their home
communities. A member of COPRECA (Comité Propaz y Reconstruccion
de Cacaopera/Committee for Peace and Reconstruction of Cacaopera) recalled that when he immigrated to the United States, he was continually
conscious of what was happening in his hometown and "every night we
begged God that the families that remained behind would not be killed." A
participant from another association began sobbing as she described the
childhood poverty that now compelled her to help others.

Consistent with this sense of service—and, though few associations were
legally registered as such, with the definition of nonprofit organizations—
participants stressed that their work was apolitical, not partisan, not for
personal gain, and not in service of a religious end. Within COMU-
NIDADES, to call something "pure *negocio*" (pure business) was to con-
demn it. The pride that they took in their work was evidenced by members'
desire to document their activities. Many had binders filled with clippings

and photos of their activities, videotapes of their work in their home communities, and careful records of their associations' meetings, membership, finances, and any bylaws, letters, or agreements. Through hometown associations, migrants sought to fill holes that the war left in people, buildings, and towns—bullet holes, lost limbs, psychological traumas, and absent people. By reconnecting internationally dispersed communities, hometown associations turned absence into presence.

The work of hometown associations was generally praised by Salvadoran officials, members of NGOs, and the general public. The Salvadoran Ministry of Foreign Affairs created a staff position within the DGACE to work with members of hometown associations. Salvadoran consulates also have officials who are responsible for community affairs, which generally means responding to and attempting to coordinate the work of community associations. The DGACE website publicizes associations' fund-raising events and describes procedures to obtain tax-exempt status for donated goods that are being brought into El Salvador as donations. The Salvadoran FISDL (Fondo de Inversión Social para el Desarrollo Local/Social Investment for Local Development Fund) supports the work of hometown associations through a program, Unidos por la Solidaridad, that permits associations to compete for government development funds. The icon for this program (see Ministerio de Relaciones Exteriores and FISDL n.d.) features a triangle whose base is "Salvadoreños en el Exterior" (Salvadorans Living Abroad) and whose two upper sides are "Gobierno Nacional" (National Government) and "Municipio Comunidad" (Municipal Community). Overarching the whole triangle (like a rainbow) are the words "Creando un Triángulo Solidario" (Creating a Solidary Triangle). Numerous NGOs, both in the United States and in El Salvador, also sought to work with hometown associations in order to promote development in El Salvador. Like officials, these NGO members perceived Salvadoran migrants as the "base" and therefore as key to development. Even international bodies, such as the Organisation for Economic Co-operation and Development (OECD), see hometown associations as having development potential: "Immigrants have a thorough knowledge of the regions and populations concerned by these [collective] projects and thus, better than external agents (national or foreign), can work out appropriate projects which the people support and finally appropriate for themselves. Moreover, these projects can be favourable to collective and democratic participation by the inhabitants" (Libercier and Schneider 1996, 47).

Although they praised hometown associations for members' dedication, self-sacrifice, and sense of service, officials, NGO members, and others who wanted to work with these groups also sought to "improve" their work. Many individuals told me of ambulances that had been sent to El Salvador by hometown associations, only to break down on Salvadoran roads, lack repair parts, or contain equipment that no one knew how to use (cf. de Laet 2002).[9] For instance, a Salvadoran official told me, "They send the town, for example, an ambulance, but it turns out that in six months, the ambulance breaks down and, as there is no money to maintain it, it's ruined and there it sits forever. Or, simply, they send the ambulance, but there is no doctor to tend [people]. Or they send the ambulance, but there are no roads on which the ambulance can circulate."

It is probably not a coincidence that these stories focused on *ambulances*. Communities were trying to provide "first aid," but such aid was seen as problematic. Associations were criticized for paternalism, for charitable approaches, for doing what felt good instead of what a community really needed, for allowing the government to evade its responsibility to provide basic services to citizens, for divisiveness, and for providing inappropriate aid.[10] Another Salvadoran official related an anecdote about an association that "was working with the school in one *cantón*. They elected a queen and raised money. With this money, they purchased schoolbooks and sent them to the school. But they didn't realize that the school didn't have a bathroom. The students had to go outside to perform their necessities. Later they realized that it might have been better for them to have built a bathroom than to have bought the books."

Officials suggested that the state could serve as an overarching institution, coordinating hometown associations' work, providing technical assistance, directing associations toward different sorts of projects (such as investing in Salvadoran businesses), and ensuring that groups provided assistance that is truly needed.[11] NGOs also appeared eager to provide such assistance (Goldring 2003). A member of a U.S.-based Salvadoran NGO suggested that by working with hometown associations, his own organization could "advance and increase these potentials in three years, in five years, in ten years, and the current benefits would quintuple enormously."

These criticisms have not gone unnoticed by hometown associations, whose members explicitly strive for transparency, accountability, and nonpaternalism. One association member recounted that "to rid ourselves of the paternalism of only giving and giving and giving, we opted for another idea, of giving them seeds that they would plant." Further, to avoid contributing to "remittance towns in which they don't work because they are waiting for the check from the relative who is in the United States," this individual said, "what we are doing as a nonprofit organization is trying to provide aid to the young people, teaching them job skills." Members of another organization, whose donations had been absconded with by an individual in their hometown, stressed the need for transparency: "We don't like things that are fraudulent (*chuecadas*), as they say. We obtain evidence [of our activities]. Such as receipts from TACA [a Central American airline]." Members of another association, Comité Pro-Mejoramiento San Miguel Tepezontes (San Miguel Tepezontes Improvement Committee), deliberately sought to avoid charitable approaches: "It's a joint effort. That is, they [hometown residents] have to work and also we [Comité Pro-Mejoramiento San Miguel Tepezontes members] work. Even when we send aid, there are times that we send [it], for example, in a form that puts the people to work so that they are not merely receiving money." Participants also critique the neoliberal notion that citizens can take over and more efficiently perform services that were previously a government responsibility (see Herbert 2005).

Such comments indicate that despite the widespread admiration for and appreciation of hometown associations, providing collective remittances is fraught work. This work was called forth by a particular set of circumstances (the Salvadoran civil war, emigration, and economic needs in El Salvador) and by particular desires (e.g., to reconnect with community members, relive better times, counter poverty, and improve migrants' communities of origin). Collective remittances, however, are being given added significance by competing yet coalescing models of development. On the one hand, neoliberal financial models encourage migrants to be generous and self-sacrificing (Baker-Cristales 2004; Hernandez and Coutin 2006). Emigrants are being told to remit and to constitute themselves as ideal emigrant citizens: emissaries for El Salvador, who serve their nation through good works, but who must absent themselves to do so. By providing collective remittances, hometown associations—like other migrants who remit—participate in the broader reconstitution of the nation of El Salvador through its dispersed citizenry. As Baker-Cristales (2004, 77) notes, "Migrants are consistently essentialized as displaced members of a nation who naturally long to reunite with the motherland, whether the reunion is physical or simply virtual." On the other hand, the more leftist notion that the poor are key to the future suggests that hometown associations are "organizaciones de base" (base organizations), as one Salvadoran activist stated. These models coalesce in their emphasis on productivity, sustainability, and local empowerment. Migrants and migrant associations—a highly informal sector—are, once again, deemed key to their country's future.

Absence and Presence

The large-scale exodus set in motion by the Salvadoran civil war produced a sizeable influx of remittances into El Salvador. This development was not inevitable. Migrants could have chosen to not send this money, or they could have sent smaller amounts. The channels through which money was sent could have remained informal. Officials could have defined this money differently, for instance, as "illicit" income. But circumstances conspired to give these transactions increased visibility within national financial accounts. On a macroeconomic level, remittances seem to have benefited El Salvador enormously, though the long-term impact of migrant remittances remains a subject of debate. Citizens who were directly or indirectly excluded from Salvadoran territory during the civil war came, through remitting, to be hailed as loyal patriots who long for their homeland, sacrifice for the greater good, and place altruistic national goals before selfish or partisan interests. Instead of repatriating within El Salvador, these migrants send emissaries: dollars that course through the Salvadoran economy and banking system, making their presence felt in the form of consumer income, good works, and financial records. Remittances' presence, however, is also linked to absence—the holes that are left in families, towns, labor forces, productive enterprises, and Salvadoranness itself, which, some argue, becomes corrupted by U.S. dollars. Traces of the political and economic violence of migration itself remain in that which returns to El Salvador.

CHAPTER 6

Productos de la Guerra (Products of War)

Nosotros somos el resultado de un pasado oscuro en El Salvador.

Salvadoran activist in Los Angeles

This country—or we Salvadorans—are standing on the bodies of thousands of compatriots who died during the war. More than one hundred thousand deaths, and there are still disappeared people about whom there is no answer. So there is a whole national tragedy, and it is on this tragedy that the democracy is built. There is a historic and ethical responsibility toward the people who gave their lives in the construction of a different reality.

Member of a Salvadoran NGO dedicated to human rights

Between remittances and gangs, one can see the two extremes of how the community [in the U.S.] continually affects the country.

Salvadoran journalist

Violence is generally considered to be destructive. Violence wounds bodies, kills people, tears apart families, destroys buildings, annihilates social orders, and, in some instances, makes nations something of a fiction. What does it mean, then, to be *produced* by a *destructive force* (Feldman 1991)? And how do *traces* of violence remain within its products?

The large-scale emigration that accompanied the onset of the Salvadoran civil war has been seen as a product of political violence and the economic disruptions associated with that violence (Mountz et al. 2002). During the war, Salvadorans experienced kidnappings, massacres, bombings, stray bullets, assassinations, torture, surveillance, forced recruitment, the confiscation of property, and the uncertainty of political terror (Binford 1996; Byrne 1996; Coutin 2001a; Green 1999; Montgomery 1995; Stephen 1997). Perpetrators justified such actions as preventing the spread of Communism, defending El Salvador, and seeking a more just future. Those who were not affected directly may have suffered indirectly, through loss of jobs or income, difficulties pursuing studies and careers, and the suffering of family members and close friends. To obtain refuge in the United States migrants had to prove that their presence was a product of political violence; that they had "a well-founded fear of being persecuted for reasons of race, religion, nationality, membership of a particular social group or political opinion"; and that they were unwilling or unable to return to their countries of origin due to such fear (1951 Convention Relating to the Status of Refugees, chap. 1, art. 1, sec. A2). This definition distinguished direct persecution from generalized violence, economic suffering, and common crimes. In reality, however, individuals' experiences of violence and their motivations for migrating were often more mixed. An individual could emigrate to the United States because her life was in danger, she had no job, and her aunt lived in Los Angeles. Similarly an act of persecution could be justified through political rhetoric but also enable perpetrators to profit financially. Nonetheless, during the Salvadoran civil war, the discourse surrounding violence focused on human rights, cold war politics, and the political subject recognized by international law.

During the postwar period, the character of violence in El Salvador changed. Homicides, gang activity, muggings, kidnappings, and robberies began to rise, making El Salvador, in 1996, the country with the highest homicide rate in Latin America (Saldomando 1998, 77; Moodie 2006). Migrants who were eligible to apply for NACARA commonly cited crime as one of the factors that would make it a hardship for them to return to El Salvador, and some argued that criminal activities could in fact be a cover for political violence (see also Dickson-Gómez 2002). The crime wave was considered at least in part a product of emigration. Analysts argued that youth who remained in El Salvador while their parents worked in the United States grew up with less supervision, authority, and moral guidance, and therefore were more susceptible to being recruited by criminal gangs. To the degree that emigration tore apart families and communities, some argued, it also destroyed the social values that had previously kept criminal activity in check. Further, in the mid-1990s, as the United States began to deport criminal aliens in larger numbers, youth gangs began to proliferate in El Salvador. These gangs reproduced U.S. gang structures and practices, even adopting names, such as 18th Street, that were coined in the United

States (Baker-Cristales 2004; Zilberg 2004). In response, the Salvadoran government adopted stringent antigang measures known as Súper Mano Dura (super heavy hand). Some of these measures, such as declaring gangs illicit associations and authorizing Salvadoran soldiers to support police in their antigang efforts, resembled tactics previously used against guerrillas. As crime escalated, some citizens began to look back on the war years as a period of relative safety, when violence was less arbitrary and therefore more predictable (Moodie 2006; Zilberg 2007a). According to polls taken in 2004, shortly after antigang policies were adopted, the majority of the Salvadoran public supported a government crackdown on gangs (Salamanca 2004). It has also become common for citizens and businesses to adopt private security measures, such has hiring armed guards, relocating within gated communities, and installing security systems.

El Salvador is not alone in experiencing rising crime, the privatization of security, and the intensification of state security forces and measures. Guatemala, Bolivia, South Africa, Venezuela, and other countries have gone through similar processes (Comaroff and Comaroff 2004b; Godoy 2002, 2004, 2005; Goldstein 2004; Wilson 2001). Some analysts attribute these developments to neoliberal economic policies that remove social supports, exacerbate poverty, and encourage privatization of state functions. Jean and John Comaroff (2004a, 822) explain:

> In postcolonial South Africa, dramatic enactments of crime and punishment . . . are a vital part of the effort to *produce* social order and to arrive at persuasive ways of representing it, thereby to construct a minimally coherent world-in-place; even more, to do so under neoliberal conditions in which technologies of governance—including technologies of detection and enforcement—are, at the very least, changing rapidly and are, in some places, under dire threat.

Others point to security concerns that increased following the hijackings of September 11, 2001, and to antiterrorism measures that are being adopted internationally (Scheppele 2004a, 2004b). Still others cite factors, such as a history of civil war, widespread availability of weapons, or the need to reintegrate former combatants, that may be unique to particular countries' histories (Wilson 2001). Although these explanations are not mutually exclusive, it is clear that a framework of crime and security is replacing that of politics and human rights as a means of accounting for violence. As "rights" take on new meanings, the products of violence are redefined, and security apparatuses are reauthorized. Defining violence as criminal rather than political in nature legitimizes state security measures and suggests that perpetrators deserve to be repressed. In such circumstances, the violence of social processes that produce migration is reinscribed in migrants themselves.[1]

War

Although the intensity of the 1980–92 Salvadoran civil war varied over time and from one location to another, few who lived through it remained untouched. Salvadorans were, of course, differentially positioned in relation to the war. Some were guerrilla combatants or soldiers, others supported one or another side in the conflict, others had relatives who were affiliated with the guerrillas, the soldiers, or both; others attempted to remain uninvolved, and still others may have lived near a military target, held an occupation (such as chauffeur) that placed them at risk, or belonged to communities that became battlegrounds. Violence was shaped by revolutionary ideals, national security doctrine, and cold war politics. Guerrillas blew up bridges and power plants, forces engaged in combat, soldiers bombed areas of supposed guerrilla support, death squads tortured and killed suspects, battalions massacred residents of allegedly hostile villages, both sides assassinated opponents, and many civilians were caught in the crossfire. Those who were not affected directly suffered indirect effects, such as surveillance, searches, roadblocks, plant closings, encountering dismembered or tortured bodies, and the confiscation of goods or services.[2] Violence and related economic problems produced a massive displacement of people, as individuals sought jobs, safety, and reunion with family members. As noted earlier, by 1984, "within El Salvador there were 468,000 displaced people (9.75 percent of the population), 244,000 in Mexico and elsewhere in Central America, and 500,000 more in the United States, for a total of more than 1.2 million displaced and refugees (25 percent of the population)" (Byrne 1996, 115). Emigration from El Salvador to the United States preceded the civil war (Menjívar 2000), and migrants' motives for migrating were mixed. Nonetheless, to a significant degree the Salvadoran immigrant population in the United States is a product of the civil war.

Almost all of the migrants (primarily NACARA applicants, members of hometown associations, and deportees) whom I interviewed regarding their immigration histories cited the civil war as a key reason for leaving El Salvador. The civil war was not their only motive. Individuals also sought jobs, better opportunities, and to rejoin family members who were already living in the United States. Stories of traumatic experiences, terrible losses, ongoing threats, and devastated communities nonetheless were common. Many, including individuals who left El Salvador as children, told of their horror at finding bodies or body parts. Carlos Pineda, who left El Salvador at eleven, felt he had had to escape the country because he "had seen so many people dead and everything. The way they got killed. And, you know, by just looking at them all destroyed, all torn up [in] pieces, because they were cut by machetes and all that other stuff . . . almost had ribs coming off." Irma Martínez, who emigrated at nine, recalled walking in the street and finding "a man hanging whose skin had been removed. Or when I went to an area where they were building houses and the houses were empty and they took us to play there and in one of those [houses] I fell and I found a hand." Alejandro Cruz worked in El Salvador as a chauffeur. One day, en route to Guazapa, he found five people hanging. Another time, on the way to San Vicente, he found decapitated bodies: "The bodies were to one side because the pigs were eating them, and the heads on the tables. . . . Very, very, very horrible that whole situation." Discarding bodies seems to have been a common practice during the civil war (see also McAllister 2003). Another migrant, George Gomez, who immigrated to the United States as a young child, said that his father wanted him and his siblings to leave because "the area right there where we lived was like the spot where they'd throw bodies."

Other emigrants fled because they happened to live in areas where battles were common. Ricardo and Ana Cuellar lived in front of a military command station where there were continual battles. Motioning to a photo on their mantelpiece, Ricardo told me, "The boy who is in that picture there and who came with us when we traveled to the U.S. has shrapnel from a grenade in his back. And her [Ana's] mother had a bullet in her arm." Arceli Ulloa lived across from an educational institute where the National Guard and the guerrillas appeared regularly. Concerned that her daughter, a student at the time, would be recruited, Ulloa commented that "it was terrible not knowing who was speaking to whom." Many of Ulloa's daughter's schoolmates were killed, she related. Amalia Martínez, who lived on the outskirts of San Salvador and who was Irma's older sister, found that daily tasks, like going home from school, endangered her life: "I remember that once we had to stop in the middle of the street. My father grabbed us— it was so sudden that we didn't even feel what had happened, and we hid behind a tree and we began to hear the shots and the shots and we [were like] what is happening, and where are we, and what happened?" Amalia and her two younger sisters regularly practiced hiding in their home so that, if an incident occurred when their parents weren't home, soldiers would not find them and rape them. Irma recalled:

> I remember one time we were in the hallway as usual when the soldiers came, always in the hallway, really quiet on the floor. We heard a really big noise outside. There was a lot of people out there, big crowd, there was some sort of commotion going on, because then I heard some screaming and I peeked outside and I saw the soldiers were trying to get this one, this guy who is running like crazy and after I saw him run by, I saw why he was screaming. They had poured boiling water or something on his back, and I can see the boils and his skin crawling in the back.

Battles, university closings, and other disruptions frustrated many young people's plans to study. Miguel López Herrera found it impossible to attend the university in which he had enrolled: "I came in '90, the [final] offensive was in '89; well, that was something—imagine, twenty years [old], one is young, one has many aspirations. I had enrolled in the university and I wanted to go forward, but because of that, it was practically a year later. So the situation was chaotic, and worse, because, if you didn't study, there were no sources of work." López Herrera also feared being forcibly recruited into either the army or the guerrilla forces. Even young children were seemingly at risk of forced recruitment. Carlos Pineda's mother was worried that, at eleven, he would be taken away to fight in the war.

The war also exposed individuals to brutal assassinations of friends, relatives, and co-workers. Javier López related that "they had already assassinated my father, my brother. The put a noose on my mother—the man, the lieutenant, the sergeant, I don't know what he was—and they told her, 'I'm going to kill you,' but with cusswords, to my mother who already was sixty years old." When the guerrillas took over the town of Berlín, Alejandro Cruz was able to enter as a reporter's chauffeur: "And there in Berlín the guerrillas were walking around like they were the authority. To a friend of mine who was my teacher, to that man there in Berlín, they gave a cruel death. Yes, they hung him, *le tasajearon*, because he shot at them when they entered Berlín, and I went to see this man, poor thing—he was a teacher, an elementary school teacher." When their friends or relatives were killed, many concluded that they could be next. Alicia Montalvo's father belonged to a union at the brewery where he worked: "They killed my dad's friend because he was sending the propaganda. And they knew that my dad was his friend. So it was kind of 'we have to go now or he's next.' " Alejandro Cruz, who was a member of the Christian Democratic political party, received death threats accusing him of being a leftist. Amalia and Irma Martínez's parents worked with the Catholic Church in El Salvador. Although they never took up arms, they learned that their names were on a blacklist, and they narrowly missed being massacred on numerous occasions.

Such experiences contributed to massive emigration from El Salvador. One interviewee described the effects of the war on his own hometown of Cacaopera:

> The town has completely become a ghost town. No people live there. Every-one emigrated to the capital, to other countries, to Mexico, Honduras, the United States. We have people in Australia. We have people in Canada, orig-inally from our town. But the majority of the people reside in California, New York, and Washington, D.C.
>
> So, the reason this occurred is that our land was practically destroyed by the invasions of the planes when they were bombing. The guerrillas would come by night, the army in the day, they even fought in the daytime. It was a highly conflictive zone. People from the countryside arrived, they arrived to populate the edges of the city, building their cardboard houses out of dis-carded industrial material, and these zones were called "refugee zones." Where the people from the countryside came, the Torola River crossed, which was the border of the war. So the situation was that these people lived without good medical attention. These people did not have drinking water. So the government of El Salvador, the government did not exist, it wasn't there. The municipal government had gone to another city due to the con-flicts.
>
> They emigrated because they were at risk of death. In fact, many people lost entire families. Children, the elderly, young people, because it was a mountainous zone. It reached such an extreme that the vegetation was com-pletely destroyed.
>
> We have people who lasted, yes, they lasted twelve years living in the town. These people did not remain well in the head. Children who were born, children of soldiers, children of guerrillas, and the parents died. We have grandmothers who are raising children because the mother is no longer there. She is in another country, and the father died in the war. The problem of trauma occurs. A psychological trauma in children, they play with weapons, they make weapons out of wood because they were born in the war.
>
> The war ends, the town is semidestroyed. The church was hit by a missile designed to knock down helicopters. The main tower is destroyed. The city

hall was a garbage dump. The town clinic was disastrous—it wasn't a clinic, it was something horrible, all dirty, with slogans and signs from the two bands [of the conflict]. There was no medicine.

Clearly the war had a long-term impact on individuals and communities (Dickson-Gómez 2002). Irma Martínez, for example, told me that she always sleeps with her shoes and clothes handy, in case something occurs during the night, and Irma's younger sister Katarina, who was only six when she left El Salvador, said that she adopts a defensive pose while walking in public, so that no one will attack her.

The civil war continued to shape the experiences of Salvadorans in the United States, as migrants, officials, and advocates debated how to characterize the Salvadoran immigrant population.

Human Rights

During the Salvadoran civil war, connections between violence and emigration were made through a discourse of human rights. In theory, international human-rights law establishes a series of rights (such as rights to life, liberty, freedom of expression, freedom of religion, due process, and freedom from torture) that are considered so basic to being human that they are supposed to be inviolable (see Ishay 1997). Nonetheless, there are important limitations, in practice, to these protections. How governments implement (or fail to implement) such rights may be very different from the guarantees provided by national constitutions and international conventions (Hayner 2001). The state's use of force, such as detention, incarceration, and even the death penalty, is not usually considered a human-rights violation. Human-rights law generally protects only civil and political rights, as opposed to economic and cultural rights (so-called second- and third-generation rights), such as the right to employment, health care, and cultural traditions (Bhabha 1996). Governments are permitted to use violence against forces that threaten the nation, therefore acts of war, such as bombings, are usually distinguished from human-rights violations. Further, common crimes—murder, kidnapping, robbery—are not usually described as human-rights violations unless perpetrated systematically by a government or by a group that the government cannot control—typically a group that has a particular political agenda (Coutin 2001a). In fact, in punishing such actions, governments situate themselves on the side of law, as protectors of citizens' basic rights.

Human-rights discourse has been linked to immigration through politi-cal asylum, which was established as a remedy for citizens who have es-caped a government that was violating or failing to protect their human rights. In the United States, asylum was restricted to individuals who were fleeing Communist countries or were citizens of certain Middle Eastern na-tions, but the 1980 Refugee Act adopted the United Nations High Commis-sion for Refugees (UNHCR) definition of refugee, thus making asylum available to any who had a well-founded fear of being persecuted due to their race, nationality, religion, social group membership, or political opin-ion (Churgin 1996; Hull 1985; Kennedy 1981). Despite this broader defini-tion, asylum continued to be envisioned as form of protection for relatively exceptional individuals, such as leaders of dissident movements, rather than for large numbers of people fleeing mass persecution (Churgin 1996; Zolberg 1990). For situations of widespread violence, the United States ad-vocated other, more temporary solutions, such as the establishment of refugee camps in neighboring countries (Fagen 1988).[3] Granting asylum to the persecuted was a way for a state to criticize regimes from which asylum seekers were fleeing. In addition to asylum, the principle of *nonrefoulement* establishes that individuals who are at risk of persecution cannot be re-turned to their countries of origin. The United States adopted this principle when it signed the United Nations Protocol Relating to the Status of Refugees in 1968, and when it passed the 1980 Refugee Act, which adopted the UNHCR definition of "refugee" as U.S. law (Churgin 1996; Fagen 1988; Kennedy 1981).

During the 1980s, refugee-rights advocates and members of the Central American solidarity movement used human-rights discourse to link vio-lence and immigration. First, advocates and solidarity workers argued that widespread violence, including the strafing of civilian areas, massacres, death squad killings, arbitrary assassinations, kidnappings, and disappear-ances, made everyone in El Salvador a potential target. According to this reasoning, anyone from El Salvador, regardless of the particular circum-stances that led them to emigrate, could be considered a refugee (Coutin 2001a). Second, advocates drew attention to cases in which Salvadoran mi-grants had been individually targeted by the army, death squads, or guerril-las. One attorney who helped to set up networks of attorneys who would take Salvadoran and Guatemalan clients on a pro bono basis described the sorts of cases that his legal clinic publicized:

So there's the case of Miguel and Angelina [surname deleted]. [Miguel] fled Huehuetenango, [Guatemala]; [their] family was massacred, they were caught by the INS, put in custody. We paid the bond, he came out. He came out of the jail, was filmed. He pointed to the wall and said, "The army came, they threw my parents against the wall. They yelled at them, 'You're subversives,' and killed them. [They said] that all of us campesinos are Communists."

And so we did cases like that. We did a case of [people from the] Mesa Grande [refugee camp]. Big case of about nine Mesa Grande refugees. They were concienticized [that is, they underwent consciousness-raising] through the liberation theology. Actually, the most conscious peasants I've ever met. And that was to dramatize the repression of these refugees after they returned to El Salvador in '87. That got quite a bit of press and we won the case too for the nine.

Publicizing cases in which individuals were singled out for persecution due to being indigenous campesinos or former refugee camp residents who repopulated their villages invoked legal definitions of "refugee" and thus was a way of arguing that Salvadorans deserved political asylum.[4]

During the 1980s, the civil war and human rights concerns provided an organizational focus for groups in the United States and in El Salvador. Numerous international organizations with offices in El Salvador developed programs that focused on refugee issues. The International Organization for Migration, for example, opened an office in El Salvador in 1983 and launched programs that allowed thousands to travel to Canada or Australia as refugees. A Catholic Charities staff member noted that during the 1980s, an Italian religious order established a network of migrant shelters throughout Central America and Mexico. The UNHCR also provided support for refugees and victims of human rights abuses, and monitored the security situation in communities that had been repopulated by returning refugees. In the United States, Central American migrants organized political committees that were focused on struggles in El Salvador. Such committees sought to support guerrillas or their political counterparts, discredit the Salvadoran government, legitimize the FMLN, draw attention to human rights abuses, and prevent U.S. military aid. These political committees soon gave rise to refugee committees that provided services to the burgeoning Central American population. While providing migrants with legal assistance, food, housing, bus tokens, medical care, and job assistance, refugee committees continued to advocate that Central Americans be granted refugee status in the United States. U.S. religious groups and other U.S.-based NGOs also provided support (see Bau 1985; Coutin 1993, 2000, 2005c; Golden and McConnell 1986; MacEoin 1985; C. Smith 1996).

Advocates argued that Salvadorans were a refugee community both as a statement of fact—many had fled situations that endangered their lives—and as a humanitarian and political strategy. Practically speaking, asylum was one of the few ways for Salvadorans who were in the United States to forestall deportations, so these migrants *had* to be refugees (which, in fact, they often were). Securing refugee status could save lives. Politically, the claim that Salvadorans were refugees was a challenge to U.S. foreign policy, as a Salvadoran activist explained:

> We promoted more directly solidarity with El Salvador, based on how we could contribute to changing the foreign policy of the United States; how we could contribute to stopping military aid to El Salvador. The work against military aid [was] based on the situation of human rights in El Salvador, which we also took as grounds for [working to change] immigration policies.

Advocates' efforts to secure refugee status and their opposition to U.S. support for the Salvadoran and Guatemalan governments were interconnected, as an attorney who was involved in the ABC lawsuit explained:

> When you file a lawsuit like this—and from a left perspective, which we definitely were doing—it wasn't just a thing of "these refugees need protection." It was "the reason you're denying this is because of your foreign policy. And the only reason this is happening is because of U.S. foreign policy in Central America and your efforts to stop 'the spread of Communism' or what you believe is groups that support the Soviet sphere." So it was definitely a political lawsuit.

Of course, this challenge did not go unmet. U.S. officials attempted to define Salvadorans as economic migrants, and Salvadoran officials rebutted contentions that human-rights abuses were prevalent in El Salvador. Nonetheless, in both the United States and El Salvador, an infrastructure that attempted to officially define Salvadoran migrants as refugees was created. This infrastructure included attorneys who provided legal services to asylum seekers, organizations that lobbied Congress for legislation that would grant Salvadorans safe haven, international organizations that documented human-rights abuses in El Salvador, and groups that attempted to meet the needs of refugees en route to the United States. Even U.S. authorities, who defined Salvadorans as economic immigrants, were forced to adopt human-rights language, such as when, in order to release military assistance to El Salvador, the Reagan administration had to certify that abuses were diminishing.

In short, though controversial at the time, by the 1990s the claim that large-scale emigration from El Salvador had been triggered by political violence had become conventional wisdom. To give a few examples, a member of a human rights NGO in El Salvador remarked, "Of course, in the decade of the '80s in particular, the migration phenomenon was marked by political reasons"; a human rights official in El Salvador commented, "The first generation of Salvadoran immigrants [was] for labor reasons. The second for political reasons. The third today in the decade of the '90s, due to the aggravation of the economic crisis in the country"; and a high-level Salvadoran official in the United States stated, "Immigration from El Salvador to the United States has a very long history, since at least the 1940s in the area of San Francisco, but also the armed conflict caused the number of immigrants to increase." Interestingly, just as at least some on the right can now acknowledge political reasons for migrating (though they may not agree with criticisms of Salvadoran officials' human-rights record), those on the left can now acknowledge that migrants had mixed, including economic, motives.

Being products of war both legitimized and stigmatized Salvadoran migrants. The violence in El Salvador enabled unauthorized Salvadoran migrants to argue that, unlike other migrants, they had had to flee their country to save their lives. This argument carried some weight. During a 2000 interview, a staff member of a Republican congressman reminded me, "If you look at it strictly as an immigration issue, then it seems like Central Americans should go back. Otherwise, you are rewarding people for getting here and staying here illegally. But it isn't strictly an immigration issue. There is also a refugee issue here." Refugees generally garner a certain amount of public sympathy. At the same time, the term "refugee" can be stigmatizing, implying that those so named are dirty, poor, desperate, and not in control of their futures (Malkki 1995).[5] A number of Salvadoran migrants I interviewed in the mid-1990s rejected the term for these reasons, preferring to simply call themselves "immigrants" (Coutin 2000). The claim that Salvadorans were refugees also led to certain erasures, as more complex motives for migrating—fear of persecution *and* need for a job— could not be publicly acknowledged (Coutin 2001a). Individuals were also somewhat sullied by their association with violence. The director of a Salvadoran cultural institution in the United States contended that because of the war, some migrants did not tell their children about El Salvador, and in fact pretended to be from somewhere else. And, of course, the war left scars, including trauma, grief, flashbacks, anxiety, family separations, fear, exile, and the impossibility of return. During a 2000 interview, a Salvadoran official who was hoping to promote tourism and investment complained, "We are still being reported as like many countries, as a country at war, a violent country."

After peace accords were signed, emigration came to be seen as not only a *product* but a *cause* of violence, as migrants were blamed for disrupting families, leaving children without adequate supervision, corrupting Salvadoran values, and introducing gangs to El Salvador. Further, the violence associated with emigration was increasingly interpreted through a frame of delinquency rather than through one of human rights.

Delinquency

With the 1992 Chapultepec Peace Accords (named after their signing place in Mexico City), violence in El Salvador did not end but rather seemingly changed character (Moodie 2006; Ramos 2000). Instead of bombings and armed confrontations, Salvadorans experienced homicides, kidnappings, robberies, and assaults, sometimes carried out by organized bands but often perpetrated by individuals.[6] As Salvadorans confronted what soon came to be characterized as a crime wave, the war came to be seen by at least some as, in retrospect, a safer time, when violence was less random and when there was greater hope that it would eventually end (see also Caldeira 2000; Moodie 2006; Zilberg 2007a). Nonetheless, contrasts between criminal and political violence were not always clear. On the one hand, crime and political violence were described as different phenomena, the former committed opportunistically, for personal gain or pleasure, and the latter carried out deliberately, with political or ideological goals in mind (Moodie 2006). On the other hand, the war was often cited as the backdrop for subsequent violence, suggesting continuity rather than a dramatic shift, and the discourse that, in the 1980s, condemned the guerrillas as subversives in some ways resembled the discourse of the 1990s and 2000s that defined delinquents as enemies of the nation. Accounts of criminal violence therefore highlight the simultaneous familiarity and novelty of this phenomenon, suggesting a sort of déjà vu that isn't; in other words, a sense that war-time violence was recurring, and yet that, in the postwar period, this violence was something other than war (Moodie 2006).[7] And in this déjà vu, migrants were situated complexly, as potential victims, should they return to El Salvador; as potential perpetrators, should they be deported to

El Salvador; and as indirectly having contributed to the societal transformations that had spawned delinquency. In such analyses, rights took on new meanings. Civil and political rights were largely seen as having been protected, but these very protections were also blamed for insecurity, leading to calls for the curtailment of civil rights in criminal cases.

The surge in criminal activity in the postwar period took many by surprise (Saldomando 1998). During the 1980s, claims that Salvadoran migrants had to remain outside of their country due to political violence implied that, if the violence ended, it would be safe for them to return.[8] Similarly, the peace accords themselves linked security to the cessation of military conflict. Hence, the accords included such measures as limiting the mission of the armed forces to national defense, demobilizing the guerrilla forces, creating mechanisms to incorporate former combatants in civilian life, decreasing the size of the armed forces, establishing the PDH, and replacing existing domestic security forces with a new body, the PNC (Córdova Macías 2001; Studemeister 2001). As violence that was explicitly political decreased, however, criminal violence increased. In 1994, the homicide rate in El Salvador reached 138 per 100,000 residents, as compared to 30 per 100,000 residents in the prewar years (Dalton 2002b, 2002a),[9] and by 1996, according to World Bank statistics, El Salvador was considered the most dangerous country in the Americas (Dalton 2001a; see also Moodie 2004). Kidnappings of businesspeople, some of whom were killed even though relatives paid ransoms, received considerable press attention (e.g., Dalton 2000f). By 2001, an average of fourteen cars were being stolen and six homicides were being committed daily (Dalton 2001b), and a survey conducted in 2002, found that 25 percent of all Salvadorans reported having been the victim of an assault or robbery in the previous four months (*El Diario de Hoy* 2002a). By 2002, an estimated twenty thousand Salvadoran youth had joined gangs (*La Opinión* 2002; Baker-Cristales 2004; Lungo and Kandel 1999; Zilberg 2004).[10] Travelers were assaulted on the highways, in some cases by individuals posing as security personnel (Dalton 2000d, 2000e; Fuentes 2002).[11] In 2000, scandal erupted when it was revealed that members of the PNC were involved in criminal bands (Dalton 2000e). A purging of the police force ensued, with some twelve hundred officers being relieved of duty (Dalton 2000d).

As public insecurity became a focus of conferences, press attention, and public concern and debate, the war served as a backdrop or point of comparison. During interviews, members of human rights–oriented NGOs were quick to contrast the present situation with the human rights violations of the war years. One attorney who specialized in human rights work told me, "Many violations of human rights that were systematically linked to the country have disappeared. The massive violations of human rights, the serious crimes that were politically motivated disappeared from the country, and that is a substantial improvement in the country." Similarly, a member of a human-rights focused NGO remarked:

> We would be unfair in saying that there are problems of systematic violation of human rights. In fact, there are not, in the sense of civil and political rights. That is, legal defense is possible. There are not systematic experiences of torture. There are not arbitrary detentions on the part of the police. The rights of the citizen are protected, there are not clandestine prisons, nor political disappearances. At least, if there are some cases, they are isolated cases. But there is not a government policy in that sense. There is respect for freedoms and respect in some measure for political rights. Today in El Salvador one can be Communist, and they would not take one prisoner for this. Fifteen years ago, if the police found a magazine from the Catholic university [the Jesuit-run University of Central America] in your house, simply for the act of having the magazine from the Catholic university, you would be arrested and you would be investigated. Today, the Catholic university is the principal adviser of the government on educational reform.

Despite such improvements, other interviewees said that they actually felt safer during the civil war. One woman, who had been active in the Salvadoran Left, told me that during the war she understood the risks associated with particular actions as well as how to minimize the chance of being detained. In the postwar period, she commented apprehensively, it was completely unclear why certain people were the targets of kidnappings. Another woman remarked that many Salvadorans were frustrated because they could not visit beautiful or tourist spots in El Salvador. "It was safer to go to those sorts of places during the war," she said. In fact, experts calculated, more people were killed annually through violence during the postwar period than during the war itself.[12] This sense that violence had ended but continued also characterized media accounts. For example, an article published in the Los Angeles–based Spanish newspaper *La Opinión* reported that "in the Central American region . . . deaths over Christmas totaled 111 people, and 490 wounded, numbers that recall the civil wars of the decades of the '70s and '80s" (Dalton 2000b). Similarly, according to an account of a police effort to rescue a kidnapped child, "witnesses reported that the [gun]battles recalled the past civil war, as there was anguish and fear in the area due to the mobilization of military force and then due to the

prolonged and severe battle" (Dalton 2001c). Criminal violence contributed to a widespread sense of insecurity (Cruz 1998). As one analyst
observed, "Although it is awful to say so, the war, with everything that it
presumes in terms of casualties and pain, has, in large measure, more sense
and logic than periods of transition" (Yerushalmi 1998, 44; see also Wilkinson 2004).

Explanations for criminal violence focused largely on historical, structural, and cultural factors, rather than on explicitly political motivations.[13]
Analysts drew attention to the war as a historic process that had both
shaped cultural values and had crimogenic effects. A staff member of a
transnational NGO commented, "The whole [Salvadoran] society is very
violent. It's not just the young people. Anybody feels like they can just pull
out a gun and kill someone. These kids are throwing grenades. How do you
think they learned how to do that?" The civil war was also blamed for leaving firearms, former combatants, demobilized soldiers, and dismissed security personnel in its wake (Cruz 1998; Godoy 2005; Lungo and Martel
2003). Some drew attention to a tradition of impunity, including the 1993
amnesty law that permitted individuals who were responsible for serious
human-rights abuses to remain at large within the Salvadoran population
(Amaya Cóbar and Palmieri 2000). Several Salvadoran community leaders
in the United States attributed juvenile delinquency—which they believed
had been exported to El Salvador through deportations—to conditions
that Salvadoran youth encountered in the United States.[14] A New York–based
community activist stressed that migrants had to work two jobs, leading
migrant youth to grow up with insufficient parental supervision, while a
Los Angeles–based scholar commented that lack of strong cultural identity
led youth to join gangs, sell drugs, and commit crimes. Other common explanations for crime included an inefficient judicial systems, links between
criminals and the police, income polarization in El Salvador, lack of public
faith in the criminal justice system, a failure to fully implement the peace
accords, disruptions and transformations associated with emigration and a
remittance-based economy, transculturation (the influence of U.S. culture
on El Salvador), and the erosion of communities and of Salvadoran values
(Costa 2001; Cruz 2000; Godoy 2005; Lungo and Martel 2003; Papadopoulos et al. 1998; Ramos et al. 2000; and interviews). Some citizens also
blamed democratization and reforms of the criminal code for granting defendants too many rights and curtailing the ability of the security forces to
combat crime (Cruz 2000; Godoy 2005; Popkin 2001). Many of these explanations have political implications—for example, the notion that impunity is to blame suggests that the amnesty law should be overturned,

while criticisms of democracy for being "weak" imply that authoritarian measures are needed—yet the motives of criminals themselves are not considered explicitly political.

Emigrants are situated complexly vis-à-vis criminal violence (Lungo and Martel 2003). The random nature of violence suggests that emigrants, like others, would be at risk in El Salvador. Indeed, when, as a volunteer, I helped to prepare NACARA applications in 1999, many applicants cited insecurity and crime as a hardship factor that they or their children would face if they returned. Javier López did return to El Salvador for a visit in 1994, only to conclude that "the situation had become too difficult. They robbed a lot, assaulted, and also killed and kidnapped. The situation was pretty hard. It was worse than in the war. In the war, they didn't go around stealing. It was war."

Emigrants also are thought to contribute directly or indirectly to the proliferation of crime in El Salvador. A former human-rights official in El Salvador cited violence as one of the social costs of migration: "It [migration] translates itself into disintegrated homes, into rebellious children, into children that don't study, even into the very same gangs because the parents have had to leave and have left their children [who are] at a formative age where family affection is determinant, and they have left them to be raised without the guidance of an adult. It is a defect of the very same violence that the youth of the country live." Emigration is blamed for disrupting family life, eroding Salvadoran values, permitting unsupervised children to join gangs, weakening work ethics, and promoting transculturation, all of which in turn are thought to contribute to delinquency. As we have seen, deportees are particularly blamed for bringing gangs, drugs, and criminal violence to El Salvador.[15] Further, the factors that contribute to delinquency are also thought to contribute to emigration. Thus, one human-rights attorney in El Salvador argued that, although no longer a direct effect of political violence, emigration was still "linked with human rights, especially with the absence or deterioration of economic, social, political conditions in the interior of countries that oblige people to seek other countries."

This shift from seeing emigration as a product of violence to also being a cause of it is associated with reinterpretations of human rights. During the 1980s, Salvadoran and solidarity activists used human rights to refer primarily to civil and political rights, such as the right to life, to freedom from torture, and to due process, that were violated by security forces. Human rights therefore had a leftist political connotation, and were associated with protecting the citizenry from governmental abuses of power. In the postwar period, state officials now also use rights language, which in turn is shorn of its leftist connotation (see also Schirmer 1998). For example, an official in the Salvadoran Ministry of Foreign Affairs told me that his office sought to defend the rights of migrants in transit: "We experience the most violations of human rights because we have the largest number of people who have emigrated." Similarly, President Tony Saca's plan for El Salvador stressed the need to protect inhabitants' "fundamental rights, particularly life, physical and moral integrity, and liberty, which are seen to be permanently threatened by criminality" (Saca 2004, 41). "Rights," however, are also associated with weakness, as in complaints that criminals have too many rights, and that laws and security forces need to be strengthened (Godoy 2002, 2004, 2005; Zilberg 2007a, 2007b). In this sense, efforts to protect the legal rights of criminal suspects appear out of touch with security concerns and the need for anticrime measures. In the postwar period, "rights"—when interpreted as legalistic conventions that hamper authorities—can become the *opposite of* security, rather than the *means to* security.

The ambiguity of violence—it is and is not a departure from the war years—and the complex ways that emigrants are situated regarding violence suggest that it is important not to accept distinctions between criminal and political violence at face value. As Godoy (2005, 114, *emphasis in original*; see also Zilberg 2007a) argues, it is important to see "*the politics in crime*" and "*the crime in politics*." During the war, property was confiscated, individuals were abducted, people were assassinated, bodies were dismembered, and many bystanders were killed in the process. After the war, property was stolen, people were kidnapped, individuals were murdered, bodies sometimes were mutilated, and many bystanders were killed or injured. The human-rights violations committed during the war were also crimes, and the crimes committed after the war also violated victims' rights (Godoy 2005). Further, during wars politics can be used as a cover to commit crimes (Ramos 2000; Paul and Demarest 1988), and during periods of peace crimes can have hidden political motives. When I helped to prepare asylum applications for ABC class members in the mid-1990s, I found that numerous applicants were baffled by legal distinctions between crime and political persecution. For example, one applicant told me of a friend who had been killed after rejecting the advances of a young man who was part of a death squad (see Coutin 2001a). It is difficult to classify such an action as exclusively political or exclusively criminal in nature (see also Farmer 2003). Moreover, if current delinquency is rooted at least partially in past political violence and in conditions associated with that violence, then crime also has political connotations. In other words, even though crime, unlike political violence, may not be designed to bring about or to prevent social change, particular forms of violence—domestic abuse, financial fraud, gang activity, corruption—may be linked to social exclusion, power relations, and institutional orders, and therefore, indirectly, to political structures (Moodie 2006).[16] Crime is not only an individual act but also a social product.

Postwar violence to some degree reinscribes the violence of emigration within migrants themselves. As Smutt (1998, 109) points out, "El Salvador lived through twelve years of armed conflict, which left numerous aftereffects. Among the most visible, one can mention more than seventy-five thousand deaths, exacerbation of poverty, internal migrations and migrations outside of the country, which generally took place in an illegal fashion." Unauthorized migrants themselves may be products of various forms of violence—the civil war, social or economic exclusion, border policing, alien-smuggling, marginalization and economic exploitation in the United States, crime and police brutality in low-income neighborhoods in the urban United States. When migrants are held to be implicated in processes (such as family separations) that contribute to violence, or when migrants (such as deportees) are considered responsible for violence itself, then the structural violence that migrants experience comes to be seen as part of migrants' own being. To the degree that absent parents are blamed for youth criminality or that deportees are blamed for gang activity, structural conditions and historical processes come to be situated in persons. My goal in making this point is neither to exonerate individual perpetrators of responsibility nor to suggest that structural conditions do not in fact produce violent people. Nor do I mean to exaggerate the degree to which emigration is held to contribute to delinquency. Rather, I seek to draw attention to the ways that traces of violence remain within its products, thus continuing to haunt present realities, as the past (or the future) sometimes seeps into the present (cf. Feldman 1991; Godoy 2002) Thus, associating migration with delinquency essentializes migrants by inverting narratives of victimization: migrants, regardless of their individual circumstances, become potential victimizers through direct or indirect contributions to criminality.[17]

If crime has political implications then so too do the security measures that are designed to put an end to criminal violence.

Security

Like crime itself, anticrime measures depart from but also in certain respects reproduce tactics used during the civil war. The postwar emphasis on democracy, transparency, civil rights, and the rule of law officially precludes repressive practices such as deploying the military against the citizenry, detaining people arbitrarily, exceeding legal limits on the use of force, or targeting individuals due to their suspected tendencies rather than their past actions. Nonetheless, current characterizations of violence as criminal in nature have authorized security measures that, if launched against political opponents rather than common criminals, could be characterized as human-rights violations. The target of these measures is no longer the guerrilla or subversive, but rather the gang member, who has become the new threat to public order. Gang members—and recall that the rise of gangs is attributed, among other things, to emigration, family disruptions, and deportation—are held to be responsible for assassinations, rape, assaults, drug dealing, robbery, theft, and terrorizing particular neighborhoods or towns. Citing the grave threat that such activities pose to citizens' rights, the Salvadoran government has launched antigang measures, including the criminalization of gang membership, increased police presence in areas of high gang activity, the mobilization of soldiers alongside police in antigang units, mass detentions, and increased prison terms for convicted suspects. These measures—some of which have been declared unconstitutional—have garnered public support (Fundación de Estudios 2004). Furthermore, citizens with the means to do so have adopted their own security measures, including hiring armed guards, installing security systems, retreating behind bars and walls, and avoiding areas believed dangerous (Godoy 2005; Caldeira 2000; Lungo and Martel 2003). Critics who warn that the privatization of security erodes social citizenship (Lungo and Martel 2003) or who call for rehabilitation and reinsertion rather than repression (Fundación de Estudios 2004) have had little influence on crime policies, though courts have refused to try individuals when evidence of criminal activity was lacking. Rather, public fears of delinquents have legitimized tactics that, in certain respects, place criminals outside the collectivity of citizens (indeed, of humans) who have rights. Migrants are linked to these measures in that they are thought to have indirectly contributed to conditions in which criminality flourishes.

The Salvadoran government's most recent anticrime initiative, Plan Súper Mano Dura, was launched 30 August 2004, by Salvadoran president Tony Saca only three months after assuming office.[18] Súper Mano Dura replaced the earlier anticrime plan, Mano Dura, and the Ley Antimaras (Antigang Law) promulgated by Saca's predecessor, Francisco Flores (see Zilberg 2007b).[19] These initiatives created a temporary special security regimen to contend with the emergency created by gangs and high crime (see also Goldstein 2007). Within this regimen, gangs were defined as illicit associations, making gang membership—as evidenced by tattoos, throwing signs, or obeying gang leaders—a crime. Soldiers joined police in the fight against gangs, resulting in the detention of 19,275 suspected gang members (Fundación de Estudios 2004). These measures were part of a broader effort to stiffen El Salvador's anticrime policies, including trying juveniles as adults, lengthening sentences for violent offenses, and calling for reinstatement of the death penalty. Both the Plan Mano Dura and the Ley Antimaras immediately confronted legal problems. Only 5 percent of the suspects detained under this plan were tried in court; the remainder were released due to lack of evidence (Iraheta and Salamanca 2004). Police blamed these releases on citizens' reluctance to testify against gang members, while critics complained that the police and prosecutors' office lacked effective investigative skills (Fundación de Estudios 2004). In April 2004, the Salvadoran Supreme Court of Justice declared the Ley Antimaras unconstitutional on the grounds that its provisions violated citizens' rights to equal treatment under the law; that citizens could only be prosecuted for criminal conduct, not merely for belonging to a group; and that throwing signs or having tattoos did not endanger third parties and therefore could not be punished (Fundación de Estudios 2004). Nonetheless, the number of people detained swelled, while the Plan Mano Dura was in effect, straining El Salvador's prison capacities (Fundación de Estudios 2004).

In this context, Saca made the Plan Súper Mano Dura a key component of his campaign platform, entitled, not insignificantly, Plan País Seguro (Secure Country). This platform drew a sharp contrast between the "systematic crazed destruction" of the war years, with which Saca sought to associate his opponent Shafik Handal, a former FMLN commander, and the progress and development that he argued would result from his election to the Salvadoran presidency (Saca 2004, 4). The Plan País Seguro contained a broad analysis of the crime problem, citing family distintegration, social exclusion, marginalization, transculturation, school attrition, and the effects of the war as causes (8). These factors are also commonly cited by scholars as key causes of postwar crime in El Salvador (e.g., Papadopoulos et al. 1998). After being elected, Saca developed a participatory approach to fleshing out his anticrime plan. Representatives of government institutions, the judicial system, the legislative assembly, human-rights groups, and NGOs participated in a series of forums that resulted in recommendations that were incorporated into the plan itself. The plan's axes of action included "prevention and citizen participation, deterrence and pursuit, rehabilitation and reinsertion" (Casa Presidencial 2004a). In line with his promise to be a "gobierno con sentido humano" (government with humane feelings),[20] Saca's announcement of the Plan Súper Mano Dura assured gang members' relatives:

> Not all of our actions are designed to deter and repress. Today, I want to say to all those mothers whose children have fallen under the perverse seduction of gangs not to lose hope.
>
> Together, with the Plan Súper Mano Dura, we will fight to rehabilitate and reinsert into society all those youth who are disposed to do so. (Casa Presidencial 2004a)

The implementation of the Plan Súper Mano Dura, at least in its initial stages, nonetheless focused largely on repressive measures and identified gang members as the primary source of El Salvador's crime problem. Although the plan was designed to fight crime in general and included measures to combat white-collar crime and the distribution of stolen goods, the president's speech announcing this initiative repeatedly cited "pandillas" (gangs) and "pandilleros" (gang members) as the plan's primary targets (Casa Presidencial 2004a).[21] In the days after the plan was launched, television and print media featured footage and photos of police arresting gang members who covered their faces but nonetheless defiantly threw gang signs with their hands. Advertisements encouraging citizens to denounce gang members announced, "¡A los pandilleros se les acabó la fiesta! Hoy sí tenemos Súper Mano Dura" ("The gang members' party is over! We now have Súper Mano Dura.").[22] The notion that gang members had intrinsic criminal tendencies was evidenced by one former high-level Salvadoran official's comment to me: "I know that gang members have completed their sentences before they were deported, but there must be some way to just detain them at the airport, when they enter the country!" Note too that this quote draws explicit connections between *gangs* and *deportation*. In part, the focus on gang members was a short-term approach (Saca 2004), presumably to be followed by plans targeting other sectors. This focus nonetheless contributed to a deep stigmatization of gang members and those who appeared to be gang members, while conflating crime with gangs. Note, in contrast, that one scholar's list of crimes common to El Salvador included numerous offenses that are not usually attributed to gangs: "minor urban crime, private and public corruption, white-collar financial embezzlement of large fraudulent financiers, organized crime (like the international bands of car thieves and drug smugglers), intrafamily and youth violence, massacres of entire families, the action of assassins and the aftermath, pseudo-political or not, of kidnappers who cling to the past" (Bejar 1998, 98).

The focus on dangerous people rather than on violations and on incarceration rather than rehabilitation epitomizes broader international criminal justice trends, including in countries such as the United States (Feeley and Simon 1992; Petersilia 2003; Zilberg 2007a, 2007b). As I have noted elsewhere, "Instead of attempting to reform socially deviant individuals, penal practices now attempt to 'manage' dangerous persons, who are then 'warehoused' as part of ever-growing prison populations. Criminality is treated more as a condition of a person, than of a particular act (though an act can be used to 'diagnose' this underlying condition)" (Coutin 2005b, 7). This shift, which Feeley and Simon term "the new penology" (see also Wacquant 1999, 2001), resembles state-sponsored repression in that each justifies extreme measures by placing certain individuals outside the bounds of the polity. Thus, the national-security doctrine adopted during the Salvadoran civil war defined guerrillas and alleged guerrilla sympathizers as depraved, violent enemies who served international Marxism and whose actions threatened the integrity of the Salvadoran nation. Similarly, gang members have been depicted as depraved, violent individuals who threaten public security and the nation itself.[23] Deported gang members are particularly stigmatized.

Given this discursive similarity—both guerrillas and gang members have occupied the position of suspect, of stigmatized other—it is perhaps not surprising that gang members are sometimes confused with the former guerrillas (see also Cruz 2000). For instance, according to a Salvadoran human-rights worker, elderly people in some rural areas referred to gang members as guerrillas, and a staff member at an NGO that worked on gang issues told me that with the antigang laws, there were rumors that gang members would go to the mountains and take up arms (see also Dickson-Gómez 2002). Security measures that target a stigmatized enemy juxtapose "rights" and "security," suggesting that such enemies are undeserving of the rights accorded to law-abiding citizens. Such measures can, however, undermine all citizens' rights, as Godoy (2005, 132) points out: "The notion that criminals can be denied their citizenship rights while noncriminals can have their rights protected assumes an ability to distinguish reliably between the two groups." Deploying the troops against suspected gang members therefore bears an uncanny resemblance to the earlier use of military force against civilians suspected of supporting or sympathizing with the guerrillas (see also Zilberg 2007a and Zilberg forthcoming).[24] In assessing social violence in El Salvador, Fundación de Estudios para la Aplicación del Derecho (2004, 44) concludes that far from combating violence, the Mano Dura plans are *part of* the violence: "The Plan Mano Dura, instead of reducing social violence, has increased it, given that the combined forces of the army and the police have been used to massively and without legal basis detain thousands of young people due to their appearance or membership in gangs."

The stiffening of public security forces has been accompanied by the securitization or militarization of private space. As Lungo and Martel (2003) note, to escape the violence that occurs in public spaces, citizens have barricaded themselves in private spaces. In postwar El Salvador, it was common for businesses, offices, banks, stores, fast food restaurants, gas stations, pharmacies, car repair shops, and even homes (in the case of well-to-do individuals) to hire security guards who stood outside with shotguns hanging around their necks (see figure 4). Owners of small, streetside shops sometimes sold their products to customers through barred windows (Godoy 2005). Homes were frequently behind a wall or, in the case of the well-to-do, behind gates with security systems and armed guards (see also Caldeira 2000). Elite individuals sometimes hired their own bodyguards, to deter assailants or kidnappers. The ubiquity of armed guards created the impression of a society at war, and, indeed, according to interviewees, *vigilantes* (security guards) were often former police officers, demobilized soldiers, or even ex-combatants. Like criminal justice policies more generally, this trend toward hiring private security is part of a broader international phenomenon (Caldeira 2000). Some analysts link this trend to neoliberalism, pointing out that just as private enterprise is now expected to provide health care, welfare, and other social services that used to be the responsibility of the state, so too are private citizens now expected to provide for their own security (Comaroff and Comaroff 2004a; Goldstein 2003).[25]

The expansion of the authority of public security forces and the privatization of security have combined to produce privatized forms of justice, ranging from lynchings—common in many parts of Latin America (Godoy 2002, 2004; Goldstein 2003)—to death squads (Zilberg 2004) to the use of violence to settle private conflicts (Bejar 1998). One deported gang member, interviewed in 2001 after he had returned (without authorization) to the United States from El Salvador, provided the following account of his battles with a paramilitary death squad, the Sombra Negra, which sought to eradicate gangs through extrajudicial killings:

> When the death squad came out, we're like "Well, the hell with this! What are they going to do? They're just another gang to us."

Fig. 4. Security guard stationed at a market for Salvadoran crafts. Photograph by author.

We knew the type of cars they drove. We knew the way they looked, not each and every one of them, but physically they were kind of militarized: short hair, square. So they weren't like civilians really; it was people that were trained to do things like this. They had these Cherokees, Range Rovers, Nissans, four-door Nissan trucks that they used to drive, with tinted windows. So what happened was the gang members sent a message saying, "You know what, if we see a truck or a car with tinted windows coming up to our neighborhood, and they're up? We're throwing the grenade. Any car. And if it's innocent people, it's going to be the death squad's fault because they started this. If people that are civilians are coming through with tinted windows, they had better have them lowered down. That's the only way they're going to save themselves. Because they're up, and we can't see who's inside, we won't care."

So that was one of the things that would happen during that time. It was like warfare.

Significantly, this interviewee puts death squads, a paramilitary institution that nonetheless seems to be on the side of (and indeed had connections with) the police, on a par with gangs, saying, "They're just another gang to us" (see also Zilberg 2007a). Singling out gang members as the source of crime ignores such similarities.

Alongside the Mano Dura plans, the privatization of security and privatized justice were—largely unheeded—calls for alternative approaches to crime. The Súper Mano Dura plan called for rehabilitation, a measure that came to be known as Mano Amigo (Friendly Hand). Numerous scholars, human-rights workers, NGO members, religious leaders, and officials in the PDH argued that crime could only be reduced by getting to the root of the problem, that is, poverty, social exclusion, unemployment, lack of educational opportunities, income polarization, lack of confidence in the justice system, a tradition of impunity, war-related trauma, domestic violence, the widespread availability of weapons—including weapons of war—in El Salvador, and programs that would permit former soldiers and former guerilla members to become reintegrated in society (see, e.g., Fundación de Estudios 2004; Papadopoulos et al. 1998). Calls for such measures were heard in that the País Seguro governmental plan insists that "the primordial objective of government action is the well-being of its population. To the degree that there is a sector that is excluded from it, the government's work is not finished" (Saca 2004, 4). Programs to fight crime nonetheless focused on increased police operations, prosecution, and incarceration.

Perhaps it is not surprising that anticrime measures generated one more practice reminiscent of the civil war: marches for peace. In 2001–2, Salvadoran communities in El Salvador responded to particularly heinous acts of violence by organizing marches featuring banners with slogans such as "Live without Violence" (Escobar and Martínez 2002) and "¡No! a la violencia" (El Diario de Hoy 2002b). The fact that these marches called for *peace* suggests that, to many, El Salvador was still experiencing a kind of war, not a war between political factions, but rather a more diffuse and therefore less comprehensible form of violence. As an attendee at a march in Santa Ana commented, "This is not living in peace. In this hell, only God [is] with one" (Escobar and Martínez 2002).

Reinscribing Violence

As products of war, many Salvadoran migrants experienced political violence, forced migration, the violence of traveling without authorization, the violence of being placed in clandestine spaces, and the economic violence that compels both migration and remitting. During the 1980–92 Salvadoran civil war, some of this violence was acknowledged through efforts to obtain refugee status for Salvadorans and Guatemalans. In the postwar period, migrants' relationship to violence shifted. Not only *products* of vio-

lence, migrants and migration were seen as contributing, directly or indirectly, to crime in El Salvador, through the deportation of gang youth,
through disrupted families that permitted children to grow up without supervision, and through the erosion of Salvadoran values. By holding individuals, rather than policies, structures, and histories, responsible for
crime, the violence that migrants experienced was thus reinscribed within
migrants themselves. At the same time, in the postwar period the nature of
violence was considered to have changed from human-rights violations
and explicitly political violence to common crime. Public concerns about
crime and increased stigmatization of gang members in particular authorized the reintroduction, under color of law, of measures that resembled
certain tactics used during the war. Human rights discourse, which had
earlier been linked to justice and which had been key to emigrants' quest to
legal status in the United States, came to be seen as an obstacle to citizens'
security.

Discourses can, however, shift in multiple ways, and that which is prohibited has a way of demanding recognition. Such was the case with efforts
to ban unauthorized migrants in the early 2000s.

CHAPTER 7

¡Sí, se puede! (Yes, it can be done!)

They want to give two hundred thousand visas . . . so that we can bring more immigrants to work in the high-tech industry. And I'm for that. That's fine. But what about the two million people who are already here working? Just because you are . . . a doctor or dentist or scientist, this work counts. But do you know what also counts? That gardener. His work counts too. Someone who goes to the harvest? His work counts too. People who clean hotels. Their work is also worthwhile. All jobs are worthwhile, because all [of us] human beings are equal, and we demand justice for them.

Representative Luis Gutierrez (D-IL), speaking in English and Spanish (translated) during a prolegalization rally on the Capitol steps in September 2000

EVIDENCE OF LAWFUL STATUS.—A State shall require, before issuing a driver's license or identification card to a person, valid documentary evidence that the person—
(i) is a citizen or national of the United States;
(ii) is an alien lawfully admitted for permanent or temporary residence in the United States;
(iii) has conditional permanent resident status in the United States;
(iv) has an approved application for asylum in the United States or has entered into the United States in refugee status;
(v) has a valid, unexpired nonimmigrant visa or nonimmigrant visa status for entry into the United States;
(vi) has a pending application for asylum in the United States;
(vii) has a pending or approved application for temporary protected status in the United States;
(viii) has approved deferred action status; or
(ix) has a pending application for adjustment of status to that of an alien lawfully admitted for permanent residence in the United States or conditional permanent resident status in the United States.

REAL ID Act of 2005, section 202

In the mid-1990s, Central American community organizations in Los Angeles regularly hosted presentations on U.S. immigration law. During these talks, attorneys described the avenues through which undocumented immigrants could become legalized and answered listeners' questions about whether they could qualify. All too often the answer was a discouraging "no," followed by the comment, "But they say that there may be another amnesty in 2000, so just wait." At the time, this statement seemed to me to be an empty promise. After all, as recently as 1994, California Proposition 187, which required teachers, doctors, and other service workers to report suspected illegal aliens, had been overwhelmingly approved by the California electorate (Martin 1995). Although this measure was largely declared unconstitutional, its passage deeply stigmatized undocumented immigrants and legitimized calls for their removal. Moreover, in 1996, federal legislation stiffened border enforcement, expanded the range of crimes that rendered noncitizens deportable, restricted means of legalization, and made even legal immigrants ineligible for numerous forms of public assistance. It seemed that, if anything, the trend in immigration policymaking was toward greater restriction. Nonetheless, in the waning days of the 2000 congressional session, President Clinton threatened to veto the Commerce-Justice-State appropriations act, at least in part, because it did not include legislation that would have permitted large numbers of immigrants to legalize (Wasem 2002). Indeed, during the first few months of the second Bush administration, immigrant rights activists spoke optimistically of securing an *amnistía* (amnesty), and in 2006 the streets of major U.S. cities filled with marchers demanding a broad-based legalization program. How did what was almost unthinkable in 1996 almost materialize in 2000 and again in 2006?

Addressing this question requires examining ways that, paradoxically, prohibition can sometimes augment or call forth rather than erase presence. In examining this paradox, this chapter picks up the story that was being told in chapter 2. Recall that the restrictive measures adopted in the mid-1990s ostensibly sought to prohibit undocumented and criminal aliens. This prohibition was to be accomplished through preventing entry, facilitating removal, and making it difficult for undocumented residents to authorize their presence. This very effort to prohibit, however, led many who were eligible for legal permanent residency or citizenship to avail themselves of these as quickly as possible. A surge in naturalization applications and in voter registration by new citizens gave immigrants an increased presence within the electorate (Baker 1997; Coutin 2003; Paral 1995; Sánchez 1997). At the same time, the 1996 immigration laws spurred undocumented and temporary residents to organize in larger numbers. By doing so, these residents drew attention to the significance of their presence—to their roles as workers, community members, relatives, and even constituents. These claims resonated in somewhat surprising quarters—for example, among business leaders in sectors that employed immigrant workers and with political leaders in migrants' countries of origin. By 2000, as the Democratic and Republican parties vied for the "Latino vote," espousing anti-immigrant rhetoric threatened to alienate instead of attract support. The September 11, 2001, attacks on the Pentagon and the World Trade Center derailed efforts to secure an "amnesty," as the figure of the terrorist and that of the immigrant—not for the first time in history—came to be conflated (Cole 2001). Nonetheless, while rationales for an amnesty, or "earned adjustment" as it is sometimes called, have come to focus on security rather than on recognizing presence, efforts to create an ongoing legalization program have gained force. Those who are forced underground, whose presence is denied, and who are suspected of being security risks are nonetheless in some ways indispensable and therefore can—at times—compel law to bend in their direction.

Resurfacing

Measures that, in the early to mid-1990s, sought to prohibit underground movement and illegal presence led immigrants, in the late 1990s to early 2000s, to resurface, in multiple ways. First, instead of leaving or going deeper underground, migrants became, in certain respects, even more visible. On being marked as outside the boundaries of the polity, ineligible for particular public services, and basically undesirable or problematic, noncitizens sought to challenge these characterizations. Legal permanent residents naturalized in record numbers (Coutin 2003; INS 2000), temporarily authorized migrants demanded permanent immigration rights, and unauthorized immigrants called for a broad-based legalization program. Thus, migrants asserted that, prohibited or not, they were part of families, communities, and the U.S. workforce, and that their social, cultural, and economic contributions warranted recognition. There is thus a sense in which prohibiting particular persons or practices in effect calls these forth (Katz 1988; Marx 1981; Žižek 1989)—and certainly, requiring identity documents makes those who *lack* such documents more visible. Second, calls to legalize undocumented workers draw attention to the pockets of clandestinity and informality that are part of U.S. territory.

In essence, this territory is "re-surfaced" as the clandestine is made visible, and as individuals point out ways that prohibited persons and practices are key to the economy. Third, as noncitizens demanded greater recognition, discourse regarding immigration underwent resurfacing, with the creation of new terms, such as "earned adjustment," and a reemphasis on the value of immigrant workers. By the 2000 presidential elections, both Democratic and Republican politicians had seemingly concluded that calls to restrict immigration were more likely to alienate than to attract voters.

While U.S. immigration policies have varied in their restrictiveness (and in the groups toward which restrictiveness was directed—see Calavita 2000), the roots of the mid-1990s legislation can perhaps be traced to the 1986 Immigration Reform and Control Act (IRCA). During the 1980s, fears that the U.S. immigration system, and U.S. society more generally, were being undermined by a growing undocumented and therefore, some assumed, lawless population gave rise to a two-pronged approach to eliminating illegal aliens (Baker 1997; Fuchs 1985; Glazer 1985). The first prong consisted of imposing sanctions on employers who failed to verify new employees' authorization to work in the United States. The employer sanctions provisions of IRCA were designed to remove the presumed "draw"—the prospect of a job—that fueled illegal immigration, thus cutting off the flow. Moreover, if undocumented immigrants already in the country could no longer find employment, presumably they would leave. The second prong of IRCA was inclusive rather than restrictive, and was an "amnesty" program that permitted certain seasonal agricultural workers (SAWs) and immigrants who had been continuously and illegally present in the United States since January 1, 1982, to legalize. The legalization program was a political trade-off that enabled IRCA to be approved, but it also sought to eliminate illegal immigration, through legalization rather than through prohibition. The program's two avenues toward legalization (SAW and regular amnesty) defined undocumented immigrants according to their status as laborers who were critical to the agricultural industry or as community members who, by 1987 when the legalization program was implemented, had lived in the United States for five years.

During the early and mid-1990s, restrictionist sentiment intensified, as economic recession contributed to calls to rid the country of illegal aliens. Immigrants were accused of being a drain on funding for public services, taking jobs away from U.S. citizens, committing crimes, failing to assimilate, ruining the environment, and destroying the fabric of the country (Chavez 2001; Perea 1997; Sánchez 1997). The English-only movement gained force, affirmative action was challenged, and even legal immigrants were regarded with suspicion. In 1994—the same year that California began denying driver's licenses to undocumented immigrants—California voters were confronted with Proposition 187, termed the "Save our State" initiative. Proposition 187 required teachers, doctors, police officers, and social service workers to report suspected illegal aliens to the U.S. Immigration and Naturalization Service.[1] Proponents argued that this measure was necessary to prevent illegal immigrants from using services to which they were not entitled. Opponents complained that the proposition would turn ordinary citizens into immigration agents. After a bitter debate, the initiative was overwhelmingly approved by the electorate, only to then be ruled largely unconstitutional in court.[2]

After Proposition 187 was approved in California, proponents of immigration reform took their battle to the federal level (Coutin and Alva 1999). Three major pieces of immigration-related legislation were signed into law in 1996. The 1996 Welfare Reform Act denied many forms of public assistance to *legal* immigrants who had previously been eligible for such aid. A fiscal measure linked to balanced budget conservatism (Calavita 1996), the Welfare Reform Act was part of a broader redefinition of immigrants as undeserving encroachers. In 1996, Congress also approved IIRIRA and the AEDPA, whose provisions stiffened border enforcement, making unauthorized entry more costly and more deadly (Andreas 2000; Nevins 2002); made it more difficult for undocumented immigrants to legalize their presence; and targeted aliens convicted of crimes.

Proposition 187 and the 1996 immigration-related legislation had at least three effects. One was to create a potentially permanent underclass of long-term residents who were not going to be able to legalize. Another was to spur those who could become naturalized citizens to do so as soon as possible, before the laws changed yet again. In 1996, the number of individuals naturalized in a single year reached a record high of 1,044,689, as individuals sought to protect their rights, restore their eligibility for public benefits, and reduce their vulnerability to deportation, and as the Clinton administration, in an election year, made naturalization a high priority (Coutin 2003; INS 2000). And a third effect, not surprisingly, was to mobilize immigrants and immigrant-rights advocates. Referring both to an anti-Republican backlash by Latino voters and to increased naturalization rates, one San Francisco immigration attorney called Proposition 187, referring to California governor Pete Wilson, "Wilson's short-term gain, the Republicans' long-term pain," and "the Pete Wilson Citizenship Promotion Act of 1994."

Following approval of the 1996 laws, calls for more restrictive policies initially declined. With an improved economy, immigrant workers seemed less threatening, and analysts began to predict that as Baby Boomers aged and Social Security became increasingly burdened, a labor shortage could result. During a 2000 interview, one Democratic staffer noted, "We are experiencing good times. There are plenty of jobs. . . . There is a need for gardeners, cleaners, waiters, etc., many of whom are Latinos." Another Democratic staffer pointed out that, by 2000, groups such as the Chamber of Commerce and the National Federation of Independent Businesses were lobbying in support of legalization: "They pointed out that they were experiencing a labor shortage. The hotel associations, the meatpacking industries complained that they couldn't find enough people to employ." Similarly, an immigration attorney in Los Angeles remarked, "I think [Federal Reserve board chairman] Alan Greenspan had a quote that essentially said 'without the support of the immigrant dollar through consumer tax as well as income tax as well as cheap labor that they provide for our economy, we're going to be in dire, dire straits.'[3] For this generation, you and I." Moreover, analysts pointed out, proponents of more restrictive policies had achieved their goals with the 1996 reforms, making additional measures unnecessary (Coutin and Alva 1999).

As anti-immigrant sentiment declined, noncitizens were increasingly recognized as part of the polity. A Democratic staffer recalled, "Whereas the '96 debate concerned a nameless, faceless group of immigrants, the discussion of NACARA and NACARA parity was different. These were longtime residents. It doesn't make sense to deport the parents of U.S. citizen children." In Los Angeles, city council members passed resolutions supporting federal legislation that would have permitted more undocumented immigrants to legalize (see, e.g., Los Angeles City Council 2001). As an aide to one city council member summarized her boss's attitude, "I don't care if you're legal or undocumented, you're my constituent, and I'll represent you like anybody else." Immigrants themselves argued that they were key components of U.S. society. An immigrant-rights activist in San Salvador argued that "the Hispanic community is a growing community, not only in terms of numbers but in that a larger number of people are accessing positions of power—not only political power but also economic power, social power. I believe that the future of the United States, in good part, resides in the Hispanic community."

It was in this context of an improved economy and declining anti-immigrant sentiment that, in February 2000, the AFL-CIO, which had long argued that immigrants lowered wages and competed with U.S. citizens for jobs, came out in favor of an "amnesty" for undocumented immigrants (see Watts 2002). Many attribute this watershed event to union organizers' discovery that many of the workers that they were trying to unionize were themselves undocumented immigrants who favored more inclusive immigration laws. An official at the Service Employees International Union (SEIU) described how this shift came about:

> When [John] Sweeny took over the AFL-CIO, he was very clear that he wanted to organize. So, he sent a bunch of people to start organizing, and they start finding out that if you want to organize, you are gonna have to confront the issue of immigration, because there are a lot of employers out there who are taking advantage of the so-called employer's sanctions, meaning when workers are trying to organize and fight for their rights [and] all of a sudden they [employers] remember that these people may be undocumented so they start threatening these people with deportation. Secondly, it was wrong to try to organize the workers without being able to be supportive on the issues that they cared [about] the most.

This interviewee argued that the shift in AFL-CIO policy had an enormous impact on the viability of a legalization program: "Before February of 2000, nobody dared mention the word 'amnesty.' It wasn't until the AFL-CIO changed their position that the word 'amnesty' started being more and more accepted. It hasn't been a week in the main newspaper or a main TV [show] that the word 'amnesty' or 'legalization' does not get mentioned." This view was echoed by numerous immigrant-rights advocates.

As the AFL-CIO changed its stance, foreign governments began to push for legalization programs. Vicente Fox, the Mexican president, made securing such a program a priority. The Central American presidents also pressed the Clinton administration to allow Central Americans to remain in the United States, where they could earn money that they would then send back home to family members.

By 2000, enormous organizing efforts were under way. Grassroots groups of individuals who had been affected by one or another provision of the 1996 legislation launched letter-writing campaigns, sent representatives to Washington, D.C., to lobby Congress, met with local officials, and held vigils and rallies. An attorney who was active in these efforts described the enthusiasm of those involved:

> You ought to interview this lady, Carmen Martínez. Maybe she's nineteen or something. She doesn't qualify [for NACARA]. She was here, [but] didn't file for ABC or TPS. So I've had her speak at NACARA trainings. We do a

mock interview [regarding whether she is eligible for NACARA]. I go through the interview and I say [to the audience], "Well, what's she eligible for?" "Nothing," [they answer]. "I guess we just have to tell her, 'There's nothing you can do.'" "Is that what you're doing, Carmen?" She says, "No! I'm active in Centro Latino Cuzcatlan. I led a delegation of young people to Washington, D.C." And that's a *particular* leadership. That's the young, bilingual, bicultural leaders that are dynamite.

The amnesty, the amnesty proposal has electrified the immigrant community. It sent a shockwave of optimism, hope, and energy.

Analysts also argued that, by 2000, Latino voters had become a force to be reckoned with, leading politicians to *court* rather than *disparage* immigrants. A Democratic congressional staffer attributed the interest in immigration legislation to the "growth of the Latino population, which can make a difference in tight elections. Look at the California model. Look what happened to Pete Wilson."[4] Salvadoran interviewees cited the Cuban community as an example to emulate in their own efforts to gain political power. Salvadoran activists also pointed to U.S. elected officials of Salvadoran descent, such as California state senator Liz Figueroa and the former deputy administrator in the U.S. Department of Transportation, Ana Sol Gutierrez, as evidence of Salvadoran immigrants' growing political clout.

Thus, only four years after restrictive policies were adopted, "amnesty" proposals went from being unthinkable to viable. As immigrants resurfaced, prohibiting those who were already here became increasingly problematic.

The Latino and Immigrant Fairness Act

In 2000, immigrants' resurfacing culminated in efforts to pass the Latino and Immigrant Fairness Act, or LIFA. Although it ultimately failed (or, some might say, was transformed), this proposed legislation became part of the contentious electoral contest of 2000 and contributed to Clinton's threat, in the waning days of his administration, to veto the Commerce-Justice-State appropriations act (Wasem 2002).[5] The fact that high-level politicians, including the president, made passage of this act a priority demonstrates how significantly public stances on immigration had changed since the mid-1990s. At the same time, an upsurge in opposition to an "amnesty" and to rewarding "lawbreakers" indicates that the taint of prohibition continued to mark those who had immigrated without authorization. The twists and turns of the effort to pass LIFA shed light on both the difficulty of denying the realities of de facto membership in U.S. communities and the importance of such denial to the integrity of U.S. territory, polity, and economic structures.

The LIFA effort was grounded in the sense that undocumented immigrants were de facto community members, that distinctions between "deserving" and "undeserving" immigrants were arbitrary, and that the 1996 reforms had gone too far. In January 1997, following what they perceived as an onslaught of immigration reform legislation, Central American activists began to campaign for residency for ABC class members. Community organizations asked the U.S. Congress and the Clinton administration for legislation that would restore suspension eligibility to ABC class members and TPS registrants (groups that overlapped). The Central American governments, fearing that the 1996 legislation would produce mass deportations, joined community groups in seeking relief. In 1997, these efforts resulted in the passage of NACARA.

Efforts to obtain immigration relief for Central Americans subsequently focused on what was known as "NACARA parity," an effort to extend the benefits that NACARA had granted to Nicaraguans to other similarly situated Central Americans (Salvadorans, Guatemalans, Hondurans, and Haitians)—and, in some versions, Liberians—and also to extend eligibility to those who entered the United States before 1995 (the date used for Nicaraguans) rather than the 1991 cutoff date used for Salvadorans and Guatemalans. The parity argument suggested that legal distinctions between Central Americans were arbitrary and motivated by political considerations rather than by meaningful differences in Central Americans' objective circumstances, as one Salvadoran immigrant-rights advocate explained:

> My opinion is that the Republicans were taking advantage of what was left of the cold war to get a benefit from the people they considered closest to them, that is the Cubans and Nicaraguans [who had fled left-wing governments]. And their argument was that because they were people who had fought for democracies in their countries, and that the Salvadorans and Guatemalans were seen as more of a threat, more leftist—and in electoral terms, were people who were more likely to vote with the Democrats than the Republicans.

Opponents of NACARA parity argued that the distinctions between Central Americans were meaningful rather than arbitrary, in that Nicaraguans were "victims of Communism" (as per the act's original title), whereas Salvadorans and Guatemalans fled governments that the United States supported. Alternatively, opponents argued that nationality-based programs were a mistake and that it had been an error to grant legal permanent residency to Nicaraguans. Interestingly, however, though parity advocates opposed disparate treatment, it was disparate treatment that created the opportunity to advocate for the inclusion of additional groups, as one immigrant-rights attorney noted: "NACARA immediately created a demand for equity that couldn't have been raised if they had granted Nicaraguans the same benefits they gave the Salvadorans and Guatemalans."

In pursuit of NACARA parity, Central American community organizations joined forces with other Latino and immigrant-rights groups lobbying for amendments to the 1996 immigration law. Through legislative proposals with such names as "Fix '96," a host of immigrant-rights issues were raised. Some groups were concerned about the effects of IIRIRA on so-called late amnesty applicants—members of class-action suits that challenged immigration officials' implementation of the 1986 legalization program. Others sought to restore the waivers that permitted criminal aliens to challenge their deportations. Others prioritized "245(i)," a provision of immigration law that allowed beneficiaries of family visa petitions to adjust their status in the United States instead of in their homelands, thus avoiding an exit that would then trigger a three- or ten-year bar on reentry. Still others sought a guest-worker program that would enable immigrants to enter the United States legally, avoiding the dangers posed by illegal entry. And some imagined a new form of legalization that would create mechanisms through which longtime illegal residents could regularize their status.

Although these efforts to secure immigration remedies took different forms, each sought to make a de facto status into a de jure one. Remedies focused largely on immigrants who, regardless of being undocumented, were already living and working in the United States, and on processes—such as the recruitment of undocumented workers—that have become key to particular industries (Sassen 1989, 1991). In essence, proponents argued that it was unfair to utilize immigrant labor without awarding immigrants the legal right to remain in the United States. Speaking at a rally in Washington, D.C., in September 2000, the director of a Los Angeles Central American community organization argued, "The present situation is unfair, it's unequal, and it separates families. And it does not recognize the contribution that immigrants make to the economy of this nation." As another speaker at the rally contended, "We [immigrants] have kept our end of the bargain. We have kept our end of the bargain in this country. What we are asking Congress to do, what we are asking the leaders of this country to do is to keep their end of the bargain!" This claim invoked the notion of an implicit contract that was betrayed by permitting undocumented workers to live in the United States without immigration rights. Granting such rights would "resurface" the United States.

During summer 2000, immigrant-rights organizations combined their efforts in a piece of legislation known as the Latino and Immigrant Fairness Act. LIFA had three main components: (1) NACARA parity, (2) the restoration of 245(i), and (3) changing the registry date (which had been 1972) such that individuals who had been in the United States since before 1986 would be able to adjust their status to that of a legal permanent resident. The third measure, changing the registry date, would permit the legalization of individuals (known as "late amnesty applicants") with pending lawsuits due to disputes over the correct interpretation of the 1986 legalization program. A Democratic congressional staffer explained the strategy behind combining these three measures: "These are different communities. NACARA helps the smaller Latino communities. Late amnesty benefits Mexicans. And if you are going to be opposed to these, you're going to be opposed whether they are single issues or they are grouped. So packaging these three doesn't strengthen the opposition. But it *does* strengthen the coalition." If approved, LIFA promised to legalize large numbers of undocumented immigrants. An estimated 680,000 Central Americans and Haitians would benefit from NACARA parity, while 500,000 immigrants of various nationalities would gain legal permanent residency from a change in the registry date (Wasem 2002).[6] LIFA immediately became highly contentious. Opponents condemned LIFA for being an amnesty and for rewarding lawbreakers for illegal behavior. Such rewards, opponents contended, would only further additional illegal immigration. Proponents hailed LIFA for redressing past errors (such as disparate treatment of Central Americans and mistakes made during the 1986 legalization process), eliminating arbitrary distinctions, and establishing policies and mechanisms that would be viable over the long term.

Given election-year competition for the Latino vote, the AFL-CIO's new support for legalization, foreign governments' calls for immigration benefits for their nationals, industry pressure to increase the legal-immigrant labor force, and continued staunch opposition to illegal immigration on the part of many members of Congress (particularly conservatives), a tremendous battle over LIFA's passage ensued. In fall 2000, proponents pursued two key strategies to pass LIFA. The first was to link LIFA to a bill that would increase the numbers of visas, known as H1–B, available to high-tech workers. Without this H1–B bill, which one proponent described as "the first moving immigra-

Fig. 5. Participant in a pro-LIFA (Latino and Immigrant Fairness Act) rally in Washington, D.C., 2000. Photograph by author.

tion bill that has come along in several years," LIFA might not have emerged as potentially viable legislation. The H1–B legislation had bipartisan support, though there was some opposition from labor unions. One Democratic staffer emphasized, "It is important to understand how big H1–B is. It's the new economy, innovation, technology, competitiveness. These are very romantic things within the Congress, and they are universally seen as good." Efforts to link H1–B and LIFA focused on the seeming disparity in increasing the number of high-tech workers who could immigrate legally while failing to award legal status to low-tech workers who were already here. One staffer summarized this argument: "We could point out that companies that have foreign ownership are pushing to bring foreign workers to the United States while families with U.S.-born children who are already here are not getting legal status." Significantly, the effort to link H1–B and LIFA defined unauthorized immigrants predominantly as workers who demonstrated American values (such as a work ethic), who were part of U.S. families, and who contributed to society, rather than as lawbreakers and illegal immigrants.

The effort to link LIFA and H1–B ultimately failed, due to pressure from the high-tech industries and to fear of voting against H1–B in an election year. According to interviewees, the Hispanic caucus had a "hold" on the H1–B legislation, in that the caucus opposed passing H1–B if LIFA were not attached. Under intense pressure from high-tech lobbyists and from colleagues who did not want to appear to be antitechnology, a second strategy for passing LIFA was devised, as an interviewee explained:

> So the only way to pass LIFA was to tie it to the H1–B bill, what we called H1–B-plus. And we didn't *oppose* H1–B—there was generally support for H1–B, but we just wanted additional things. And we managed to slow the bill down. The Democratic leadership didn't want to dis the high- tech industry, but they didn't want to dis Latinos either. So the Hispanic Caucus met with the president, and the president said, "If you can show me that you have the political clout to sustain a veto of the [Commerce-Justice-State] appropriations bill, then I'll veto it." So they collected signatures, and they told him that they did have the votes to sustain a veto. That allowed H1–B to go to the floor. By reassuring the Hispanic Caucus, the Hispanic Caucus relinquished its hold on H1–B.

As 2000 was an election year, LIFA supporters reasoned that the desire of most members of Congress to adjourn early would create pressure for LIFA opponents to simply accede to attaching LIFA to the Commerce-Justice-State appropriations bill.

These strategies did not play out as anticipated. Instead of pushing to adjourn early, Republican members of Congress were willing to stay in session. Democrats, in an effort to claim the Latino vote, argued that immigration was a partisan issue and that they were the party in favor of more open policies. Republicans disputed this contention, arguing that they too favored legal immigration, but that they opposed "amnesties" for lawbreakers, as such measures merely fueled additional illegal immigration. As one Republican staffer commented during an interview, "It is a bad idea to give amnesties, because they create the impression that if you go to the U.S. illegally and stay long enough, then you will eventually be able to get legal status." Republicans responded to LIFA with their own bill, the Legal Immigration Family Equity Act, or LIFE Act, which (1) permitted immigrants who were part of certain "late amnesty" lawsuits charging that the INS had administered the 1986 legalization program incorrectly to legalize, (2) created temporary visas for spouses and children of legal permanent residents, (3) temporarily extended 245(i), and (4) corrected a technical problem regarding the reinstatement of old deportation orders in NACARA cases (Wasem 2002). Speaking in the U.S. Senate in October 2000, Senator Orrin G. Hatch, a proponent of LIFE, stated:

> I rise again today to urge President Clinton not to veto the Commerce, Justice, State appropriations bill that the Senate passed yesterday.
>
> President Clinton has threatened a veto because we did not include his so-called Latino fairness act. But we have included something much better— the Legal Immigration Family Equity Act, the LIFE Act. This act reunites families and restores due process to those who have played by the rules. Our proposal does not pit one nationality against another, nor does it pit one race against another. Our legislation provides relief to immigrants from all countries. A veto of CJS would be a blow against immigrant fairness. (*Congressional Record* 2000a, S11307.)

As the 2000 election results played out and as opponents of LIFA refused to budge, Clinton signed the appropriations bill—and LIFE—into law. Although many Central American organizations regarded LIFE as largely a defeat, Democratic congressional staffers argued that the LIFA effort had contributed to the passage of LIFE, which benefited some immigrants. One staffer commented, "We were starting from zero, so to have gotten what we did get is a success."

The difficulties in passing LIFA demonstrate how much was at stake in denying de facto realities. Opponents of LIFA depicted undocumented immigrants as "encroachers," "lawbreakers," people who had not abided by the rules or waited their turn. They were "undeserving." For instance, during Senate debates over LIFA, Senator Robert Byrd (D-WV) commented that both LIFA and LIFE were "an affront to those immigrants who have played by the rules" (Congressional Record 2000a, S11280). Such comments placed the blame for illegality solely on immigrants, rather than on their employers or on industries (such as agriculture and services) that utilize immigrant labor (Lamphere et al. 1994; Martin 1990; Walker et al. 1992).[7] Failing to pass LIFA would not actually remove such immigrants (though obviously, if individual immigrants were apprehended, they could be deported) but would only keep them undocumented. Preventing legalization of the unauthorized privileges the de jure over the de facto, and maintains the integrity of U.S. territory and polity by positioning unauthorized immigrants "elsewhere."

At the same time, using the term "amnesty" was also problematic in the view of some proponents of legalization. During a November 2000 interview, a Salvadoran activist in northern California told me:

> We are not in agreement with the term "amnesty" because to accept the term amnesty is to accept that we have committed some crime. Why do we have to ask for pardon? . . . Do we have to ask for pardon for having come to contribute to the economic development of this country? What we need is a program that permits us to legalize or adjust the status of every single person who is contributing in a positive manner in economic, social, and cultural terms to North American society. That is why we insist on the term "legalization."

These comments, which were echoed by other Central American activists, reject the term "amnesty" for both strategic and moral reasons. In contrast, "legalization," this activist suggested, would bring the de facto (immigrants' contributions to U.S. society) and the de jure (immigrants' legal status) into alignment.

In sum, in 2000–2001, immigrants who had earlier been condemned as "merely economic" migrants were instead being praised by some powerful groups for their contributions to society and for their "low-skilled" work. During the early days of his presidency, George Bush met with Vicente Fox to discuss legalization, and a few months later, in a historic speech, Fox urged the U.S. Congress to create a new guest-worker program that would benefit Mexican immigrants. These developments suggested that earlier forms of prohibition were on the verge of giving way to recognized presence. In an

August 2001 interview, an immigration attorney who had been involved in the effort to pass LIFA predicted:

> There will be an expansion of the essential workers through the H-visas [in other words, an expansion of employment-based visas], with a proviso to allow those workers to become permanent. And that's going to happen very soon. Second, 245(i) will come back, which is pro-family unity, and also more money for the INS. That will come back I think even this year. Third, I think [Bush is] talking about increasing family-based immigration visa numbers. He's going to make little fixes here and there. And I think there's some sort of deal that's going on with President Fox, whether it's trade, oil— something. But something that the general public, we don't know about. Because he's absolutely wed to the idea of allowing for the Mexican immigrants, and then later, depending on how he maneuvers through the first phase of the temporary-worker programs, there'll be something that's a little bit more broad.

Before the accuracy of these predictions could be tested, however, terrorists hijacked and crashed airplanes into the World Trade Center, the Pentagon, and a field in Pennsylvania. In the process, they also drew the legalization momentum to a halt.

Exposure

If prohibited immigrants resurfaced during the years leading up to the 2000 and 2001 amnesty efforts, the events of September 11, 2001, left them exposed. On that date, a small group of noncitizens carried out an unprecedented terrorist attack against the United States, resulting in the deaths of 2,973 people. Although some prior terrorist actions, such as the bombing of the Oklahoma City Federal Building, had been carried out by U.S. citizens, after September 11, 2001, the presence of "foreign elements" inside U.S. territory came to be perceived as a risk, and the U.S. immigration system appeared to be deeply flawed. Subjected to increased scrutiny and more pervasive requests for identity documents, immigrants (particularly from the Middle East) became more visible. As accounts of the events leading to the terrorist attacks emerged, strategies through which migrants and visitors gained entry, temporary legal status, or false documents were exposed. In the wake of the attacks, the U.S. economy worsened, which, coupled with heightened security concerns, again fueled calls for more

restrictive immigration measures. Immigrants' exposure—to increased surveillance, accusations of disloyalty and lawlessness, and calls for removal—
took a toll on immigrant communities and on legalization efforts alike.

Central Americans, like other immigrant groups, found their priorities
and strategies redefined by the 2001 terrorist attacks. On September 14,
2001, I attended a previously scheduled meeting of immigrants with pending NACARA applications. At this meeting, which was designed to incorporate NACARA applicants into community organizations' advocacy
work, those present concluded that, in the wake of the attacks, it would be
much more difficult to obtain NACARA parity or a general legalization
program. Applicants nevertheless decided that they had to try, so they
spent most of the meeting discussing strategies. Organizing a march was
ruled out in fear that, in the present circumstances, it might appear "anti-
American." One elderly Salvadoran woman suggested that the tragedies of
September 11 might make the U.S. public more sympathetic to the plight of
Salvadorans and Guatemalans who had fled civil war and political violence.
Such parallels were echoed at an October 2001 regional meeting of Central
American community organizations. During this regional meeting, Central
American activists argued that terrorism was not limited to the violence of
September 11 but also included civil-rights violations and anti-immigrant
actions, as these also generate fear. Activists predicted that, in the wake of
the attacks, there would be a rise in anti-immigrant sentiment, an economic downturn, a rise in nativism, and an erosion of civil liberties. Such
developments, they worried, would make their own work more difficult.
Not only would their legislative proposals be less likely to win approval but
migrants who were unemployed and more fearful might be more difficult
to organize. Activists nonetheless vowed to continue their work, and some
suggested that they might argue that legalization would enhance security by
promoting documentation (see also J. Smith 2001).

As they revised their strategies, Central American activists contended
with a sense of increased vulnerability. In an interview that occurred
shortly after the attacks, one activist acknowledged, "Obviously right now
the focus of the entire nation is national security. That's defense of the land,
of the nation, and that's in preparation of war. And, any country that is
preparing for war is not going to think about any other issue, whether it is
international or domestic." A Washington, D.C.–based activist recalled:

> [After the attacks] we also met and participated in many religious events for
> the victims. Many of us suffered the impact. We had that feeling of grief, and
> we also had to recover. Because we suffered alongside all the rest of Americans.

For many, it was a moment of conversion. Because we realized what it meant to be American, to be linked to the safety of the United States, and, well, we didn't want things like that to happen. It was a very emotional moment.

Indeed, this sense of vulnerability and solidarity appeared to be widespread. At the 2001 Central American Independence Day parade in Los Angeles, U.S. flags, which were not normally a prominent component of the event, far outnumbered Central American flags (see also Grewal 2005). Recovery entailed asserting loyalty.

Immigrants' fears were not unfounded. Following the attacks, public concerns about a potential terrorist threat posed by noncitizens (particularly those who were Muslim) grew. Muslim and other minority communities experienced increases in hate crimes and discriminatory behavior, while individuals whose name, country of origin, or physical appearance fit the profile of a terrorist were subjected to additional security clearances at airports and sometimes were denied access to flights (Grewal 2005; Moore 2002). In one tragic case, a Sikh man who wore a turban was murdered in vengeance for the September 11, 2001, attacks, even though there was no Sikh involvement whatsoever (Anton 2001). Even the U.S. government singled out citizens of nations that were considered suspicious. Following the September 11, 2001, attacks, aliens from twenty-five countries were required to register with immigration officials through what has come to be known as "special alien registration" (U.S. Department of Homeland Security 2003; U.S. Customs and Immigration Enforcement n.d.). Some of those who did so were arrested and detained, even if they were about to become eligible for an immigration remedy (such as a family visa petition) (American Civil Liberties Union 2003). Following September 11, 2001, immigration officials also argued that they had the right to hold secret deportation hearings when a security risk existed. Some of the detainees who were placed in such hearings were held for lengthy periods due to minor immigration violations that would not previously have been prosecuted (Fainaru 2003; Lichtblau 2003). Additionally, many of the suspects held in the aftermath of the 2001 attacks on the Pentagon and World Trade Center were charged with violations of immigration law rather than with crimes, and thus were subjected to proceedings in which fewer civil liberties were observed (Cole and Dempsey 2002; Human Rights Watch 2002; Lawyers Committee for Human Rights 2003).

Increased exposure made visibility a liability for undocumented immigrants, who, during the 2000 legalization drive, had sought to draw attention to ways that their presence contributed to society. Particular immigrant strategies—such as obtaining false documents, overstaying one's tourist visa, applying for asylum, obtaining U.S. identity documents such as driver's licenses, studying at U.S. schools, and entering the country clandestinely—were exposed as mechanisms through which terrorists or others who posed a threat could enter the country or deceive authorities. Security measures adopted after September 11, 2001, focused on invalidating these strategies through increased scrutiny of visa applicants (particularly those from "suspect" nations), subjecting student visa holders to additional reporting and verification requirements, restricting political asylum, making proof of legal presence a prerequisite for obtaining driver's licenses, further militarizing U.S. borders, and enhancing security and passenger-screening procedures at airports. These measures have led to a new reformulation of the discourse, laws, and policies regarding immigration, even as migrants themselves have sought to recuperate from heightened suspicion and decreased rights.

Recovery

In relation to immigration issues, the post–September 11, 2001 period has been a time of recovery, in multiple senses. First, as the discourse surrounding immigration has come to focus more on security, migrants find themselves on a terrain that has shifted, in which migrants are seen as potential terrorists, enforcement is prioritized, the federal government has assumed increased surveillance and policing powers, immigration rights have been curtailed, and popular calls for more restrictive immigration policies are on the rise. These developments strengthen borders around the unauthorized, setting them further apart, and thus "resurface" or "re-cover" the national terrain in key ways. Second, proposals for various forms of legalization have had to take this newly re-covered terrain into account. Proposals therefore stress the improved security that could come from enabling migrants to come "out of the shadows" and from undermining the black market in labor. These proposals suggest that the boundary around the undocumented is unstable and potentially permeable—that, in fact, these immigrants are in our midst, performing vital functions, and that it is a flawed immigration system, rather than the behavior of individual migrants, that produces illegality and disorder. Third, migrants have had to recover from the setbacks that they experienced in the aftermath of the September 2001 terrorist attacks. Recovery has entailed insisting that the undocumented deserve legal rights at a time when, due to the "war on terrorism," "rights" themselves are seen by some as problematic.

With the September 2001 terrorist attacks, immigration came to be defined, as Central American activists had predicted, primarily as a matter of *security* rather than of labor or justice. Following the attacks, the much-maligned INS, which had previously been housed in the Department of Labor and then in the Department of Justice, was reorganized into three bureaus within the new Department of Homeland Security.[8] As a result, all immigration services—including naturalization and green card approval—became matters of homeland security. The attacks also led to reassessments of vulnerability in the area of immigration. Previously, immigration enforcement prioritized the U.S.-Mexico border rather than the interior of the country (Nevins 2002). Mexicans were presumed to be the "typical" undocumented immigrants, reflected in the fact that Border Patrol officers developed the category "other than Mexican" (OTM) to refer to their less-typical detainees (Heyman 1995). In the post-9/11 climate, there has been an increased focus on immigrants from the Middle East, and criminal background checks have become a higher priority within immigration proceedings. Shortly after September 11, 2001, immigration officials announced that they would seek to apprehend "absconders," people who had been ordered deported but who had remained in the United States. Previously, such individuals had been a low enforcement priority. Both airports and the U.S.-Canadian border also became areas of increased focus, with the USA Patriot Act tripling the number of Border Patrol officers posted along the northern border of the United States (Doyle 2001). Existing immigration laws were scrutinized for loopholes that could permit terrorists to enter the country, posing as immigrants. For instance, section 101 of the REAL ID Act of 2005 is entitled, "Preventing Terrorists from Obtaining Relief from Removal," implying that, in the past, terrorists succeeded in avoiding removal.[9]

Enforcement strategies adopted after September 11, 2001, have attempted to once again sharpen distinctions between individuals who are present in the United States legally and those who are in an unlawful and therefore suspect status. The title of the 2005 REAL ID Act is instructive in this regard—identity documents are to be made *real*. The act accomplishes this task by requiring all states to verify an applicant's lawful presence in this country before issuing a driver's license. Driver's licenses issued by states that fail to comply with the new requirements will not be accepted by federal officials as proof of identity. This strategy appears designed to make unauthorized immigrants stand out due to their lack of documents. The president's Military Order of November 13, 2001, goes further, exacerbating distinctions between citizens and noncitizens, regardless of lawful status (see 66 *Fed. Reg.* 57833, 57834, Nov. 16, 2001). This order "allows the Secretary of Defense to detain designated alien terrorist suspects, within the United States or elsewhere, without express limitation or condition except with regard to food, water, shelter, clothing, medical treatment, religious exercise, and a proscription on invidious discrimination" (Doyle 2001, 35). In 2003 the U.S. Supreme Court ruled that, because they are not citizens, aliens who are in deportation proceedings can be held indefinitely and without bond, even if such aliens pose neither a security nor a flight risk (*Demore v. Kim* 2003; see also *In re D-J-* 2003). At the same time, the citizen-alien distinction is eroded by treating U.S. citizens as "enemy combatants" who have violated the terms of their citizenship and who can therefore be deprived of certain rights (Lichtblau 2005).[10]

The sense that unauthorized migrants may be enemies has been taken up by some private citizens, who have sought to make the U.S. government enforce the control of U.S. borders more effectively. In 2005, a group calling themselves the Minutemen positioned themselves along the U.S.-Mexico border in order to assist the U.S. Border Patrol (Chavez 2007). According to a Minutemen spokesperson, this campaign drew on both patriotic imagery (the Minutemen of revolutionary days) and that of Martin Luther King Jr., who advocated nonviolent action. A newspaper article about this group featured a photo of one member posting a sign that read "Terrorists (heart) open borders," implying that unauthorized migrants might be terrorists (Kelly 2005). After President Bush denounced this group as vigilantes, they in turn denounced him as the "co-president of Mexico" and therefore presumably in service of foreign interests (Kelly 2005, A23). Organizations such as the Federation for American Immigration Reform (FAIR) also promote the notion that unauthorized migrants are a threat to the United States. A statement posted on the FAIR website asserts that "whatever terminology is used, granting legal status to illegal aliens is amnesty for millions of people who flouted the law, and will be seen as an invitation by countless millions more people to violate our laws" (FAIR 2005, 3). This statement, like the opposition to LIFA, suggests that unauthorized immigrants are essentially lawbreakers and that legalization undermines the rule of law by inviting further lawlessness.

Proponents of legalization, in contrast, have attempted to invert security discourse by arguing that it is current law, rather than illegal behavior per se, that has produced disorder and given rise to an undocumented population of some seven million. The American Immigration Lawyers Association, for example, complains that the REAL ID Act *weakens* security: "Preventing immigrants from obtaining driver's licenses undermines national security by pushing people into the shadows and fueling the black market for fraudulent identification documents. It is clear from the 9/11 and Terrorist Travel staff report that the proposed restrictions would not have prevented a single hijacker from obtaining a driver's license or boarding a plane" (2005, 6). Testifying before a U.S. Senate judiciary subcommittee, Kathleen Campbell Walker of AILA asserted, "*Our current system has made illegality the norm.* Our current 'hard' border has spurred the growth of a black market that profits from undocumented workers, as migrants increasingly have come to rely on professional smugglers to find their way past border guards" (U.S. Senate, Committee on the Judiciary 2006, 63; see also Rosenblum 2005).

As they blamed overzealous enforcement tactics for producing disorder and illegality, advocates also minimized distinctions between undocumented immigrants and legal U.S. citizens and residents. To do so, advocates stressed, as they did during the LIFA effort, that undocumented immigrants were *workers*. For instance, in 2003, the AILA website featured the slogan "Immigration Works!" along with a mug, T-shirts, and tote bags displaying an "Immigration Works!" logo. 2003 was also the year of the Immigrant Workers Freedom Ride (IWFR), in which some one thousand immigrants and their supporters caravanned across the United States from west to east, converging on the nation's capital. Modeled after the freedom rides of the civil rights movement, the IWFR was designed to "expose the injustice of current policies toward immigrants" (IWFR 2003). In contrast to imagery suggesting that the undocumented were in the "shadows," IWFR organizers asserted that "immigrant workers work hard, pay taxes, and sacrifice for their families. They work as construction workers, doctors, nurses, janitors, meat packers, chefs, busboys, engineers, farm workers, and soldiers. They care for our children, tend to our elderly, pick and serve our food, build and clean our houses, and want what we all want: a fair shot at the American Dream." IWFR organizers also disputed the contention that undocumented immigrants were lawbreakers, and instead advocated policies that "*reward work* by granting legal status to hardworking, taxpaying, law-abiding immigrant workers already established in the United States" (IWFR 2003).

The titles of post-9/11 immigration legislation reflect the renewed focus on security. For instance, a 2004 proposal that included a legalization program was entitled the Safe, Orderly Legal Visas and Enforcement Act (SOLVE). The title of this proposed legislation makes no mention of rights or of legalization per se, and in fact, from the title it would be possible to conclude that the proposed legislation would restrict immigration. Similarly a 2005 proposal, sponsored by Senators John McCain (R-AZ) and Edward

Fig. 6. "Immigration Works!" slogan and logo. Reprinted with permission of the American Immigration Lawyers Association.

Kennedy (D-MA) and Representatives Luis Gutierrez (D-IL), Jeff Flake (R-AZ), and Jim Kolbe (R-AZ), was entitled the Secure America and Orderly Immigration Act. Legalization proponents argued that such measures would lead immigrants to be identified, subjected to security checks, and documented. For instance, proponents of the SOLVE Act stated, "This measure enhances our security by: bringing immigration under the rule of law, enabling our law enforcement agencies to focus on terrorists and criminals rather than workers and families; encouraging legality at our borders; and strengthening our intelligence capacity and ability to verify the validity of documents and determine individuals' identity" (National Council of La Raza [NCLR] 2004, 1; see also Coalition for Humane Immigrant Rights of Los Angeles 2005). Similarly, proponents of "AgJobs," which would permit undocumented agricultural workers to obtain temporary legal status, asserted that this legislation "would improve national security by encouraging illegal farmworkers to step forward, identify themselves and undergo background checks to achieve temporary residency" (Curtius 2005, A14). Even the NACARA parity legislation has been renamed the Central American Security Act, whose stated purpose is to "identify and register certain Central Americans residing in the United States" (108th Congress, 1st session, HR 1300 IH, 17 March 2003).

President Bush's proposal for a temporary-worker program illustrates the tensions inherent in seeking to incorporate the prohibited. Bush's proposal, which resembles the proposals put forth by legalization advocates (Allen 2004), would "match willing foreign workers with willing U.S. employers when no Americans can be found to fill the jobs. . . . This new program would allow workers who currently hold jobs to come out of hiding and participate legally in America's economy while not encouraging further illegal behavior" (White House 2004b). The conditions that create "willingness"

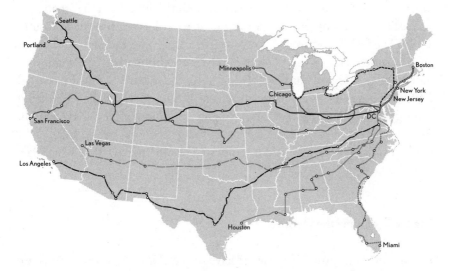

Fig. 7. "Legalization and a Road to Citizenship" route map. Based on a map on the Immigrant Workers Freedom Ride website. Reproduced with permission of the Immigrant Workers Freedom Ride/UNITE Here.

are not addressed in the proposal, though advocates of restrictionist policies have contended that lawful U.S. citizens and residents would take available jobs if pay and work conditions improved, and that it is only the presence of illegal immigrants that permits employers to lower wages and take advantage of workers (see FAIR 2005). The White House (2004b) stressed that the president's new program would promote "compassion for unprotected workers," without "unfairly rewarding those who came here unlawfully or hope to do so." "Following the rules" was singled out as a moral virtue, as in the statement that the new program "should not permit undocumented workers to gain an advantage over those who have followed the rules." Again, the proposal contained no discussion of the context or incentives that might have led some to "follow the rules" by waiting for a visa, and others, who might never become eligible for a visa, to enter without authorization. Descriptions of this new program characterized the immigrants who would benefit as "decent, hard-working people" who "only seek to earn a living" *and* as "illegal immigrants" (White House 2004c). The proposal thus attempted to treat the undocumented as morally deserving and *un*deserving at the same time. Like other contemporaneous proposals, Bush's emphasized security, stating that this program "would allow workers . . . to come out of hiding" (White House 2004a). In contrast to the IWFR organizers' statements, such references to "hiding" or being in the "shadows" suggest that even workers who are already here are located elsewhere (Coutin 2000). The "shadows" are thus constituted through law, rather than through any overt behavior of migrants themselves. By eliminating "the shadows," indeed by encompassing illegality, an "orderly system" would be created (White House 2004a). Previously illegal behavior would be eliminated through legalization, rather than through prohibition of the behavior itself. Rather than being unique to Bush's rhetoric or proposal per se, such a taking in of illegality is intrinsic to embracing both law and that which law prohibits.

The De Facto and the De Jure

Recent efforts to prohibit presence have fueled claims that immigrants are integral to U.S. society. This assertion of presence has taken two forms. First, immigrants have attempted to establish a more significant *legal presence*, through naturalization, voter registration drives, and the political mobilization of immigrant voters. Second, instead of complying with prohibition measures by leaving or staying in their countries of origin, immigrants have attempted to *redefine illegal presence.* To do so, they have depicted themselves as de facto legal residents, individuals who live in the United States, contribute to the economy through their labor, pay taxes, form families, and participate in communities. If undocumented immigrants are de facto legal residents, then law, rather than immigrants themselves, is out of order. Calls for an "amnesty"—ranging from provisions of LIFA to "earned adjustment" to the temporary-worker program contemplated in the early months of the Bush administration—are attempts to correct this situation by changing law. The fact that some form of broad-based legalization became viable attests to the significance of immigrants' legal presence and to the redefinition of immigrants as constituents rather than as aliens who lack a basis to make claims on public officials. This redefinition inverted earlier arguments for more restrictive policies. During the 1990s, advocates of immigration reform contended that migrants were taking jobs from Americans, lowering wages, and putting a strain on public services. By 2000, the need for low-skilled workers was being touted as a rationale for facilitating legal immigration, some asserted that there was a shortage of low-skilled workers, and alliances between service-industry representatives, labor unions, and immigrant advocates had become possible. Politicians began to argue that it was not fair to benefit from migrants' labor without granting them legal status. Migrants' labor and economic contributions had become grounds for deserv-ingness rather than rationales for deportation.

Recent shifts from restriction to inclusion to suspicion demonstrate the interconnection between immigration and foreign policies. The restrictive immigration policies that were adopted in 1996 generated alarm on the part of immigrant-sending nations. Central American governments feared that the immigrant remittances that had stabilized Central American currencies would evaporate and that mass deportations would fuel unemployment and political unrest. These governments therefore made NACARA a high prior-ity. Similarly, Vicente Fox attempted to secure a humane means of permit-ting Mexican workers to enter the United States, without having to endure risky border crossings or illicit status. His 2001 speech to the U.S. Congress gave this effort high visibility. In the post-9/11 political climate, foreign-policy considerations have promoted a return to more restrictive measures. Immigration policies have become linked to the war on terrorism, leading to increased scrutiny of all immigrants, with immigrants from the Middle East bearing the greatest brunt of new reporting and detention requirements.

In 2006, efforts to criminalize and thus prohibit illegal immigration once again gave rise to increased visibility, as immigrants and others took to the streets in record-breaking numbers, advocating legalization (see Ca-ble News Network 2006). The changed demographics—specifically, larger numbers of naturalized immigrants—that made LIFA viable militate against more restrictive policies. At the same time, sharp lines between the civil rights that are accorded to citizens and noncitizens are being drawn. For instance, U.S. cities have passed local ordinances against hiring or rent-ing to unlawful residents (though note that, following protests, some such ordinances have been rescinded) (Barry 2006; Los Angeles Times 2006). These lines work against mutual recognition of deservingness, even as the erosion of aliens' rights on security grounds can ultimately erode citizens' rights as well. Increased nationalism and nativism are likely to obscure ways that the United States, El Salvador, and other countries have become intermingled as nations of emigrants.

Conclusion

In August 2006, as I was completing this book, the U.S. Supreme Court reached its decision in the case of *Fernandez-Vargas v. Gonzales*. Humberto Fernandez-Vargas had entered the United States from Mexico during the 1970s, only to be deported and reenter repeatedly. In 1982, he reentered the United States for the last time and subsequently started a trucking business, fathered a child, and, in 2001, married a U.S. citizen. When his wife petitioned for him to become a legal permanent resident, he came to the attention of immigration authorities, who deported him once again. The issue before the Supreme Court concerned the retroactivity of IIRIRA. Prior to 1996, Fernandez-Vargas would have been eligible to apply for permission to remain in the country permanently, given his long period of residence and his strong ties to U.S. citizens. In 1996, however, IIRIRA made individuals who had returned to the United States illegally after being removed ineligible for any form of relief. Did this new provision of immigration law apply to immigrants such as Fernandez-Vargas, who had been in the country prior to 1996? In an 8–1 decision, the Supreme Court ruled that it did. For the majority, Justice Souter wrote, "He claims a right to continue illegal conduct indefinitely under the terms on which it began, an entitlement of legal stasis for those whose lawbreaking is continuous" (*Fernandez-Vargas v. Gonzales* 2006, 000; Savage 2006, A10). Through this decision, acts that might have been considered grounds for deservingness were defined as continuous lawbreaking. Unauthorized or temporarily authorized migrants remain vulnerable to such definitions. As prohibited persons, they can be subject to abductions. Their presence is an absence, a space and time from which legality is erased. Though the path of law can bend to incorporate them, it can also be redrawn to exclude them, such that they were never on this path at all.

Meanwhile, as the U.S. Supreme Court rendered its decision, Salvadoran authorities were preparing to issue national ID cards (DUI) within the United States. The DUI, which had been designed in 2001 as a more secure identity document, was initially available only in El Salvador. After Salvadorans living abroad complained that they lacked access to this document, Salvadoran authorities created a new bilingual version and on September 15, 2006, Salvadoran Independence Day, began to issue the DUI in Los Angeles, California; Woodbridge, Virginia; and Long Island, New York. The president of El Salvador visited Long Island to officially inaugurate this new endeavor (López 2006). Through such initiatives, the very individuals who were in some ways a present absence within the United States also became an absent presence in El Salvador, with the nation stretching beyond its territorial boundaries to include emigrants living abroad. In El Salvador, Independence Day could be celebrated in part by acknowledging a form of dependence, a need for Salvadorans outside of the country to continue to identify with and remain involved in El Salvador, particularly through remittances, tourism, consumption, and business opportunities. Although their official stances toward emigrants might differ, both El Salvador and the United States were nations of emigrants, made up of people who, like Fernandez-Vargas, had gone or come from elsewhere. Through emigrants, nations came to intersect.

In this book, I have attempted to show how standard notions of citizenship, nations, and movement give rise to forms that belie official accounts and yet are also, in some sense, true. Nations, for example, are thought to be unique entities, made up of distinct and bounded territories, citizenries, and economies. Creating this boundedness requires sorting through persons and transactions, and removing those who do not belong. Such removals create holes in national territories, while also extending nations outside national boundaries. Thus, Salvadorans bring something of El Salvador to the United States, while Salvadoran deportees and returnees bring something of the United States to El Salvador. As their citizens, residents, and economies travel, nations leak. For instance, currency that is transferred clandestinely or that is transformed into a good may not be incorporated into national balance-of-payment statements. Leakages nonetheless make possible the claimings and rejections through which boundaries are constituted and through which nations are distinguished from one another. Thus, when looked at one way, the cartographic version of the international order is correct. Yet, when looked at another way, national territories are interrupted through alien presences, enabling nations to intermingle. Nations, like emigrants, are en route.

Being en route entails experiencing both visitations and hauntings. Like movement, time is multidirectional, moving backward and sideways, as well as forward. Thus, deportees find themselves abducted from one present to another, in which they must assume identities that they are held to have always already had. Celebrations of migration, whether through judgments of deservingness or through praise of emigrant remittances, are haunted by the figures of the deportee and the unauthorized migrant en route. Reclaimings—through legalization, attention to migrants living abroad, or incorporating informal transactions within formal accounts—entail a return to the past, a return that reconstitutes the past as something else, such that prohibited presence becomes "setting down roots," the "international" becomes a source of expertise rather than of subversion, and payments to family members become contributions to national well-being. Paradoxically, such returns to the past can produce a new present. For instance, Salvadorans who were considered "economic immigrants" and therefore deportable were reconstituted as deserving, as "people we knew" whose temporary identity documents had placed them on the path of the law all along. Such alterations may be incomplete, however, enabling alternative pasts to again reshape the present. Thus seemingly "deserving" immigrants, such as Fernandez-Vargas, can suddenly become deportable once again, their lives in the United States reconstituted as continuous illegal activity.

The subjects of such temporal movements assume multiple forms. They are Salvadorans, Americans, encroachers, contributors, corrupting, saviors, sources of national dissipation and of national development. Present in multiple places simultaneously, absented citizens become conduits of national movement. In the process, distinctions between persons and objects are eroded. Emigrants come to bear national essences, distributing Salvadoranness throughout the world. At the same time, unauthorized immigrants who are long-term residents are in some sense de facto citizens of the United States who, if deported, bring the United States to El Salvador. As products of the documents that ascertain legal identity, unauthorized immigrants come to embody illegality and thus to occupy a space from which legality is vacated. The disjuncture between legal absence and social and physical presence can be overcome by making these coincide, either through legalization or through deportation. This disjuncture can, however, pull immigrants apart, as they attempt to occupy spaces (in cargo holds, on top of trains) outside of normal travel corridors. As they occupy multiple temporalities and social and legal spaces, emigrants can appear and disappear, living in above-board communities and in an underground at the same time. As one emigrant who had temporary legal status was quoted previously, "You're like invisible to everything else. Everybody else is solid but you're not."

As subjects, emigrants are both sources and products of investment. Emigrants are said to invest in nations, contributing to U.S. society through their labor, supporting the Salvadoran economy through their remittances, and promoting development through their community associations. Their desires—for citizenship, for their hometowns, for selves that they once were—enchant nations, giving these the power to pull emigrants in multiple directions. At the same time, what appear to be investments are also products of power-laden processes. Emigrants' contributions to the U.S. economy are made possible by employers' desire for migrant labor, a desire that derives, at least in part, from migrants' exploitability (Calavita 2005). Remitting is, among other things, a strategy for coping with a lack of economic opportunity in migrants' home countries and is consistent with neoliberal financial policies (Hernandez and Coutin 2006; Schiller, Basch, and Szanton Blanc 1995). Collective remittances, much like family remittances, are blamed by some for promoting dependency and thus preventing rather than promoting development. Desire for citizenship and nostalgia for one's country of origin may be fueled, in part, by exclusionary policies that make citizenship a prerequisite for opportunities or that prevent international travel. Material and emotional investments therefore take multiple forms and can shift between being *investments* and *signs of subjugation*.

Investments in emigrants are potentially violent. Salvadorans emigrants were produced, to a significant degree, by the violence of the civil war. Fears of subversives and of guerrillas constituted the Salvadoran citizenry as suspect, leading many to flee the country. As most lacked authorization to enter the United States, these emigrants confronted enforcement practices that pushed them into uninhabitable places, such as deserts, mountains, and cargo holds. If apprehended, emigrants experienced the coercion of detention and possibly deportation. In El Salvador, deportees were stigmatized as criminals and as in some sense alien, as the gang member replaced the guerrilla as the focus of Salvadoran security measures. Violence, however, has also been interpreted as nonviolence. For instance, during the 1980s U.S. authorities attributed immigration from El Salvador to poverty rather than war. The violence of U.S. border enforcement is in many cases nonagentive, making border deaths appear to be due to accident or to the elements rather than the result of immigration policies. Deportation is not generally considered an act of violence, but rather merely a means of locating unauthorized aliens in their countries of legal residency. Although they in some ways resemble tactics formerly used against guerrillas, measures adopted to fight gangs in El Salvador are seen as enforcing law rather than as repressing dissidents. Violence that is massive in scope, carried out by authorities, embedded in structures and policies, or directed against a socially stigmatized group can be seen as something other than violence. Like emigrants, such violence appears and disappears.

The shifting nature of space, time, subjectivity, investment, and violence suggests that official accounts give rise to an "outside" that is both necessary and impossible. This outside is necessary in that accounts are compelled by the as-yet-unassessed, the "undiscovered," as it were, made up of unknown persons, transactions that have not yet been counted, and versions of history that are not official. An "outside" is also impossible in that nations should not be made up of unauthorized residents or of citizens who cannot be present; financial reports should take all transactions into account; and multiple histories cannot exist. The "outside" can be both another space and another time, for example, the time when individuals were unauthorized or when a monetary transfer had not yet been counted as a remittance—the time *before* an account was produced (cf. Benjamin 1978; Derrida 1992). Accounting requires entering this outside in order to narrate a prior history. At the same time, the "outside" contains gaps that cannot be traversed, as when no record of an individual's presence exists, or when payments are made in kind rather than in cash. Entering the "outside" therefore incorporates a certain fuzziness or sleight of hand into an account. Accounts that lack this element may appear false (e.g., asylum officials sometimes suggest that stories that lack inconsistencies may have been invented) even as opaqueness seems to undermine an account (too many inconsistencies also undermine asylum applicants' credibility) (Robertson and Camerini 2000). Truth therefore relies on an element of fiction, the narration of the moment "before" the record begins.

Ethnographic accounts are no exceptions.[1] The notion of the as-yet-unstudied or of a "gap" in knowledge motivates academic work, and is often used as a justification in research proposals (Riles 2000; Maurer 2002; Strathern 1999). According to this "gap" rationale, knowledge, though ideally complete, is intrinsically partial, as a new perspective can always add to existing accounts.[2] Ethnography is thus propelled by (and dependent on) the ethnographic unknown, the idea that there are social realities that have not yet been studied and research questions that have not yet been posed. At the same time, there is a sense in which such an "outside" is impossible, given that the "field" *as an object of inquiry* comes into being in relation to ethnographers (Coutin 2005a). Ethnographers bring this field into being through data collection—through interview transcripts, field notes, surveys, and other sorts of records. There is therefore a gap between the field that, in a sense, materializes through fieldwork, and the field that is imagined to be "beyond" or temporally "before" this record is created (Axel 2004). These two fields are imagined to be the same, otherwise the ethnographic endeavor would have no validity. At the same time, these fields are known to differ in that no account can perfectly represent the reality that it purports to describe (in statistics, this difference is referred to as a "margin of error"). If an ethnographic account were identical in every respect to some exterior or preexisting social reality, then this account would cease to be ethnographic and would become an instance of what is sometimes referred to as "going native." To be scientifically valid, then, ethnographic accounts must maintain an element of fiction, that is, the notion that gaps can be traversed, that the "unknown" can be narrated, that "data" can bring ethnographers into a reality that is outside of "the field" that ethnographers construct.

In this particular ethnography, I have attempted to enter a space that is not fully there, a space occupied by emigrants who are legally excluded from territories where they are physically present, where absent citizens extend national territories, where nations are en route. To do so, I have constructed an account that doubles back, returning to reconsider the significance of violence, of presence, and of being "outside." This account moves in both time and space, returning to the period of civil war as both a foundation that set in motion that which followed and as a series of events whose meaning was produced at least in part after the fact. Thus, the civil war caused emigration, which in turn produced remittance flows. At the same time, remittances permitted emigrants to be reconstituted as absent citizens, which in turn redefined the war as a source of commonality ("something we all lived through") rather than division. This book therefore has proceeded nonlinearly, opening with an account of departure and return (deportation) rather than, as is more typical, arrival.[3]

In drawing attention to the fictions that make ethnography possible and to the form of my own account, I do not wish to suggest that ethnographies are merely constructions, products of the social position of ethnographers while in the field, and therefore, to a large degree, literary devices rather than social science. Nor do I wish to suggest that the structure of my account somehow subverts power relations between ethnographers and research subjects (though note that in my case such power relations run in multiple directions—the metaphor of studying "up" or "down" does not work—see also Coutin and Hirsch 1998). Rather, my goal is to explore the relationship between social reality and the tools used to measure that reality (Callon 1998). As Barbara Yngvesson and I point out elsewhere (n.d.), ethnographic accounts work, paradoxically, precisely because of the fictions that otherwise would seem to undermine their validity. Just as accounting procedures both measure remittances and imbue them with particular qualities, and just as legal determinations derive from and produce legal facts (such as NACARA applicants' presumed hardship), so too do ethnographies constitute and reflect social realities. They do so not by *overcoming* gaps, but rather by *positing* a gap in the first place. Thus, at the moment that the fieldworker embarks on data collection, the field is constituted as another order of reality, an "unknown" that can only be accessed through the records that the ethnographer produces. The field thus becomes an elsewhere, reflected in and thus constituted by the ethnographer's account (see also Strathern 1999).

The gap between the field as an unknown and the field as depicted ethnographically makes ethnographic accounts shimmer. The "elsewhereness" of the field may be difficult to maintain, such that there are moments during fieldwork when the field ceases to be an object of study. Such moments permit other sorts of accounts to enter ethnographies, as that which is not (or not yet) data pulls the ethnographer in unanticipated directions. This pull of the "before" or the "outside" compels ethnographers to return, via field notes, to the moment of fieldwork, and to redefine incidents and statements in light of a developing analysis. Such returns give ethnographies a dual quality: ethnographies can convey searing truths about social realities, even as they are in some sense inventions.

This dual quality is particularly sharp in the ethnography of emigration, given that the field that it is meant to describe both is and isn't there, and that its subjects assume multiple forms. Instead of focusing on a particular place or group of people, the ethnography of emigration entails following departures from the status quo into the clandestine routes traveled by the unauthorized, the transnational nationalism practiced by emigrant nations, and the alternative presents that deportees are made to occupy. The ethnography of emigration requires holding incompatible realities in juxtaposition simultaneously, such that "deserving immigrants" can also be engaged in "continuous illegal behavior" and that "national identity documents" can be issued to "expatriate citizens." Emigration pulls ethnographers in multiple directions, both physically, in that multiple sites (e.g., the United States, El Salvador) must be visited, but also analytically, in that ethnographers must visit sites (e.g., the clandestine) to which they lack access, that they can only visit ethnographically, through their data. Such inaccessible sites include the erased prior histories of migrants who have been deported and the spaces occupied by migrants who are not there. When such in essence nonexistent sites cease to be elsewhere, then the "aboveboard" becomes illusory, giving ethnography a surreal quality.

In 2006, as I drafted this conclusion, the U.S. Congress passed legislation that enlarged the Border Patrol, authorized an additional 700 miles of fencing along the U.S.-Mexico border, improved border sensors, and provided for additional detention center space (Gaouette 2006a) A 2006 Arizona gubernatorial candidate (who lost the primary) went so far as to propose housing illegal immigrants in a "tent city" and putting them to work constructing border fencing and picking up trash in the desert (Barabak 2006). Such measures sharpen distinctions between legal and unauthorized residents and situate the latter outside, as fugitives from the police, subject to detention and deportation if apprehended, and as expendable labor, perhaps akin to the garbage the gubernatorial candidate wanted them to collect. Stiffening border enforcement makes crossings more costly and more dangerous, potentially increasing the numbers of deaths along the border as well as the violence of smugglers seeking to evade authorities (Andreas 2000). Facilitating detention and deportation elevate legal status above other measures of belonging, leading to dislocations and erasures. Exclusionary policies constitute the unauthorized as an underclass whose long-term residence poses dilemmas for the United States. Should legal avenues of immigration be increased, as proposed by the guest-worker and AgJobs legislation? Will unauthorized migrants be redefined as deserving, with eventual eligibility for naturalization, as has happened for the majority of NACARA applicants? And will efforts to prohibit the unauthorized give rise to calls for a new legalization program, as occurred through the immigrant rights marches of 2006? As these questions are answered, U.S. communities, which are composed of both legal and unauthorized residents, will be reshaped.

Emigrants' absent presence in El Salvador is also increasingly being realized. In October 2006, the Salvadoran government hosted its second

Presidential Forum with Salvadorans Living Abroad. The two-day meeting included panels on tourism, development, retirement, education, technology, cultural identity, business and investment opportunities, and migration (Ministero de Relaciones Exteriores, El Salvador 2006). This event was clearly designed to, among other things, promote economic links between El Salvador and Salvadorans living abroad. Such events define emigrants as potential tourists and investors who may also choose to purchase housing and retire in El Salvador. Such economic opportunities position emigrants outside of and yet within El Salvador. They are outside, in the exterior, in that living in the United States or in other parts of the world has enabled them to hold jobs, develop businesses, and acquire funds that could presumably be spent in El Salvador. They are inside, in that they are compatriots, hailed through the creation of government offices to attend to their needs, recognized as eligible for national identity documents, and encouraged to strengthen their cultural identities as Salvadoran. Such absent presences also pose dilemmas. Will Salvadorans living abroad continue to identify with El Salvador? Do economic initiatives that depend on emigrants also depend on the violence associated with unauthorized immigration? Will conditions in El Salvador change such that fewer Salvadorans seek to emigrate? How do emigrant citizens reconfigure the Salvadoran nation?

One possible response to these dilemmas is to recognize that both the United States and El Salvador are nations of emigrants. By this statement, I do not mean to promote emigration, which clearly has social consequences and can come at great personal cost. Rather, my point is to draw attention to de facto realities that are currently prohibited. Immigrating without authorization, an act that is condemned in the United States, is a normal part of life in many places. Recall the question posed by an adolescent girl in rural El Salvador in response to a presentation on immigration: "If they say it's a crime for us to travel to the United States without papers, then why don't they give us papers?" This question depicts the U.S. decision to criminalize unauthorized immigration as arbitrary and illogical, given the normalcy of immigrating, with or without authorization. Of course, there *is* a logic to prohibiting unauthorized border crossings—it could prevent illegal immigration or, some argue, can be key to creating an undocumented and therefore more expendable workforce (Bach 1978; Jenkins 1978). Defining the United States and El Salvador as nations of emigrants, however, draws attention to the interconnections presumed by the girl who posed this question. The United States, El Salvador, and many other nations are interconnected through families, markets, and histories; they look toward each other in many respects. Perhaps it is time to acknowledge such interconnections, and to permit individuals, communities, and nations to span boundaries, not by abandoning notions of the nation-state, sovereignty, or citizenship, but rather by permitting these to include the multiple spaces occupied by emigrants.

Epilogue

"Frutos de la Guerra" by Marvin Novoa Escobar (AKA Bullet)

Frutos de la Guerra

En nombre de Dios pues y en nombre de este sufrido pueblo,
cuyos lamentos suben hasta el cielo cada día mas tumultuosos,
les suplico, les ruego, les ordeno en nombre de Dios,
cese la represión . . .[1]

Saludando a mi patria y a mi gente nativa,
me dejo caer, con una rola alternativa
Guanacos de corazón, pipiles de el salvador
ayudando a mi pueblo mejor que embajador,
empezando esta ves desde la raíz de una historia de guerra
que arruino nuestro país,
doce años fueron, los que se sufrieron,
almas inocentes que la vida perdieron,
por gente demente que sin pensar combatieron
varias familias tuvieron que dividir,
buscando otra forma de sobrevivir
de su patria así mismo obligados a salir
a otro país con cultura diferente,

algo que no era usual para nuestra gente,
adaptándose al sistema sin ninguna opción,
trabajando como burros sin tener decisión,
descuidando al igual la comunicación,
dejando a los hijos sin orientación,
empezando esto fue como una semilla
trayendo como fruto la formación de pandillas,
tratemos este tema con mucha seriedad
algo sin sentido pero esto es realidad
la realidad que se vive como frutos de la guerra.

Fue más de una década la que vivió El Salvador,
momentos duros que todo fue aterrador,
la paz llego y se firmaron los acuerdos,
dejando que lo pasado se quedara en recuerdos
trayendo por consiguiente la deportación,
abuso masivo de parte de inmigración,
obligando a los guanacos a regresar a su nación
asiéndolos victimas de la explotación,
regresando a su país con un estilo nuevo,
la gente queriendo que se cambie por huevo . . .
la policía abusando y como siempre buscando
forma eficaz para tenerte tabiando,[2]
la sociedad tiende a temer y desconfiar
y ni quisiera intentando la situación analizar,
sociedad radical eso es lo que son
viviendo la ignorancia desde el corazón,
muchos de los que anduvieron combatiendo
hoy en día en las calles se encuentran poniendo
para poder obtener, el pan de cada día
muchos de ellos viviendo a puro queso y tortillas,
él que a la guerra los mando después los abandono
sí sabemos que es cierto no digamos que no,
lo que hacen es lo que les enseñaron
sin tener otra opción fue la vida que agarraron
esto es algo que todos tenemos que cambiar
y por esa razón lo venimos a rapear,
esta gente, de la sociedad se siente fuera,
todo consecuencia de los frutos de la guerra

No podemos imaginar lo que se sintió
en los momentos duros que la gente vivió,
muchas vidas que, estuvieron en un hilo
y por salvarse muchas de ellas pidieron asilo,
yo no estoy ni con la izquierda ni con la derecha
solo digo en verdad lo que la guerra cosecha,
esto es algo que ahora la gente lamenta
nunca pensando que traería en cuenta
todo lo que ahora se esta padeciendo
la maldad que día a día sigue creciendo,
los derechos humanos no han sido respetados,
mas bien lo que yo veo siguen siendo violados,
esta en nosotros cambiar este mundo,
lo digo yo no soy primero ni tampoco segundo,
pongamos stop a la maldad que hay en la tierra
y démosle un fin a los frutos de la guerra
Frutos de la guerra

Fruits of the War

In the name of God and in the name of this suffering people
Whose ever more tumultuous cries rise to heaven
I beg you, I plead to you, I order you in the name of God
Stop the repression . . .

Greeting my country and my native people,
I get down with this alternative rhyme
Guanacos from the heart, Pipiles de El Salvador,[3]
helping out my people better than an ambassador.
Starting this time from the roots of a history of war
that ruined our country.
Twelve years it was that they suffered.
Innocent souls who lost their lives,
because of unconscious people who fought without thinking
Many families had to be divided,
searching for another way to survive.
And from their homeland they were forced to leave,
to another country with a different culture,

something that was strange to our people.
Adapting themselves to the system without any option,
working like mules without having a choice.
Neglecting equally communication,
that left their children without orientation.
Starting this was like a seed,
bringing as its fruit the formation of the gangs
Let's treat this topic with much seriousness
something that doesn't make sense but it is reality,
The reality that lives in the fruits of the war

It was more than a decade that El Salvador lived,
tough times in which everything was terrifying.
Peace came and the accords were signed,
leaving that which had passed to remain in memories.
Bringing in its wake deportation,
massive abuse from Immigration.[4]
Forcing Guanacos to return to their nation,
making them victims of exploitation.
Returning to the country with a new style,
the people wanting to change them through force.
The police abusing and always looking for,
an effective way to keep you doing time.
Society tends to fear and to distrust,
not even trying to analyze the situation.
Radical society is what they are,[5]
Living in ignorance to the very core.
Many of those who went around fighting [during the war],
now days, are found "jacking it" in the street.
In order to obtain their daily bread,
many of them living on just cheese and tortilla.
The one [who] sent them to war, abandoned them afterwards,
if we know this is true, we shouldn't say "no."[6]
What they do is what they were taught,
Without having another option, it was the life that they clung to
It's something that all of us have to change,
and for this reason, I come to rap.
These people, felt put aside from society,
They are the consequences of the fruits of the war.

We can't imagine what was felt
in those difficult moments that the people lived.
Many lives were hanging by a thread,
and in order to save themselves many of them petitioned for asylum.
I'm not with the left or the right,
I just tell the truth about what the war reaped.
Something that the people now lament,
never thinking what it would bring about.
All that we are now suffering,
the madness that day by day keeps growing.
Human rights have not been respected,
Rather as I see it, they continue to be violated.
It's up to us to change this world,
I'm not the first nor the second to say it.
Let's put a "STOP" to the madness in this land,
And let's put an end to the "Fruits of the War."

Translated by Marvin Nova Escobar and Elana Zilberg
Transcription provided by Elana Zilberg

Note: Lyrics of "Frutos de la Guerra" were provided by Luis Romero of Homies Unidos El Salvador and are reprinted by permission of Homies Unidos El Salvador. Elana Zilberg checked the lyrics against her audiotape of Bullet's performance of this song and made minor corrections. Spelling and punctuation have been left as in the original Spanish, as, due to Bullet's untimely death, it is impossible to consult with him regarding changes. Elana Zilberg, an anthropologist who did fieldwork in El Salvador and who knew Bullet, also provided a transcription of an English translation that she and Bullet made prior to his death. I use this translation here with only very minor changes, as it conveys the author's own interpretation of his lyrics. I am grateful to Luis Romero and Elana Zilberg for their assistance, and for permission to reproduce their transcriptions of Bullet's song.

References

1951 Convention Relating to the Status of Refugees. Available at http://www.unhcr
.org/cgi-bin/texis/vtx/protect/opendoc.pdf?tbl=PROTECTION&id=3b66c2aa10.
Accessed 17 March 2006.

Ábrego, Geovanny. 2004. "El monumento que sólo ha sido renombrado en papel."
La Prensa Gráfica, 3 August. Available at http://www.laprensagrafica.com/
gransansalvador/gransansalvador1.asp. Accessed 3 August 2004.

Agamben, Giorgio. 1998. *Homo Sacer: Sovereign Power and Bare Life.* Translated by
Daniel Heller-Roazen. Stanford: Stanford University Press.

Aguayo, Sergio, and Patricia Weiss Fagen. 1988. *Central Americans in Mexico and
the United States: Unilateral, Bilateral, and Regional Perspectives.* Washington,
D.C.: Georgetown University, Center for Immigration Policy and Refugee Assistance.

Allen, Mike. 2004. "Bush to Seek Immigrant Benefit Protection." *Washington Post*,
4 January, A5.

Amaya Cóbar, Edgardo A., and Gustavo Federico Palmieri. 2000. "Debilidad insti-
tucional, impunidad y violencia." In *Violencia en una sociedad en transición: Ensayos*, edited by Carlos Guillermo Ramos et al., 75–114. San Salvador: Programa
de las Naciones Unidas para el Desarrollo.

American Baptist Churches v. Meese. 1987. No. C-85–3255 RFP, United States District Court for the Northern District of California, 666 F. Supp. 1358.

———. 1989. No. C-85–3255 RFP, United States District Court for the Northern
District of California, 712 F. Supp. 756.

American Baptists Churches v. Thornburgh. 1991. No. C-85–3225–RFP, United
States District Court for the Northern District of California, 760 F. Supp. 796.

American Civil Liberties Union. 2003. "ACLU and Coalition of Immigrants' Rights Groups 'Register Discontent' with Government's Immigration Registration Program." 10 January. Available at http://www.aclu.org. Accessed 10 February 2006.

American Embassy San Salvador. 1998. "Emigrants and Remittances: A Vital Factor in El Salvador's Economy." Antiguo Cuscatlán, El Salvador. Embajada Americana.

American Immigration Lawyers Association (AILA). 2003. "Immigration Works! It's Who We Are: National Awareness Campaign." Available at http://sequoia .forest.net/tshirts/aila/action.lasso?-database=ashaorder.fp5&response=welcome2 .lasso&-add. Accessed 30 September 2003.

——. 2005. "The REAL ID Act of 2005: Summary and Selected Analysis of Provisions Included in the Emergency Supplemental Appropriations Package (H.R. 1268)." Available at http://www.nclr.org/files/33168_file_AILA_REAL_ID_ Summary_of_Selected_Provisions_as_Passed_in_Emergency_Supplemental_ H_R_1268.pdf. Accessed 4 October 2006.

Anderson, Benedict. 1983. *Imagined Communities: Reflections on the Origin and Spread of Nationalism*. Rev. ed. London: Verso.

Andrade-Eekhoff, Katharine. 2003. *Mitos y realidades: El impacto económico de la migración en los hogares rurales*. San Salvador: FLACSO Programa El Salvador.

Andreas, Peter. 2000. *Border Games: Policing the US-Mexico Divide*. Ithaca: Cornell.

Anton, Mike. 2001. "Collateral Damage in War on Terrorism: A Sikh Immigrant Is Killed at His Gas Station." *Los Angeles Times*, 22 September. Available at http://www.latimes.com. Accessed 15 February 2006.

Appadurai, Arjun. 1986. "Introduction: Commodities and the Politics of Value." In *The Social Life of Things: Commodities in Cultural Perspective*, edited by A. Appadurai, 3–63. Cambridge: Cambridge University Press.

Arendt, Hannah. 1966. *The Origins of Totalitarianism*. New York: Harcourt, Brace.

Aretxaga, Begoña. 1995. "Dirty Protest: Symbolic Overdetermination and Gender in Northern Ireland Ethnic Violence." *Ethos* 23, no. 2: 123–48.

Arnson, Cynthia J. 1989. *Crossroads: Congress, the Reagan Administration, and Central America*. New York: Pantheon Books.

Asch, Beth J., and C. Reichmann, eds. 1994. *Emigration and Its Effects on the Sending Country*. Santa Monica, Calif.: Rand Corporation, Center for Research on Immigration Policy.

Athukorala, Premachandra. 1992. "The Use of Migrant Remittances in Development: Lessons from the Asian Experience." *Journal of International Development* 4, no. 5: 511–29.

Axel, Brian Keith. 2004. "The Context of Diaspora." *Cultural Anthropology* 19, no. 1: 26–60.

Bach, Robert L. 1978. "Mexican Immigration and the American State." *International Migration Review* 12, no. 4: 536–58.

——. 1990. "Immigration and U.S. Foreign Policy in Latin America and the Caribbean." In *Immigration and U.S. Foreign Policy*, edited by Robert W. Tucker, Charles B. Keely, and Linda Wrigley, 123–49. Boulder: Westview Press.

Bailey, Adrian J., and Joshua G. Hane. 1995. "Population in Motion: Salvadorean

Refugees and Circulation Migration." *Bulletin of Latin American Research* 14, no. 2: 171–200.

Baker, Susan González. 1997. "The 'Amnesty' Aftermath: Current Policy Issues Stemming from the Legalization Programs of the 1986 Immigration Reform and Control Act." *International Migration Review* 31, no. 1: 5–27.

Baker-Cristales, Beth. 2004. *Salvadoran Migration to Southern California: Redefining El Hermano Lejano*. Gainesville: University Press of Florida.

Banco Central de Reserva de El Salvador. 2003. "U.S. $1,935.2 Millones: Remesas Familiares en 2002." Comunicado de Prensa No. 1/2003. Available at http://www.bcr.gob.sv/publicaciones/comunicados.html. Accessed 10 July 2003.

———. 2006. "Remesas familiares acendieron a US $2,830.2 millones en 2005." Comunicado de Presa No. 1/2006. Available at http://www.bcr.gob.sv/ingles/publicaciones/comunicados.html. Accessed 12 January 2006.

Banco Interamericano de Desarrollo (BID). 2001. "Expertos proponen mayor esfuerzo para incrementar competitividad de servicios de infraestructura en América Latina." Press release, 25 April. Available at http://www.iadb.org/exr/PRENSA/2001/cp7501c.htm. Accessed 27 July 2004.

———. 2002a. "BID celebrará en El Salvador foro regional sobre competitividad." Press release, 5 April. Available at http://www.iadb.org. Accessed 27 July 2004.

———. 2002b. *Guía operativa para programas de competitividad para la pequeña y mediana empresa*. Serie de buenas prácticas del Departamento de Desarrollo Sostenible. Washington, D.C.: Banco Interamericano de Desarrollo.

———. 2003. "BID aprueba préstamo de 100 millones de dólares para apoyar reformas para la competitividad en El Salvador." Press release, 12 November. Available at http://www.iadb.org. Accessed 27 July 2004.

Barabak, Mark Z. 2006. "Arizona Race Doesn't Dwell on Immigration." *Los Angeles Times*, 27 September, A17.

Barbalet, J. M. 1988. *Citizenship: Rights, Struggle and Class Inequality*. Milton Keynes, Eng.: Open University Press.

Barham, Bradford, and Stephen Boucher. 1998. "Migration, Remittances, and Inequality: Estimating the Net Effects of Migration on Income Distribution." *Journal of Development Economics* 55, no. 2: 307–31.

Barry, Deborah, Raúl Vergara, and José Rodolfo Castro. 1988. " 'Low Intensity Warfare': The Counterinsurgency Strategy for Central America." In *Crisis in Central America: Regional Dynamics and U.S. Policy in the 1980s*, edited by Nora Hamilton et al., 77–96. Boulder: Westview Press.

Barry, Ellen. 2006. "It's 'Get These People Out of Town.' " *Los Angeles Times*, 16 August. Available at http://www.latimes.com/. Accessed 11 September 2006.

Basch, Linda, Nina Glick Schiller, and Cristina Szanton Blanc. 1994. *Nations Unbound: Transnational Projects, Postcolonial Predicaments, and Deterritorialized Nation-States*. Langhorne, Penn.: Gordon and Breach.

Battaglia, Debbora. 1995. "On Practical Nostalgia: Self-Prospecting among Urban Trobrianders." In *Rhetorics of Self-Making*, edited by D. Battaglia, 77–97. Berkeley: University of California Press.

Bau, Ignatius. 1985. *This Ground Is Holy: Church Sanctuary and Central American Refugees*. New York: Paulist Press.

Bauböck, Rainer, ed. 1994. *From Aliens to Citizens: Redefining the Status of Immigrants in Europe*. Aldershot, Eng.: Avebury.

Bejar, Rafael Guido. 1998. "El Salvador de posguerra: Formas de violencia en la transición." In *Violencia en una sociedad en transición*, edited by Renos Papadopoulos et al., 96–105. San Salvador: Programa de las Naciones Unidas para el Desarrollo.

Bellah, Robert N. 1975. *The Broken Covenant: American Civil Religion in Time of Trial*. New York: Seabury.

Bellah, Robert N., Richard Madsen, William M. Sullivan, Ann Swidler, and Steven M. Tipton. 1985. *Habits of the Heart: Individualism and Commitment in American Life*. New York: Harper and Row.

Benítez, Raúl. 1990. "El Salvador 1980–1990: Guerra, política y perspectivas." In *El Salvador: El proceso de democratización*. Cuaderno de Trabajo No. 13. December. Mexico City: Centro de Investigación y Acción Social.

Benjamin, Walter. 1978. "Critique of Violence." In *Reflections: Essays, Aphorisms, Autobiographical Writing*, edited by Peter Demetz, 277–300. Translated by Edmund Jephcott. New York: Schocken Books.

Bercovitch, Sacvan. 1978. *The American Jeremiad*. Madison: University of Wisconsin Press.

Beyer, Gregg A. 1994. "Reforming Affirmative Asylum Processing in the United States: Challenges and Opportunity." *American University Journal of International Law and Policy* 9, no. 4: 43–78.

Bhabha, Jacqueline. 1996. "Embodied Rights: Gender Persecution, State Sovereignty, and Refugees." *Public Culture* 9, no. 1: 3–32.

Bienvenidos a Casa. Programa de Atención a los Inmigrantes Salvadoreños. 2001. "Información al 31 de Julio 2001." San Salvador: Catholic Relief Services.

Binford, Leigh. 1996. *The Mozote Massacre: Anthropology and Human Rights*. Tucson: University of Arizona Press.

———. 1999. "Hegemony in the Interior of the Salvadoran Revolution: The ERP in Northern Morazán." *Journal of Latin American Anthropology* 4, no. 1: 2–45.

Blum, Carolyn Patty. 1991. "The Settlement of *American Baptist Churches v. Thornburgh*: Landmark Victory for Central American Asylum Seekers." *International Journal of Refugee Law* 3, no. 2: 347–56.

Bosniak, Linda S. 2000. "Citizenship Denationalized." *Indiana Journal of Global Legal Studies* 7, no. 2: 447–510.

Boudreaux, Richard. 2004. "Businessman Wins Salvadoran Presidency." *Los Angeles Times*, 22 March, A3.

Brizuela de Ávila, María Eugenia. 2003. "Atención a los Salvadoreños en la Internet." Editorial, *La Prensa Gráfica*, 14 June. Available at http://www.comunidades.gob.sv/comunidades/comunidades.nsf/pages/editorial140603. Accessed 14 October 2003.

Bureau of Citizenship and Immigration Services. N.d. "Glossary." Available at http://www.immigration.gov/graphics/glossary3.htm. Accessed 23 July 2003.

Bush, George H. W. 1990. *Public Papers of the Presidents of the United States, George*

Bush 1990, Book 2—July 1 to December 31, 1990. Washington, D.C.: U.S. Government Printing Office.

Byrne, Hugh. 1996. *El Salvador's Civil War: A Study of Revolution*. Boulder: Lynne Rienner.

Cable News Network (CNN). 2003. "California Recall Focused on Immigration." 8 September. Available at http://www.cnn.com/2003/ALLPOLITICS/09/07/california.recall/. Accessed February 24, 2007.

———. 2005. "Officials Say New Orleans Is Completely Destroyed." *Lou Dobbs Tonight*, 5 September. Available at http://transcripts.cnn.com/TRANSCRIPTS/0509/05/ldt.01.html. Accessed 17 March 2006.

———. 2006. "Thousands March for Immigrant Rights." 1 May. Available at http://www.cnn.com. Accessed 11 September 2006.

Calavita, Kitty. 1990. "Employer Sanctions Violations: Toward a Dialectical Model of White-Collar Crime." *Law and Society Review* 24, no 4: 1041–69.

———. 1996. "The New Politics of Immigration: 'Balanced-Budget Conservatism' and the Symbolism of Proposition 187." *Social Problems* 43, no. 3: 284–305.

———. 2000. "The Paradoxes of Race, Class, Identity, and 'Passing': Enforcing the Chinese Exclusion Acts, 1882–1910." *Law and Social Inquiry* 25, no. 1: 1–40.

———. 2005. *Immigrants at the Margins: Law, Race, and Exclusion in Southern Europe*. New York: Cambridge University Press.

Calavita, Kitty, Henry N. Pontell, and Robert H. Tillman. 1997. *Big Money Crime: Fraud and Politics in the Savings and Loan Crisis*. Berkeley: University of California Press.

Caldeira, Teresa P. R. 2000. *City of Walls: Crime, Segregation, and Citizenship in São Paulo*. Berkeley: University of California Press.

Calderón Sol, Armando. 2002. *Anhelos y desafíos del Presidente : por el nuevo El Salvador, en paz, progreso y libertad*. El Salvador.

Callon, Michel. 1998. "Introduction: The Embeddedness of Economic Markets in Economics." In *The Laws of the Markets*, edited by M. Callon, 1–57. Oxford: Blackwell.

Callon, Michel, Cécile Méadel, and Vololona Rabeharisoa. 2002. "The Economy of Qualities." *Economy and Society* 31, no. 2: 194–217.

Carruthers, Bruce G., and Wendy Nelson Espeland. 1998. "Money, Meaning, and Morality: Changing Forms of Payment." *American Behavioral Scientist* 41, no. 10: 1384–1409.

Casa Presidencial. República de El Salvador. 2004a. "Discurso Sr. Elias Antonio Saca Presidente de la Republica lanzamiento del Plan 'Super Mano Dura' Lunes, 30 de agosto de 2004." Available at http://www.casapres.gob.sv/discursos/disp200408/disp040830_2.htm. Accessed 25 August 2005.

———. 2004b. "Transmisión de mando presidencial 2004: Gabinete de Gobierno 2004–2009." Available at http://www.transmisonpresidencialelsalvador.com/gabinete.htm. Accessed 18 August 2004.

Chami, Ralph, Connel Fullenkamp, and Samir Jahjah. 2005. "Are Immigrant Remittance Flows a Source of Capital for Development?" *IMF Staff Papers* 52, no. 1: 55–81. Available at http://www.imf.org/External/Pubs/FT/staffp/2005/01/pdf/chami.pdf. Accessed 15 March 2006.

Chavez, Leo R. 2001. *Covering Immigration: Popular Images and the Politics of the Nation.* Berkeley: University of California Press.

———. 2007. "Spectacle in the Desert: The Minuteman Project on the U.S.-Mexico Border." In *Global Vigilantes: Anthropological Perspectives on Justice and Violence,* edited by David Pratten and Atreyee Sen. London: C. Hurst.

Child Citizenship Act of 2000. P.L. 106–395, 114 Stat. 1631, 30 October 2000.

Chi Thon Ngo v. INS. 192 F. 3d 390 (1999).

Chiswick, Barry R. 1988. *Illegal Aliens: Their Employment and Employers.* Kalamazoo, Mich.: W. E. Upjohn Institute for Employment Research.

Churgin, Michael J. 1996. "Mass Exoduses: The Response of the United States." *International Migration Review* 30, no. 1: 310–24.

Clinton, William J. 1997. *Public Papers of the Presidents of the United States: William J. Clinton, 1997, Book 2—July 1 to December 31, 1997.* Washington, D.C.: U.S. Government Printing Office.

Coalition for Humane Immigrant Rights of Los Angeles. 2005. "Press Statement: The Potential for Genuine Comprehensive Immigration Reform." 12 May. Los Angeles: CHIRLA.

Cole, David, and James Dempsey. 2002. *Terrorism and the Constitution: Sacrificing Civil Liberties in the Name of National Security.* New York: New Press.

Cole, Simon. 2001. *Suspect Identities: A History of Fingerprinting and Criminal Identification.* Cambridge: Harvard University Press.

Comaroff, Jean, and John Comaroff. 2004a. "Criminal Obsessions, after Foucault: Postcoloniality, Policing, and the Metaphysics of Disorder." *Critical Inquiry* 30 (Summer): 800–824.

———. 2004b. "Policing Culture, Cultural Policing: Law and Social Order in Postcolonial South Africa." *Law and Social Inquiry* 29: 556–88.

Comisión Económica para América Latina y el Caribe (CEPAL), Naciones Unidas. 2000. "El Salvador: Evolución económica durante 1999." Mexico: CEPAL.

Comisión Nacional de Desarrollo. 1999. *Temas claves para el Plan de Nación: Consulta Especializada.* San Salvador: Comisión Nacional de Desarrollo.

Commission on the Truth for El Salvador. 1993. *From Madness to Hope: The 12–Year War in El Salvador; Report of the Commission on the Truth for El Salvador.* New York: United Nations.

Compton, Daniel. 1987. "Recent Development: Asylum for Persecuted Social Groups; A Closed Door Left Slightly Ajar. *Sanchez-Trujillo v. INS,* 801 F. 2d 1571 (9th Cir. 1986)." *Washington Law Review* 62: 913–39.

Congressional Record. 2000a. "The Commerce-Justice-State Bill." U.S. Senate, 27 October, S11279–S11281. Available at http://www.gpoaccess.gov/crecord/. Accessed 15 February 2006.

———. 2000b. "Fighting for Fundamental Fairness." U.S. Senate, 28 October, S11307. Available at http://www.access.gpo.gov. Accessed 17 May 2003.

———. 2004. "Speech of Hon. Thomas G. Tancredo of Colorado in the House of

Representatives, Wednesday, March 17, 2004." E389. Available at http://thomas .loc.gov/. Accessed 5 October 2004.

Conway, Dennis, and Jeffrey H. Cohen. 1998. "Consequences of Migration and Remittances for Mexican Transnational Communities." *Economic Geography* 74, no. 1: 26–44.

Córdova Macías, Ricardo. 1993. *El Salvador: Las negociaciones de paz y los retos de la postguerra.* San Salvador: Instituto de Estudios LatinoAmericanos.

——. 2001. "Demilitarizing and Democratizing Salvadoran Politics." In *El Salvador: Implementation of the Peace Accords*, edited by Margarita S. Studemeister, 27–32. Washington, D.C.: United States Institute of Peace.

Costa, Gino. 2001. "Demilitarizing Public Security: Lessons from El Salvador." In *El Salvador: Implementation of the Peace Accords*, edited by Margarita S. Studemeister, 20–27. Washington, D.C.: United States Institute of Peace.

Coutin, Susan Bibler. 1993. *The Culture of Protest: Religious Activism and the U.S. Sanctuary Movement.* Boulder: Westview Press.

——. 1995. "Smugglers or Samaritans in Tucson, Arizona: Producing and Contesting Legal Truth." *American Ethnologist* 22, no. 3: 549–71.

——. 2000. *Legalizing Moves: Salvadoran Immigrants' Struggle for U.S. Residency.* Ann Arbor: University of Michigan Press.

——. 2001a. "The Oppressed, the Suspect, and the Citizen: Subjectivity in Competing Accounts of Political Violence." *Law and Social Inquiry* 26, no. 1: 63–94.

——. 2001b. "Questionable Transactions as Grounds for Legalization: Immigration, Illegality, and Law." *Crime, Law and Social Change* 37: 19–36.

——. 2003. "Cultural Logics of Belonging and Movement: Transnationalism, Naturalization, and U.S. Immigration Politics." *American Ethnologist* 30, no. 4: 508–26.

——. 2005a. "Being en Route." *American Anthropologist* 107, no. 2: 195–206.

——. 2005b. "Contesting Criminality: Illegal Immigration and the Spatialization of Legality." *Theoretical Criminology* 9, no. 1: 5–33.

——. 2005c. "The Formation and Transformation of Central American Community Organizations in Los Angeles." In *Latino Los Angeles: Transformations, Communities, and Activism*, edited by Gilda Ochoa and Enrique Ochoa, 155–77. Tucson: University of Arizona Press.

Coutin, Susan Bibler, and Susan Alva. 1999. "Advocating for Immigrants' Rights: An Interview with Susan Alva." *PoLAR: Political and Legal Anthropology Review* 22, no. 2: 110–19.

Coutin, Susan Bibler, and Susan F. Hirsch. 1998. "Naming Resistance: Dissidents, States, and Ethnographers." *Anthropology Quarterly* 71, no. 1: 1–17.

Coutin, Susan Bibler, Bill Maurer, and Barbara Yngvesson. 2002. "In the Mirror: The Legitimation Work of Globalization." *Law and Social Inquiry* 27, no. 4: 801–43.

Coutin, Susan Bibler, and Barbara Yngvesson. N.d. "Schroedinger's Cat and the Ethnography of Law." Unpublished manuscript available from authors, University of California, Irvine, and Hampshire College.

Cruz, José Miguel. 1998. "Los factores posibilitadores de la violencia en El Salvador." In *Violencia en una sociedad en transición*, edited by Renos Papadopoulos et al., 88–95. San Salvador: Programa de las Naciones Unidas para el Desarrollo.

———. 2000. "Violencia, democracia y cultura política en América Latina." *ECA: Estudios Centamericanos* 55, nos. 619–620 (May–June): 511–25.

Cubías, Elizabeth, and Luis Monzón. 2005. "La Conferencia Regional sobre Migración o Proceso Puebla como proceso consultivo regional." Expert Group Meeting on International Migration and Development in Latin America and the Caribbean, Population Division, Department of Economic and Social Affairs, United Nations Secretariat, Mexico City, 30 November—2 December 2005. UN/POP/EGM-MIG/2005/03, 17 November. Available at http://www.un/org/esa/population/publications/IttMigLAC/P0c_LMonzon.pdf. Accessed 8 March 2006.

Curtius, Mary. 2005. "Illegal Immigration Policy Is at Crossroads in Senate." *Los Angeles Times*, 19 April, A1.

Dalton, Juan José. 2000a. "Asesinan en El Salvador a empleados de encomiendas." *La Opinión*, 24 October. Available at http://www.laopinion.com.

———. 2000b. "El Salvador acaba el año con altos índices de violencia." *La Opinión*, 29 December. Available at http://www.laopinion.com. Accessed 5 September 2002.

———. 2000c. "Mueren cinco por robo de envíos de dinero en El Salvador." *La Opinión*, 19 June, 3A.

———. 2000d. "Policía de El Salvador purga más de 1,200 miembros." *La Opinión*, 9 October. Available at http://www.laopinion.com.

———. 2000e. "Policías salvadoreños involucrados en secuestro." *La Opinión*, 25 July. Available at http://www.laopinion.com. Accessed 5 September 2002.

———. 2000f. "Secuestran a empresario en El Salvador." *La Opinión*, 10 July, 3A.

———. 2001a. "Endurecen condenas por delitos graves en El Salvador." *La Opinión*, 20 July. Available at http://www.laopinion.com.

———. 2001b. "Pobreza, violencia y corrupción son una realidad en El Salvador." *La Opinión*, 8 July. Available at http://www.laopinion.com.

———. 2001c. "Secuestradores asesinan a un niño de 9 años en El Salvador." *La Opinión*, 22 June. Available at http://www.laopinion.com.

———. 2002a. "Armas y muerta van de la mano en El Salvador." *La Opinión*, 25 April. Available at http://www.laopinion.com. Accessed 5 August 2002.

———. 2002b. "Reportaje: La violencia no cede en El Salvador." *La Opinión*, 11 March. Available at http://www.laopinion.com. Accessed 9 August 2002.

De Genova, Nicholas P. 2002. "Migrant 'Illegality' and Deportability in Everyday Life." *Annual Review of Anthropology* 31: 419–47.

de Goede, Marieke. 2003. "Hawala Discourses and the War on Terrorist Finance." *Environment and Planning D: Society and Space* 21, no. 5: 513–32.

de Laet, Marianne. 2002. "Patents, Knowledge, and Technology Transfer: On the Politics of Positioning and Place." In *Research in Science and Technology Studies: Knowledge and Technology Transfer*, edited by M. de Laet, 213–37. Amsterdam: JAI.

Demore, District Director, San Francisco District of Immigration and Naturalization Service, et al. v. Kim. 538 U.S. 510 (2003).

Derrida, Jacques. 1992. "Force of Law: The 'Mystical Foundation of Authority.' " In

Deconstruction and the Possibility of Justice, edited by Drucilla Cornell, Michel Rosenfeld, and David Gray Carlson, 3–67. New York: Routledge.

——. 2004. "Saca confirma extensión TPS para centroamericanos." 4 February. Available at http://www.elsalvador.com. Accessed 8 March 2006.

El Diario de Hoy. 2002a. "El 25% tiene al menos un familiar asaltado." 24 June. Available at http://www.elsalvador.com. Accessed 24 June 2002.

——. 2002b. "No al crimen." 18 April. Available at http://www.elsalvador.com. Accessed 7 May 2002.

Díaz-Briquets, Sergio, and Jorge Pérez-López. 1997. "Refugee Remittances: Conceptual Issues and the Cuban and Nicaraguan Experiences." *International Migration Review* 31, no. 2: 411–37.

Dickson-Gómez, Julia. 2002. "The Sound of Barking Dogs: Violence and Terror among Salvadoran Families in the Postwar." *Medical Anthropology Quarterly* 16, no. 4: 415–38.

——. 2004. " 'One Who Doesn't Know War, Doesn't Know Anything': The Problem of Comprehending Suffering in Postwar El Salvador." *Anthropology and Humanism* 29, no. 2: 145–58.

Dougherty, Mary, Denise Wilson, and Amy Wu. 2006. "Immigration Enforcement Actions: 2005." *Annual Report. November 2006*. Washington, D.C.: U.S. Department of Homeland Security, Office of Immigration Statistics, Policy Directorate. Available at http://www.dhs.gov/ximgtn/statistics/. Accessed February 17, 2007.

Doyle, Charles. 2001. "Terrorism: Section by Section Analysis of the USA PATRIOT Act." *CRS Report for Congress*. Order Code RL31200. Washington, D.C.: Congressional Research Service, Library of Congress.

Duany, Jorge. 2000. "Nation on the Move: The Construction of Cultural Identities in Puerto Rico and the Diaspora." *American Ethnologist* 27, no. 1: 5–30.

Durand, Jorge, and Douglas S. Massey. 1992. "Mexican Migration to the United States: A Critical Review." *Latin American Research Review* 27, no. 2: 3–42.

Durand, Jorge, Emilio A. Parrado, and Douglas S. Massey. 1996. "Migradollars and Development: A Reconsideration of the Mexican Case." *International Migration Review* 30, no. 2: 423–44.

Edwards, Beatrice, and Gretta Tovar Siebentritt. 1991. *Places of Origin: The Repopulation of Rural El Salvador*. Boulder: Lynne Reinner.

El-Sakka, M. I. T., and Robert McNabb. 1999. "The Macroeconomic Determinants of Emigrant Remittances." *World Development* 27, no. 8: 1493–1502.

Escobar, Antolín, and Wenceslao Martínez. 2002. "¡Ya no más violencia!" *El Diario de Hoy*, 4 May. Available at http://www.elsalvador.com. Accessed 5 June 2002.

Fagen, Patricial Weiss. 1988. "Central American Refugees and U.S. Policy." In *Crisis in Central America: Regional Dynamics and U.S. Policy in the 1980s*, edited by Nora Hamilton et al., 59–76. Boulder: Westview Press.

Fainaru, Steve. 2003. "Report: 9/11 Detainees Abused." *Washington Post*, 3 June, A1.

Farmer, Paul. 2003. *Pathologies of Power: Health, Human Rights, and the New War on the Poor*. Berkeley: University of California Press.

Federation for American Immigration Reform (FAIR). 2005. "An Immigration Reform Agenda for the 109th Congress." January. Available at http://www.fairus

.org/site/PageServer?pagename=iic_immigrationissuecentersb025. Accessed 20 March 2006.

Feeley, Malcolm M., and Jonathan Simon. 1992. "The New Penology: Notes on the Emerging Strategy of Corrections and Its Implications." *Criminology* 30, no. 4: 449–74.

Feldman, Allen. 1991. *Formations of Violence: The Narrative of the Body and Political Terror in Northern Ireland*. Chicago: University of Chicago Press.

Ferguson, James. 1994. *The Anti-Politics Machine: "Development," Depoliticization, and Bureaucratic Power in Lesotho*. Minnesota: University of Minnesota Press.

Fernandez-Vargas v. Gonzales. 126 S. Ct. 2422 (2006).

Ferrell, Jeff, and Clinton R. Sanders. 1995. *Cultural Criminology*. Boston: Northeastern University Press.

Flores, William V., and Rina Benmayor. 1997. *Latino Cultural Citizenship: Claiming Identity, Space, and Rights*. Boston: Beacon.

Florida v. Nixon. 543 U.S. 175 (2004).

Foucault, Michel. 1977. *Discipline and Punish: The Birth of the Prison*. Translated by Alan Sheridan. New York: Pantheon.

Fox, Jonathan, and Gaspar Rivera-Salgado, eds. 2004. *Indigenous Mexican Migrants in the United States*. La Jolla: University of California at San Diego, Center for U.S.-Mexican Studies.

Frohmann, Lisa. 1997. "Convictability and Discordant Locales: Reproducing Race, Class, and Gender Ideologies in Prosecutorial Decisionmaking." *Law & Society Review* 31, no. 3: 531–56.

Fuchs, Lawrence H. 1985. "The Search for a Sound Immigration Policy: A Personal View." In *Clamor at the Gates: The New American Immigration*, edited by Nathan Glazer, 17–48. San Francisco: Institute for Contemporary Studies.

Fuentes, Rosa. 2002. "Asaltos en vías a oriente señalan." *El Diario de Hoy*, 29 May. Available at http://www.elsalvador.com. Accessed 5 June 2002.

Fundación de Estudios para la Aplicación del Derecho (FESPAD). 2005. *Estado de la Seguridad Pública y la Justicia Penal en El Salvador. Enero-agosto 2005*. San Salvador: FESPAD.

Fundación de Estudios para la Aplicación del Derecho (FESPAD) and Centro de Estudios Penales de El Salvador (CEPES). 2004. *Informe Anual Sobre Justicia Penal Juvenil El Salvador 2004*. San Salvador: FESPAD.

Gammeltoft, Peter. 2002. "Remittances and Other Financial Flows to Developing Countries." *International Migration* 40, no. 5: 181–209.

Gaouette, Nicole. 2006a. "Border Barrier Approved." *Los Angeles Times*, 30 September, A 1.

———. 2006b. "Bush Signs Fence Bill, Pushes Back." *Los Angeles Times*, 27 October, A 26.

Garcia, Dawn. 1987. "Local Sanctuary Groups Oppose Duarte Request." *San Francisco Chronicle*, 7 May, 18.

García, Juan José. 1994. "Hacia una interpretación del impacto económico y sociocultural de las migraciones a Estados Unidos y las remesas familiares." *Política económica* 26: 1–29.

——. 1997. "El futuro de las remesas familiares: Crisis económica y política migratoria." *Propuestas* 1, no. 4: 12–16.

Gelbspan, Ross. 1991. *Break-ins, Death Threats, and the FBI: The Covert War against the Central America Movement.* Boston: South End Press.

Glazer, Nathan, ed. 1985. *Clamor at the Gates: The New American Immigration.* San Francisco: Institute for Contemporary Studies.

Godoy, Angelina Snodgrass. 2002. "Lynchings and the Democratization of Terror in Postwar Guatemala: Implications for Human Rights." *Human Rights Quarterly* 24: 640–61.

——. 2004. "When 'Justice' is Criminal: Lynchings in Contemporary Latin America." *Theory and Society* 33: 621–51.

——. 2005. "Democracy, 'Mano Dura,' and the Criminalization of Politics." In *(Un)Civil Societies: Human Rights and Democratic Transitions in Eastern Europe and Latin America*, edited by Rachel May and Andrew Milton, 109–37. Lanham, Md.: Lexington Books.

Golden, Renny, and Michael McConnell. 1986. *Sanctuary: The New Underground Railroad.* Maryknoll, N.Y.: Orbis Books.

Goldring, Luin. 2003. "Re-thinking Remittances: Social and Political Dimensions of Individual and Collective Remittances." CERLAC Working Paper Series. New York: Centre for Research on Latin America and the Caribbean.

Goldstein, Daniel M. 2003. " 'In our own hands': Lynching, Justice, and the Law in Bolivia." *American Ethnologist* 30, no. 1: 22–43.

——. 2004. *The Spectacular City: Violence and Performance in Urban Bolivia.* Durham: Duke University Press.

——. 2007. "The Violence of Rights: Human Rights as Culprit, Human Rights as Victim." In *The Practice of Human Rights: Tracking Law between the Global and the Local*, edited by Mark Goodale and Sally Engle Merry. Cambridge: Cambridge University Press.

Gordon, Sara. 1989. *Crisis política y guerra en El Salvador.* Federal District, Mexico City: Siglo veintiuno.

Green, Linda. 1999. *Fear as a Way of Life: Mayan Widows in Rural Guatemala.* New York: Columbia University.

Greenhouse, Carol J. 1996. *A Moment's Notice: Time Politics across Cultures.* Ithaca. Cornell University Press.

Grewal, Inderpal. 2005. *Transnational America: Feminisms, Diasporas, Neoliberalisms.* Durham: Duke University Press.

Gubert, Flore. 2002. "Do Migrants Insure Those Who Stay Behind? Evidence from the Kayes Area (Western Mali)." *Oxford Development Studies* 30, no. 3: 267–87.

Gusterson, Hugh. 1996. *Nuclear Rites: A Weapons Laboratory at the End of the Cold War.* Berkeley: University of California Press.

Hafetz, Jonathan L. 1998. "The Untold Story of Noncriminal Habeas Corpus and the 1996 Immigration Acts." *Yale Law Journal* 107, no. 8: 2509–44.

Hagan, Jacqueline Maria. 1994. *Deciding to Be Legal: A Maya Community in Houston.* Philadelphia: Temple University Press.

Hagedorn, John M. 1991. "Gangs, Neighborhoods, and Public Policy." *Social Problems* 38, no. 4: 529–42.

Haitian Refugee Center v. Smith. 676 F. 2d 1023 (1982).

Hale, Edward Everett. 1917. *The Man without a Country.* Vol. 10, pt. 6. Harvard Classics Shelf of Fiction. New York: P. F. Collier and Son.

Hamdi v. Rumsfeld. 124 S. Ct. 2633 (2004).

Hamilton, Nora, and Norma Stoltz Chinchilla. 1991. "Central American Migration: A Framework for Analysis." *Latin American Research Review* 26, no. 1: 75–110.

——. 2001. *Seeking Community in a Global City: Guatemalans and Salvadorans in Los Angeles.* Philadelphia: Temple University Press.

Hamilton, Nora, Jeffrey A. Frieden, Linda Fuller, and Manuel Pastor Jr., eds. 1988. *Crisis in Central America: Regional Dynamics and U.S. Policy in the 1980s.* Boulder: Westview Press.

Hamm, Mark S. 1995. *The Abandoned Ones: The Imprisonment and Uprising of the Mariel Boat People.* Boston: Northeastern University Press.

Hammar, Tomas. 1990. *Democracy and the Nation-State: Aliens, Denizens, and Citizens in a World of International Migration.* Aldershot, Eng.: Avebury.

Haney López, Ian F. 1996. *White by Law: The Legal Construction of Race.* New York: New York University Press.

Hansen, Thomas Blom, and Fin Stepputat, eds. 2005. *Sovereign Bodies: Citizens, Migrants, and States in the Postcolonial World.* Princeton: Princeton University Press.

Harwood, Edwin. 1985. "How Should We Enforce Immigration Law?" In *Clamor at the Gates: The New American Immigration,* edited by Nathan Glazer, 73–91. San Francisco: Institute for Contemporary Studies.

——. 1986. *In Liberty's Shadow: Illegal Aliens and Immigration Law Enforcement.* Stanford: Stanford University Press.

Hayden, Tom. 2004. *Gangs and the Future of Violence.* New York: New Press, W.W. Norton.

Hayner, Priscilla B. 2001. *Unspeakable Truths: Facing the Challenge of Truth Commissions.* New York: Routledge.

Herbert, Steve. 2005. "The Trapdoor of Community." *Annals of the Association of American Geographers* 95, no. 4: 850–65.

Hernandez, Ester, and Susan Bibler Coutin. 2006. "Remitting Subjects: Migrants, Money, and States." *Economy and Society* 35, no. 2: 185–208.

Heyman, Josiah McC. 1995. "Putting Power in the Anthropology of Bureaucracy: The Immigration and Naturalization Service at the Mexico–United States Border." *Current Anthropology* 36, no. 2: 261–87.

——. 1998. *Finding a Moral Heart for U.S. Immigration Policy: An Anthropological Perspective.* Arlington, Va.: American Anthropological Association.

——. 1999. "United States Surveillance over Mexican Lives at the Border: Snapshots of an Emerging Regime." *Human Organization* 58, no. 4: 430–38.

Hobsbawm, Eric. 1990. *Nations and Nationalism since 1780: Programme, Myth, Reality.* New York: Cambridge University Press.

Hobsbawm, Eric, and Terence Ranger. 1992. *The Invention of Tradition*. Cambridge: Cambridge University Press.

Holmes, Douglas R., and George E. Marcus. 2005. "Cultures of Expertise and the Management of Globalization: Toward the Re-functioning of Ethnography." In *Global Assemblages: Technology, Politics, and Ethics as Anthropological Problems*, edited by Aihwa Ong and Stephen J. Collier, 235–52. Oxford: Blackwell.

———. 2006. "Fast Capitalism: Para-Ethnography and the Rise of the Symbolic Analyst." In *Frontiers of Capital: Ethnographic Reflections on the New Economy*, edited by Greg Downey and Melissa Fisher, 33–57. Durham: Duke University Press.

House of Representatives. 1984. "Temporary Suspension of Deportation of Certain Aliens." Hearing before the Subcommittee on Immigration, Refugees, and International Law of the Committee on the Judiciary, House of Representatives, 98th Congress, 2nd sess., on H.R. 4447. 12 April. Washington, D.C.: U.S. Government Printing Office.

Hull, Elizabeth. 1985. *Without Justice for All: The Constitutional Rights of Aliens*. Westport, Conn.: Greenwood.

Human Rights Watch. 2002. *Presumption of Guilt: Human Rights Abuses of Post–September 11th Detainees*. New York: Human Rights Watch.

Immigrant Legal Resource Center (ILRC). N.d. "California Nonresident Tuition Exemption (AB 540)." Available at http://www.ilrc.org/ab540summary.html. Accessed 10 March 2006.

Immigrant Workers Freedom Ride. 2003. "Immigrant Workers Freedom Ride: September 20–October 4, 2003." Available at http://www.immigrantworkers-freedomride.com/about.asp. Consulted 30 September 2003.

Immigration Act of 1990. P.L. 101–649, 104 Stat. 4978, November 29, 1990.

Immigration and Nationality Act. Section 276 (8 U.S.C. 1326). "Reentry of Removed Alien." Available at http://uscis.gov/lpBin/lpext.dll/inserts/slb/slb-1/slb-22/slb-8402?f=templates&fn=document-frame.htm#slb-act276.

Immigration and Naturalization Service. 2000. *1999 Statistical Yearbook of the Immigration and Naturalization Service*. Washington, D.C.: INS.

Immigration and Naturalization Service v. St. Cyr. 533 U.S. 289 (2001).

Illegal Immigration Reform and Immigrant Responsibility Act. P.L. 104–208, 110 Stat. 3009, September 30, 1996.

In re D—J—, Respondent. Interim Decision #3488. 17 April. 23 I & N Dec. 572 (A.G. 2003).

Instituto de los Mexicanos en el Exterior. 2006. "Consejo Nacional para las Comunidades Mexicanas en el Exterior." Available at http://portal.sre.gob.mx/ime/. Accessed 16 August 2006.

International Monetary Fund (IMF). 1977. *Balance of Payments Manual*. 4th ed. Washington, D.C.: IMF.

———. 1999. "El Salvador: Statistical Annex." IMF Staff Country Report No. 99/145. Washington, D.C.: IMF.

Iraheta, Óscar, and Wilfredo Salamanca. 2004. "Plan sufre primer revés." *El Diario de Hoy*, 3 September. Available at http://www.elsalvador.com. Accessed 25 August 2005.

Isgro, Francesco. 1997. "New Immigration Law Raises Many Questions and Uncertain Future for Aliens Residing Illegally in the United States." *Migration World Magazine* 25, no. 3: 35–38.

Ishay, Micheline R., ed. 1997. *The Human Rights Reader: Major Political Writings, Essays, Speeches, and Documents from the Bible to the Present.* New York: Routledge.

Itzigsohn, José. 1995. "Migrant Remittances, Labor Markets, and Household Strategies: A Comparative Analysis of Low-Income Household Strategies in the Caribbean Basin." *Social Forces* 74, no. 2: 633–57.

Janzen, David. 1994. "Christian Community: A Visit with Our Companion Community in El Salvador." *Communities* 84 (Fall): 13.

Jenkins, Janis H. 1998. "The Medical Anthropology of Political Violence: A Cultural and Feminist Agenda." *Medical Anthropology Quarterly* 12, no. 1: 122–31.

Jenkins, Janis H., and Martha Valiente. 1994. "Bodily Transactions of the Passions: *El calor* among Salvadoran Women Refugees." In *Embodiment and Experience: The Existential Ground of Culture and Self,* edited by Thomas J. Csordas, 163–82. Cambridge: Cambridge University Press.

Jenkins, J. Craig. 1978. "The Demand for Immigrant Workers: Labor Scarcity or Social Control?" *International Migration Review* 12, no. 4: 514–35.

Jones, Luce. 2000. "LA's Deportees Send Murder Rate Soaring in El Salvador." *Guardian,* 29 February. Available at http://www.guardian.co.uk. Accessed 17 July 2003.

Kamheangpatiyooth v. Immigration and Naturalization Service. 597 F.2d 1253 (1979).

Kanstroom, Daniel. 1999. "Crying Wolf or a Dying Canary? Citizens, Strangers, and In-Betweens: Essays on Immigration and Citizenship by Peter Schuck." *New York University School of Law Review of Law & Social Change* 25: 435–77.

——. 2000. "Deportation, Social Control, and Punishment: Some Thoughts about Why Hard Laws Make Bad Cases." *Harvard Law Review* 113, no. 8: 1890–1935.

Kapur, Devesh, and John McHale. 2003. "Migration's New Payoff." *Foreign Policy* 139 (November–December): 49–57.

Katz, Jack. 1988. *Seductions of Crime: Moral and Sensual Attractions in Doing Evil.* New York: Basic Books.

Kaye, Mike. 1997. "The Role of Truth Commissions in the Search for Justice, Reconciliation and Democratisation: The Salvadorean and Honduran Cases." *Journal of Latin American Studies* 26, no. 3: 693–716.

Keely, Charles B., and Bao Nga Tran. 1989. "Remittances from Labor Migration: Evaluations, Performance, and Implications." *International Migration Review* 23, no. 3: 500–525.

Kelly, David. 2005. "Border Watchers Capture Their Prey—the Media." *Los Angeles Times,* 5 April, A1.

Kennedy, Edward M. 1981. "Refugee Act of 1980." *International Migration Review* 15, nos. 1–2: 141–56.

Kopytoff, Igor. 1986. "The Cultural Biography of Things: Commoditization as Process." In *The Social Life of Things: Commodities in Cultural Perspective,* edited by A. Appadurai, 64–91. Cambridge: Cambridge University Press.

Krueger, Carl. 2005. "In-State Tuition for Undocumented Immigrants." *ECS State Notes: Education Commission of the States.* April 2005. Available at http://www.ecs.org/clearinghouse/61/00/6100.doc. Accessed 10 March 2006.

Lamphere, Louise, Alex Stepick, and Guillermo Grenier, eds. 1994. *Newcomers in the Workplace: Immigrants and the Restructuring of the U.S. Economy.* Philadelphia: Temple University Press.

Landolt, Patricia. 2003. "Building Communities in Transnational Social Fields: The Case of Salvadoran Refugees, Migrants, and Returnees." *Estudios Migratorios Latinoamericanos* 17, no. 52 (December): 627–50.

Lawyers Committee for Human Rights. 2003. *Imbalance of Powers: How Changes to U.S. Law and Policy since 9/11 Erode Human Rights and Civil Liberties.* New York: Lawyers Committee for Human Rights.

Levine, Susan. 2000. "On the Verge of Exile: For Children Adopted from Abroad, Lawbreaking Brings Deportation." *Washington Post,* 5 March, A1.

Lewis, Libby. 2005. "Genital Mutilation Can Be Grounds for Asylum Status." *All Things Considered,* National Public Radio. 11 March. Available at http://www.npr.org/templates/story/story.php?storyId=4531744. Accessed 17 March 2006.

Lianos, Theodore P. 1997. "Factors Determining Migrant Remittances: The Case of Greece." *International Migration Review* 31, no. 1: 72–87.

Libercier, Marie-Hélene, and Harmut Schneider. 1996. *Migrants: Partners in Development Co-operation.* Paris: Development Centre of the Organisation for Economic Co-operation and Development.

Lichtblau, Eric. 2003. "U.S. Report Faults the Roundup of Illegal Immigrants after 9/11: Many with No Ties to Terror Languished in Jail." *New York Times,* 3 June, A1.

——. 2005. "In Legal Shift, U.S. Charges Detainee in Terrorism Case." *New York Times,* 23 November, A1.

López, Keny. 2006. "DUI se emitirá el 15 de septiembre." *La Prensa Gráfica,* 7 September. Availlable at http://www.laprensagrafica.com. Accessed 11 September 2006.

Los Angeles City Council. 2001. "Salvadoran Nationals Residing in US." File number 01–0002–S56, approved February 23. Available at http://cityclerk.lacity.org/CFI/Record_Preview.cfm?Document=109571&arraypos=69&LastRecord=61. Accessed 13 February 2006.

Los Angeles Times. 2006. "Ban on Renting to Illegal Immigrants is Reversed." 15 December. Available at http://www.latimes.com. Accessed February 21, 2007.

Lungo, Mario, Katharine Eekhoff, and S. Baires. 1996. "Migración internacional y desarrollo local en El Salvador." Occasional Paper No. 8. San Salvador: Fundación Nacional para el Desarrollo.

Lungo, Mario, and S. Kandel, eds. 1999. *Transformando El Salvador: Migración, sociedad y cultura.* San Salvador: Fundación Nacional para el Desarrollo.

Lungo, Mario, and Roxana Martel. 2003. "Ciudadanía social y violencia en las ciudades centroamericanas." *Realidad: Revista de Ciencias Sociales y Humanidades* 94 (July–August): 485–511.

MacEoin, Gary. 1985. *Sanctuary: A Resource Guide for Understanding and Participating in the Central American Refugees' Struggle*. San Francisco: Harper and Row.

Mahler, Sarah J. 1995. *American Dreaming: Immigrant Life on the Margins*. Princeton: Princeton University Press.

———. 2000a. "Constructing International Relations: The Role of Transnational Migrants and Other Non-State Actors." *Identities* 7, no. 2: 197–232.

———. 2000b. *Migration and Transnational Issues: Recent Trends and Prospects for 2020*. CA 2020: Working Paper #4. Hamburg: Institut für Iberoamericka-Kunde.

Malinowski, Bronislaw. 1922. *Argonauts of the Western Pacific*. London: Routledge and Sons.

Malkki, Liisa. 1995. *Purity and Exile: Violence, Memory, and National Cosmology among Hutu Refugees in Tanzania*. Chicago: University of Chicago Press.

Marosi, Richard. 2006. "2 Border Agents Tied to Migrant Movers." *Los Angeles Times*, 10 March. Available at http://www.latimes.com. Accessed 10 March 2006.

Martin, Philip L. 1990. "Harvest of Confusion: Immigration Reform and California Agriculture." *International Migration Review* 24: 69–95.

———. 1995. "Proposition 187 in California." *International Migration Review* 29, no. 1: 255–63.

Marx, Gary T. 1981. "Ironies of Social Control: Authorities as Contributors to Deviance through Escalation, Nonenforcement, and Covert Facilitation." *Social Problems* 28, no. 3: 231–46.

Massey, Douglas S., and Emilio Parrado. 1994. "Migradollars: The Remittances and Savings of Mexican Migrants to the USA." *Population Research and Policy Review* 13: 3–30.

Mathews v. Diaz. 426 U.S. 67 (1976).

Matter of Chen. Int. Dec. 3104 at 3, (BIA 1989), 20 I&N Dec. 16.

Maurer, Bill. 1997. *Recharting the Caribbean: Land, Law, and Citizenship in the British Virgin Islands*. Ann Arbor: University of Michigan Press.

———. 2002. "Anthropological and Accounting Knowledge in Islamic Banking and Finance: Rethinking Critical Accounts." *Journal of the Royal Anthropological Institute* 8: 645–67.

———. 2003. "Uncanny Exchanges: The Possibilities and Failures of 'Making Change' with Alternative Monetary Forms." *Environment and Planning D: Society and Space* 21: 317–40.

McAllister, Carlota. 2003. "The Science of Harm: Forensic Anthropology and the Making of Human Rights Facts in Guatemala." Paper presented at the Science and Technology Studies Program Speaker Series, Massachusetts Institute of Technology, September.

McAuley, John. 2002. "Immigrants Keep U.S. Economy Supple." Associated Press, *Minnesota Star Tribune*. 4 September. Posted at http://www.numbersusa.com/text?ID=1259. Accessed 13 February 2006.

McClintock, Michael. 1985. *The American Connection*. Vol. 1 of *State Terror and Popular Resistance in El Salvador*. London: Zed Books.

McCormick, Barry, and Jackline Wahba. 2000. "Overseas Employment and Remittances to a Dual Economy." *Economic Journal* 110: 509–34.

McKinley, Michelle. 1997. "Life Stories, Disclosure, and the Law." *PoLAR: Political and Legal Anthropology Review* 20, no. 2: 70–82.

Mendez v. Reno. No. CV-88–04995–TJH, C.D. Cal., Aug. 12, 1993.

Menjívar, Cecilia. 2000. *Fragmented Ties: Salvadoran Immigrant Networks in America.* Berkeley: University of California Press.

——. 2006. "Liminal Legality: Salvadoran and Guatemalan Immigrants' Lives in the United States." *American Journal of Sociology* 111, no. 4: 999–1037.

Menjívar, Cecilia, Julie DaVanzo, Lisa Greenwell, and R. Burciaga Valdez. 1998. "Remittance Behavior among Salvadoran and Filipino Immigrants in Los Angeles." *International Migration Review* 32, no. 1: 97–126.

Ministerio de Economía, Gobierno de El Salvador. 2005. "Indicadores Económicos 1999–2002." Available at http://www.minec.gob.sv/default.asp?id=17&mnu= 17.html. Accessed 13 February 2006.

Ministerio de Relaciones Exteriores. República de El Salvador. N.d.(a). "Ley de Inversiones." Decreto No. 732. Available at http://www.minec.gob.sv. Accessed 22 May 2001.

——. N.d.(b). *Política exterior de El Salvador, 1999–2004: Hacía una nueva alianza internacional.* Available at http://www.rree.gob.sv. Accessed 2 January 2001.

——. N.d.(c). "Salvadoreños en el Exterior." Available at http://www.comunidades.gob.sv/sitio/Img.nsf/vista/Documentos/$file/DATOS.doc. Accessed July 10, 2003.

——. 2006. "Segundo Foro Presidencial con Salvadoreños en el Exterior: Proyecto de Agenda." Available at http://www.rree.gob.sv. Accessed 28 September 2006.

Ministerio de Relaciones Exteriores and Fondo de Inversión Social para el Desarrollo Local (FISDL). N.d. "Programa de Apoyo a las Comunídades Salvadoreñas en el Exterior: Intipucá." Available at http://www.rree.gob.sv.sitio/img.nsf/vista/documentos02/$file/intipuca.pdf. Accessed 16 March 2006.

Montes, Segundo. 1990. *El Salvador 1989: Las remesas que envían los salvadoreños de Estados Unidos; consecuencias sociales y económicas.* San Salvador: UCA Editores.

Montes Mozo, Segundo, and Juan José García Vasquez. 1988. *Salvadoran Migration to the United States: An Exploratory Study.* Washington, D.C.: Georgetown University, Center for Immigration Policy and Refugee Assistance, Hemispheric Migration Project.

Montgomery, Tommie Sue. 1995. *Revolution in El Salvador: From Civil Strife to Civil Peace.* 2nd ed. Boulder: Westview Press.

Moodie, Ellen. 2004. " 'El Capitán Cinchazo': Blood and Meaning in Postwar San Salvador." In *Landscapes of Struggle: Politics, Society, and Community in El Salvador,* edited by Aldo Lauria-Santiago and Leigh Binford, 226–44. Pittsburgh: University of Pittsburgh Press.

——. 2006. "Microbus Crashes and Coca-Cola Cash: The Value of Death in 'Free-Market' El Salvador." *American Ethnologist* 33, no. 1: 63–80.

Moore, Kathleen M. 2002. " 'United We Stand': American Attitudes toward (Muslim) Immigration Post-September 11th." *Muslim World* 92, nos. 1–2: 39–58.

Morawetz, Nancy. 2000. "Understanding the Impact of the 1996 Deportation Laws and the Limited Scope of Proposed Reforms." *Harvard Law Review* 113, no. 8: 1936–62.

Moss, Daniel. 1995. "Resettling El Salvador." *Witness* 78, no. 4: 14.

Mountz, Alison, Richard Wright, Ines Miyares, and Adrian J. Bailey. 2002. "Lives in Limbo: Temporary Protected Status and Immigrant Identities." *Global Networks* 2, no. 4: 335–56.

National Commission on Terrorist Attacks upon the United States. 2004. *The 9/11 Commission Report: Final Report of the National Commission on Terrorist Attacks upon the United States*. Washington, D.C.: U.S. Government Printing Office.

National Council of La Raza (NCLR). 2004. "The SOLVE Act of 2004: Safe, Orderly Legal Visas and Enforcement Act of 2004." Available at http://www.nclr.org/files/2614_file_SOLVE_one_papers_English.pdf. Accessed 11 September 2006.

Nazario, Sonia. 2002. "Enrique's Journey: Chapter Three." *Los Angeles Times*, 2 October. Available at http://www.latimes.com/news/specials/enrique/la-fg-thirdsoniaoct02.story. Accessed 17 February 2004.

Nelson, Barbara J. 1984. "Women's Poverty and Women's Citizenship: Some Political Consequences of Economic Marginality." *Signs* 10, no. 2: 209–31.

Nelson, Diane M. 1999. *A Finger in the Wound: Body Politics in Quincentennial Guatemala*. Berkeley: University of California Press.

Nevins, Joseph. 2002. *Operation Gatekeeper: The Rise of the "Illegal Alien" and the Making of the U.S.-Mexico Boundary*. New York: Routledge.

Ngai, Mae M. 2004. *Impossible Subjects: Illegal Aliens and the Making of Modern America*. Princeton: Princeton University Press.

Nicaraguan Adjustment and Central American Relief Act. P.L. 105–100, 111 Stat. 2193, November 19, 1997.

O'Callaghan, Erin M. 2002. "Expedited Removal and Discrimination in the Asylum Process: The Use of Humanitarian Aid as a Political Tool." *William and Mary Law Review* 43, no. 4: 1747–76.

O'Malley. Pat. 2000. "Uncertain Subjects: Risks, Liberalism, and Contract." *Economy and Society* 29, no. 4: 460–84.

La Opinión. 2002. "Proponen rehabilitar a pandilleros salvadoreños." 25 April. Available at http://www.laopinion.com. Accessed 5 August 2002.

Orantes-Hernandez v. Meese. 685 F. Supp. 1488 (C.D. Cal. 1988).

Orellana Merlos, Carlos. 1992. "Migración y remesas: Una evaluación de su impacto en la economía salvadoreña." *Política Económica* 1, no. 11: 2–23.

Orozco, Manuel, Rodolfo de la Garza, and Miguel Baraona. 1997. *Inmigración y remesas familiares*. San José, Costa Rica: FLACSO.

Papadopoulos, Renos, et al. 1998. *Violencia en una sociedad en transición*. San Salvador: Programa de las Naciones Unidas para el Desarrollo.

Paral, Rob. 1995. "Naturalization: New Demands and New Directions at the INS." *Interpreter Releases* 72, no. 27: 937–43.

Passel, J. S. 2005. "Unauthorized Migrants: Numbers and Characteristics." Pew Hispanic Center. Available at http://pewhispanic.org/files/reports/46.pdf. Accessed 26 January 2006.

Paul, Benjamin D., and William J. Demarest. 1988. "The Operation of a Death Squad in San Pedro la Laguna." In *Harvest of Violence: The Maya Indians and the Guatemalan Crisis*, edited by Robert M. Carmack, 119–54. Norman: University of Oklahoma Press.

Pedersen, David. 2004. "In the Stream of Money: Contradictions of Migration, Remittances, and Development in El Salvador." In *Landscapes of Struggle: Politics, Society, and Community in El Salvador*, edited by Aldo Lauria-Santiago and Leigh Binford, 245–62. Pittsburgh: University of Pittsburgh Press.

Perea, Juan F., ed. 1997. *Immigrants Out! The New Nativism and the Anti-Immigrant Impulse in the United States*. New York: New York University Press.

Pérez-López, Jorge, and Sergio Díaz-Briquets. 1998. "The Determinants of Hispanic Remittances: An Exploration Using U.S. Census Data." *Hispanic Journal of Behavioral Sciences* 20, no. 3: 320–49.

Petersilia, Joan. 2003. *When Prisoners Come Home: Parole and Prisoner Reentry*. New York: Oxford University Press.

Popkin, Eric. 1995. "Guatemalan Hometown Associations in Los Angeles." In *Central Americans in California: Transnational Communities, Economies, and Cultures*. Monograph Paper No. 1:35039. Los Angeles: University of Southern California, Center for Multiethnic and Transnational Studies.

——. 1999. "Guatemalan Mayan Migration to Los Angeles: Constructing Transnational Linkages in the Context of the Settlement Process." *Ethnic and Racial Studies* 22, 2: 267–89.

Popkin, Margaret. 2000. *Peace without Justice: Obstacles to Building the Rule of Law in El Salvador*. University Park: Pennsylvania State University Press.

——. 2001. "Building the Rule of Law in Post-War El Salvador." In *El Salvador: Implementation of the Peace Accords*, edited by Margarita S. Studemeister, 10–19. Washington, D.C.: United States Institute of Peace.

Portes, Alejandro. 1978. "Toward a Structural Analysis of Illegal (Undocumented) Immigration." *International Migration Review* 12, no. 4: 469–84.

Povoledo, Elisabetta. 2006. "Italy Vote to Include Expatriates." *International Herald Tribune*, 31 May. Available at http://www.iht.com/articles/2006/03/06/news/vote-5811193.php. Accessed 16 August 2006.

Quan, Adán. 2005. "Through the Looking Glass. U.S. Aid to El Salvador and the Politics of National Identity." *American Ethnologist* 32, no. 2: 276–93.

Ramos, Carlos Guillermo. 2000. "Marginación, Exclusión Social y Violencia." In *Violencia en una sociedad en transición: Ensayos*, edited by Carlos Guillermo Ramos et al., 7–48. San Salvador: Programa de las Naciones Unidas para el Desarrollo.

Ramos, Carlos Guillermo, Jenny Lissette E. Miranda, Edgardo A. Amaya Cóbar, Gustavo Federico Palmieri, Miguel Huezo Mixco, and Lillian Moncada Davidson. 2000. *Violencia en una sociedad en transición: Ensayos*. San Salvador: Programa de las Naciones Unidas para el Desarrollo.

Reagan, Ronald. 1981. *Public Papers of the Presidents of the United States, 1981–1988/89*. Washington, D.C.: U.S. Government Printing Office.

——. 1982. *Public Papers of the Presidents of the United States, 1981–1988/89*. Washington, D.C.: U.S. Government Printing Office.

——. 1983. *Public Papers of the Presidents of the United States, 1981–1988/89.* Washington, D.C.: U.S. Government Printing Office.

Real ID Act of 2005. Public Law 109–13–May 11, 2005. 119 Stat. 302.

Richman, Joe. 1999. "Deported: Weazel's Diary." Produced by Joe Richman, *This American Life*, May 1999. Available at http://www.radiodiaries.org/transcripts/OtherDocs/weasel.html.

Riles, Annelise. 2000. *The Network Inside Out.* Ann Arbor: University of Michigan Press.

Rivera Campos, Roberto. 1996. "La potencial contraccíon de las remesas y el financimiento de la economía salvadoreña." *Cuadernos Socioeconómicos del BCIE*, no. 19. Tegucigalpa, Honduras: Banco Centroamericano de Integración Economica.

Robertson, Shari, and Michael Camerini, producers and directors. 2000. "Well-Founded Fear." Video recording. New York: Epidavros Project.

Rosenblum, Marc R. 2000. *At Home and Abroad: The Foreign and Domestic Sources of U.S. Immigration Policy.* PhD diss., University of California, San Diego.

——. 2005. "Border Brief: The Guest Worker Approach to U.S. Immigration Reform." San Diego: Center for Comparative Immigration Studies, University of California, San Diego; Center for Latin American Studies, San Diego State University; Trans-Border Institute, University of San Diego.

Ruggles, Patricia, Michael Fix, and Kathleen M. Thomas. 1985. *Profile of the Central American Population in the United States.* Washington, D.C.: Urban Institute.

Saca, Tony. 2004. "País Seguro: Plan de Gobierno 2004–2009." Available at http://www.casapres.gov.sv/descargaplan/plangobierno.doc. Accessed 20 March 2006.

Salamanca, Wilfredo. 2004. "Las fallas del primer plan." *El Diario de Hoy*, 31 August. Available at http://www.elsalvador.com/noticias/2004/8/31/nacional/nac17.asp. Accessed 17 March 2006.

Saldomando, Angel. 1998. "Violencia e inseguridad en América Central: De la guerra a la gestión cotidiana de la violencia." In *Violencia en una sociedad en transición*, edited by Renos Papadopoulos et al., 72–87. San Salvador: Programa de las Naciones Unidas para el Desarrollo.

San Francisco Chronicle. 1987a. "Salvadorans in the U.S.: Duarte's Plea on Illegal Aliens." 27 April, 11.

——. 1987b. "U.S. Snubs Duarte on Alien Issue." 13 May, 16.

Sánchez, George J. 1997. "Face the Nation: Race, Immigration, and the Rise of Nativism in Late Twentieth Century America." *International Migration Review* 31, no. 4: 1009–30.

Sanchez-Trujillo v. INS. 801 F. 2d 1571 (9th Cir. 1986).

Sapiro, Virginia. 1984. "Women, Citizenship, and Nationality: Immigration and Naturalization Policies in the United States." *Politics and Society* 13, no. 1: 1–26.

Sassen, Saskia. 1989. "America's Immigration 'Problem': The Real Causes." *World Policy Journal* 6, no. 4: 811–31.

——. 1991. *The Global City: New York, London, Tokyo.* Princeton: Princeton University Press.

Savage, David G. 2006. "Supreme Court Upholds Strict Deportation Law." *Los Angeles Times*, 23 June, A10.

Scalia, John, and Marika F. X. Litras. 2002. *Immigration Offenders in the Federal Criminal Justice System, 2000. Bureau of Justice Statistics Special Report.* Washington, D.C.: Office of Justice Programs, U.S. Department of Justice.

Scarry, Elaine. 1985. *The Body in Pain: The Making and Unmaking of the World.* New York: Oxford University Press.

Scheppele, Kim Lane. 2004a. "Law in a Time of Emergency: States of Exception and the Temptations of 9/11." *University of Pennsylvania Journal of Constitutional Law* 6, no. 5: 1001–83.

——. 2004b. "Other People's PATRIOT Acts: Europe's Response to September 11." *Loyola Law Review* 50: 89–148.

Schiller, Nina Glick, Linda Basch, and Cristina Szanton Blanc. 1995. "From Immigrant to Transmigrant: Theorizing Transnational Migration." *Anthropological Quarterly* 68, no. 1: 48–63.

Schirmer, Jennifer G. 1998. *The Guatemalan Military Project: A Violence Called Democracy.* Philadelphia: University of Pennsylvania Press.

Schwarz, Benjamin C. 1991. *American Counterinsurgency Doctrine and El Salvador: The Frustrations of Reform and the Illusions of Nation Building.* Santa Monica, Calif.: Rand Corporation, National Defense Research Institute.

Select Commission on Intelligence, U.S. Senate. 1989. *The FBI and CISPES.* Washington, D.C.: U.S. Government Printing Office.

Sklar, Helen, Bill Ong Hing, and Mark Silverman, eds. 1985. *Salvadoran and Guatemalan Asylum Cases: A Practitioner's Guide to Representing Clients in Deportation Proceedings.* San Francisco: Immigrant Legal Resource Center.

Smith, Christian. 1996. *Resisting Reagan: The U.S. Central America Peace Movement.* Chicago: University of Chicago Press.

Smith, James F. 2001. "Mexico Seeks Shared Border Security Plan." *Los Angeles Times*, 19 November, A4.

Smith, Marian L. 2006. "Overview of INS History." Available at http://uscis.gov/graphics/aboutus/history/articles/OVIEW.htm. Accessed 10 February 2006. Originally published in *A Historical Guide to the U.S. Government*, edited by George T. Kurian (New York: Oxford University Press, 1998).

Smith, Robert C. 1998. "Transnational Localities: Community, Technology, and the Politics of Membership within the Context of Mexico and U.S. Migration." In *Transnationalism from Below*, edited by Michael Peter Smith and Luis Eduardo Guarnizo, 196–238. New Brunswick, N.J.: Transaction.

Smutt, Marcela. 1998. "El fenómeno de las pandillas en El Salvador." In *Violencia en una sociedad en transición*, edited by Renos Papadopoulos et al., 146–61. San Salvador: Programa de las Naciones Unidas para el Desarrollo.

Sollis, Peter. 1993. *Reluctant Reforms: The Cristiani Government and the International Community in the Process of Salvadoran Post-War Reconstruction.* Washington, D.C.: Washington Office on Latin America.

Soriano, Antonio. 2004. "Demócrata de EEUU, en misión a favor de FMLN." *El*

Diario de Hoy, 9 March. Available at http://www.elsalvador.com. Accessed 9 March 2004.

Soysal, Yasemin Nuhoglu. 1994. *Limits of Citizenship: Migrants and Postnational Membership in Europe*. Chicago: University of Chicago Press.

State of Arizona 2004 Official Canvass. Available at http://www.azsos.gov/election/2004/General/Canvass2004General.pdf. Accessed 30 January 2006.

Stephen, Lynn. 1997. "Women's Rights Are Human Rights: The Merging of Feminine and Feminist Interests among El Salvador's Mothers of the Disappeared (CO-MADRES)." In *Women and Social Movements in Latin America: Power from Below*, 29–55. Austin: University of Texas Press.

Strathern, Marilyn. 1999. *Property, Substance and Effect: Anthropological Essays on Persons and Things*. London: Athlone Press.

——. 2004. *Commons and Borderlands: Working Papers on Interdisciplinarity, Accountability and the Flow of Knowledge*. Oxon, Eng.: Sean Kingston.

Studemeister, Margarita S., ed. 2001. *El Salvador: Implementation of the Peace Accords*. Washington, D.C.: United States Institute of Peace.

Taylor, J. Edward. 1999. "The New Economics of Labour Migration and the Role of Remittances in the Migration Process." *International Migration* 37, no. 1: 63–88.

Taylor, J. Edward, Joaquín Arango, Graeme Hugo, Ali Kouaouci, Douglas S. Massey, and Adela Pellegrino. 1996. "International Migration and National Development." *Population Index* 62, no. 2: 181–212.

Traven, Bruno. 2002. *The Death Ship*. Miami: Synergy International of the Americas.

USAID (U.S. Agency for International Development). 2006. "Central America and Mexico Gang Assessment, Annex 1: El Salvador Profile." Available at http://www.usaid.gov. Accessed February 17, 2007.

U.S. Census Bureau. 2000. "Table FBP-1. Profile of Selected Demographic and Social Characteristics: 2000. Population Universe: People Born in El Salvador." Available at http://www.census.gov/population/cen2000/stp-159/stp159–el_salvador.xls. Accessed 12 January 2006.

U.S. Citizenship and Immigration Services. 2001. "INS 'Global Reach' Initiative Counters Rise of International Migrant Smuggling." 27 June. Available at http://uscis.gov/text/publicaffairs/factsheets/globalreach.htm. Accessed 10 March 2006.

——. 2003. "2003 Yearbook of Immigration Statistics. Table 43: Aliens Removed by Criminal Status and Region and Country of Nationality. Fiscal Years 1993–2003." Available at http://uscis.gov/graphics/shared/aboutus/statistics/ENF03yrbk/ENFExcel/Table43D.xls. Accessed 1 February 2006.

——. N.d. "Estimates of the Unauthorized Immigrant Population Residing in the United States: 1990–2000." Available at http://uscis.gov/graphics/shared/aboutus/statistics/Ill_Report_1211.pdf. Accessed 26 January 2006.

U.S. Committee for Refugees (USCR). 1986. *Despite a Generous Spirit: Denying Asylum in the United States*. Washington, D.C.: American Council for Nationalities Service.

U.S. Customs and Immigration Enforcement. N.d. "Public Information: Special Registration Archives." Available at http://www.ice.gov/pi/specialregistration/archive.htm#special. Accessed February 21, 2007.

U.S. Department of Homeland Security. 2003. "8 CFR Part 264. Suspending the 30–Day and Annual Interview Requirements from the Special Registration Process for Certain Non-Immigrants; Interim Rule." *Federal Register* 68 (231, Dec. 2): 67578–584.

U.S. Department of Homeland Security, Office of Immigration Statistics. 2004. *Yearbook of Immigration Statistics.* Available at http://uscis.gov/graphics/shared/statistics/yearbook/index.htm. Accessed 13 February 2006.

———. 2006. *2005 Yearbook of Immigration Statistics.* Washington, D.C.: U.S. Department of Homeland Security, Office of Immigration Statistics.

U.S. Department of Justice. Immigration and Naturalization Service. 1998. "Suspension of Deportation and Special Rule Cancellation of Removal for Certain Nationals of Guatemala, El Salvador, and Former Soviet Bloc Countries." *Federal Register* 63, no. 226: 64895–913.

———. 1999. "Institutional Removal Program." *Fact Sheet.* Available at http://www.immigration.gov/graphics/pulicaffairs/factsheets/removal.htm. Accessed 15 July 2003.

———. 2000. "Questions and Answers: The 208 Final Rule." 6 December. Available at http://uscis.gov/graphics/publicaffairs/questsans/asylum208.htm. Accessed 17 March 2006.

———. N.d. "Statement: Keeping Our Communities Safe Is INS' Top Priority." Available at http://www.immigration.gov/graphics/publicaffairs/statements/article.htm. Accessed 15 July 2003.

U.S. Department of State. 1999. "1998 Country Report on Economic Policy and Trade Practices: El Salvador." Available at http://www.state.gov. Accessed 22 May 2001.

United States Embassy, San Salvador. 1998. "Emigrants and Remittances: A Vital Factor in El Salvador's Economy." Antiguo Cuscatlán, El Salvador: U.S. Embassy.

U.S. Federal Reserve. "Testimony of Chairman Alan Greenspan. February 17, 2000." *The Federal Reserve's Semiannual Report on the Economy and Monetary Policy.* Before the Committee on Banking and Financial Services, U.S. House of Representatives. Available at http://www.federalreserve.gov/boarddocs/hh/2000/February/Testimony.htm. Accessed 30 January 2006.

U.S. General Accounting Office (GAO). 1988. "Illegal Aliens: Influence of Illegal Workers on Wages and Working Conditions of Legal Workers." Briefing Report to Congressional Requestors. GAO/PEMD-88–13BR. Gaithersburg, Md.: GAO.

———. 2000. *Illegal Aliens: Opportunities Exist to Improve the Expedited Removal Process.* Washington, D.C.: U.S. Government Printing Office.

U.S. Senate, Committee on the Judiciary, Subcommittee on Immigration, Border Security, and Citizenship. 2006. *Strengthening Border Security between the Ports of Entry: The Use of Technology to Protect the Borders: Joint Hearing before the Subcommittee on Immigration, Border Security, and Citizenship and the Subcommittee on Terrorism, Technology, and Homeland Security of the Committee on the Judiciary, United States Senate, One Hundred Ninth Congress, first session, April 29, 2005.* Washington, D.C.: U.S. Government Printing Office.

Vargas Uribe, Guillermo, Pedro Mata Vázquez, and Odón García García. 1998. "Migración internacional y desarrollo regional en México." *Carta Económica Regional* (July–August 1998): 3–9.

Vigil, James Diego. 2002. *A Rainbow of Gangs: Street Cultures in the Mega-City.* Austin: University of Texas Press.

Vo v. Greene. 63 F. Supp. 2d 1278, 1285 (D. Colo. 1999).

Wacquant, Loïc. 1999. *Les prisons de la misère.* Paris: Raisons d'agir.

——. 2001. "The Penalisation of Poverty and the Rise of Neo-liberalism." *European Journal on Criminal Policy and Research* 9: 401–12.

Walker, Robert, Mark Ellis, and Richard Barff. 1992. "Linked Migration Systems: Immigration and Internal Labor Flows in the United States." *Economic Geography* 68, no. 3: 234–48.

Wasem, Ruth Ellen. 1997. "Central American Asylum Seekers: Impact of 1996 Immigration Law." No. 97–810 EPW. Washington, D.C.: Congressional Research Service, Library of Congress.

——. 2002. "Immigration Legalization and Status Adjustment Legislation." Order Code RL30780. Washington, D.C.: Congressional Research Service, Library of Congress.

Washington Office on Latin America. 2007. "Executive Summary: Transnational Youth Gangs in Central America, Mexico and the United States." Available at http://www.wola.org. Accessed February 17, 2007.

Watts, Julie R. 2002. *Immigration Policy and the Challenge of Globalization: Unions and Employers in Unlikely Alliance.* Ithaca: Cornell University Press.

Weiner, Tim. 2004. "U.S.-Backed Rightist Claims Victory in Salvador Election." *New York Times,* 22 March. Available at http://www.nytimes.com. Accessed 22 March 2004.

White House. Office of the Press Secretary. 1999. "Remarks by the President to Legislative Assembly, San Salvador, El Salvador." 10 March. Available at http://clinton2.nara.gov/WH/New/html/19990311–2348.html. Accessed 5 March 2006.

White House. 2004a. "Fact Sheet: Fair and Secure Immigration Reform." Available at http://www.whitehouse.gov/news/releases/2004/01/20040107–1.htm. Accessed 6 July 2004.

——. 2004b. "Immigration: Fair and Secure Immigration Reform." Available at http://www.whitehouse.gov/infocus/immigration. Accessed 1 June 2005.

——. 2004c. "President Bush Proposes New Temporary Worker Program. Remarks by the President on Immigration Policy. The East Room." Available at http://www.whitehouse.gov/news/releases/2004/01/20040107–3.html. Accessed 5 October 2006.

Williams, Brackette, ed. 1996. *Women out of Place: The Gender of Agency and the Race of Nationality.* New York: Routledge.

Wilkinson, Daniel. 2004. *Silence on the Mountain: Stories of Terror, Betrayal, and Forgetting in Guatemala.* Durham: Duke University Press.

Wilson, Richard. 2001. *The Politics of Truth and Reconciliation in South Africa: Legitimizing the Post-Apartheid State.* Cambridge: Cambridge University Press.

Yerushalmi, Hanoch. 1998. "La inseguridad y el temor en la vida cotidiana de los individuos en una sociedad en transición." In *Violencia en una sociedad en transición*, edited by Renos Papadopoulos et al., 34–45. San Salvador: Programa de las Naciones Unidas para el Desarrollo.

Yngvesson, Barbara, and Susan Bibler Coutin. 2006. "Backed by Papers: Undoing Persons, Histories, and Return." *American Ethnologist* 33, no. 2: 177–90.

Zadvydas, Kestutis v. Christine G. Davis and Immigration and Naturalization Service et al. 533 U.S. 678 (2001).

Zilberg, Elana. 2004. "Fools Banished from the Kingdom: Remapping Geographies of Gang Violence between the Americas (Los Angeles and San Salvador)." *American Quarterly* 56, no. 3: 759–79.

———. 2007a. "Gangster in Guerilla Face: A Transnational Mirror of Production between the U.S. and El Salvador." *Anthropological Theory* 7, no. 1: 37–57.

———. 2007b. "Refugee Gang Youth: Zero Tolerance and the Security State in Contemporary U.S.-Salvadoran Relations." In *Youth, Globalization and the Law*, edited by Sudhir Venkatesh and Ron Kassimir, 61–89. Palo Alto: Stanford University Press.

———. Forthcoming. "Inter-American Ethnography: Tracking Salvadoran Transationality at the Borders of Latino and Latin American Studies." In *Companion to Latino Studies*, edited by Juan Flores and Renato Rosaldo. Oxford: Blackwell.

Zilberg, Elana, and Mario Lungo. 1999. "¿Se han vuelto haraganes? Jóvenes salvadoreños, migración e identidades laborales." In *Transformando El Salvador: Migración, sociedad y cultura*, edited by M. Lungo and S. Kandel, 39–94. San Salvador: Fundación Nacional para el Desarrollo.

Žižek, Slavoj. 1989. *The Sublime Object of Ideology*. London: Verso.

Zolberg, Aristide R. 1990. "The Roots of U.S. Refugee Policy." In *Immigration and U.S. Foreign Policy*, edited by Robert W. Tucker, Charles B. Keely, and Linda Wrigley, 99–120. Boulder: Westview Press.

Notes

Introduction

1. It is perhaps appropriate that such notions of rebirth draw on religious imagery, given claims that Americans are a covenant people. See Bellah 1975, Bellah et al. 1985, and Bercovitch 1978.

2. Unless otherwise noted, all translations of Spanish sources are by the author.

3. According to the 2000 U.S. Census, which is notorious for undercounting undocumented immigrants, the number of Salvadorans who entered the United States between 1980 and 1989 was 369,615, compared to 119,145 before 1980 (U.S. Census Bureau 2000).

4. Sanctuary activities included religious services, marches, a caravan, public testimonials by refugees, asylum hearings, committee meetings, potluck dinners, and regional and national gatherings. As a volunteer, I performed a variety of tasks, such as answering phones, translating, accompanying Central Americans to doctors' appointments, and locating supporting documentation (e.g., human rights reports, news clippings) for asylum applications.

1. Los Retornados (Returnees)

1. Pseudonyms have been used for all interviewees quoted in this manuscript.

2. See the Child Citizenship Act of 2000, which grants U.S. citizenship to foreign-born adopted children on admission to the United States.

3. For relevant U.S. Supreme Court cases on the issue of indefinite detentions, see *Demore v. Kim*, 2003, 538 U.S. 510; *Zadvydas v. Davis*, 2001, 533 U.S. 678; *Chi Thon*

Ngo v. INS, 192 F. 3d 390, 392 (3d Cir. 1999), and *Vo v. Greene*, 63 F. Supp. 2d 1278, 1285 (D. Colo. 1999).

4. In order to promote efficiency and public safety, the INS created the Institutional Removal Program, designed to identify and deport criminal aliens at the conclusion of their criminal sentences (U.S. Department of Justice 1999). The U.S. General Accounting Office (GAO) regularly audits the IRP program and chides immigration officials for inefficiency in removing criminal aliens (see U.S. GAO 2000).

5. See, for example, *Immigration and Naturalization Service v. St. Cyr*, 2001, 533 U.S. 289. In *St. Cyr*, the court provided limited relief to aliens who pled guilty prior to 1996 on the grounds that the immigration consequences of a guilty plea were altered retroactively. In this case, the court reasoned, "Now that prosecutors have received the benefit of plea agreements, agreements that were likely facilitated by the aliens' belief in their continued eligibility for 212(c) relief, it would be contrary to 'familiar considerations of fair notice, reasonable reliance, and settled expectations' to hold that IIRIRA's subsequent restrictions deprives them of any possibility of such relief" (p. 2292).

6. U.S. immigration authorities estimate that the total undocumented population residing in the United States was 7.0 million as of January 2000 (USCIS n.d.). However, a report by the Pew Hispanic Center estimates the number of undocumented migrants to be 10.3 million (Passel 2005).

7. Antinuclear activists have also used shadows to represent individuals killed in a nuclear attack. According to Gusterson (1996, 198), "In 1985, on the fortieth anniversary of Hiroshima, protestors painted shadows on the sidewalks of Livermore [location of a nuclear weapons laboratory] and all over the San Francisco Bay Area: after the bombing of Hiroshima all that remained of some people were their shadows, burned into buildings and sidewalks by the extraordinary heat of the bomb. The shadows were symbols, arrested somewhere between a presence and an absence."

8. Some interviewees were known by gang monikers. In such instances, I have used invented monikers as pseudonyms. I am grateful to Cheryl Maxson and Diego Vigil for assistance in inventing monikers.

9. King says that the former INS regarded him as a terrorist threat because his case, like that of many other noncitizens with criminal convictions, was affected by the Anti-Terrorism and Effective Death Penalty Act. To my knowledge, he was never, in fact, accused of a terrorist offense. He says that he was regarded as a flight risk because he was detained without possibility of bail. In fact, detention in many removal cases was mandatory, making it unnecessary for immigration officials to determine that detainees were a flight risk.

10. Strikingly, deportees' experiences are not unlike novelist B. Traven's account of a sailor who lost his papers and thus his country. Early in the novel, the sailor is told, "You have no passport. In any civilized country he who has no passport is nobody. He does not exist for us or for anybody else" (Traven 2002, 23).

11. There is some variation in how individuals are deported. Some individuals are returned to the United States without shackles, on commercial flights, alongside other passengers.

12. According to a member of a Salvadoran NGO, when deportees reenter the United States illegally, they rub their thumbs in an attempt to alter their thumbprints and prevent identification. It is interesting that they must be physically altered (through the erased thumbprint) in order to reenter U.S. territory.

13. According to the Ministerio de Economía of El Salvador (2005), the minimum wage between 1999 and 2002 was 1,260 colones or 144 dollars per month, at an exchange rate of 8.75 colones per dollar.

14. The MS-13 or Mara Salvatrucha gang originated in Los Angeles during the 1980s, as between 2–10% of Salvadoran immigrant youth, who had experienced violence in El Salvador and poverty and school overcrowding in Los Angeles, took to the streets to form gangs. The MS-13 and the 18th Street gang, which was originally Chicano, are the two largest gangs made up of Salvadorans. The 18th Street gang has 20,000 members in Los Angeles county, approximately half of whom are Salvadoran (Vigil 2002). See Vigil 2002 and Hayden 2004 for a history of Salvadoran gangs. Although estimates of gang membership are unreliable, the Salvadoran National Police estimated that in 2002 there were 10,500 gang members and 309 gang cliques in El Salvador, and that 55% of these were affiliated with Mara Salvatrucha and 33% with 18th Street (Washington Office on Latin America 2007).

15. Zilberg points out that "unauthorized return to the United States is in some ways a self-instigated deportation from El Salvador"(2007a).

16. Small percentages—5–8%—of returnees were women. Interviewees attributed this fact to the greater likelihood that men would be charged with crimes and become deportable and to the fact that many immigrant women perform domestic labor in individuals' homes, making it less likely that they would be caught in a raid on a workplace. The relationship between gender and deportation requires further study.

17. In contrast, according to USCIS (2003) statistics, 48% of the individuals deported to El Salvador in 1999 and 2000 (a period that overlaps with that covered by the Bienvenidos a Casa report) were criminals. According to the U.S. Department of Homeland Security (2004), 8,580 people were removed to El Salvador in 1999 and 2000 (and statistics that were updated in 2006 indicate that 8,666 were removed —see table 1.2), and the Bienvenidos a Casa program claims to have assisted 8,864 people between April 1999 and July 31, 2001. Given that deportations were temporarily suspended at the beginning of 2001, due to the Salvadoran earthquakes, these figures indicate that the Bienvenidos a Casa program met with almost all the individuals who were deported from the United States to El Salvador.

2. La Ley NACARA (Nicaraguan Adjustment and Central American Relief Act)

1. This differentiation is made possible by the fiction of legal equality, the idea, for instance, that having a licensed and minimally competent attorney adequately fulfills the constitutional right to legal representation, though in fact the skill of particular attorneys varies. See, for example, *Florida v. Nixon*, 543 U.S. 175 (2004).

2. Asylum approval rates for Nicaraguans are not much higher than for Salvadorans and Guatemalans. But such figures are misleading, because the 1987 Nicaraguan Review Program permitted Nicaraguans to remain in the United States even if they were not granted asylum. As Wasem explains:

Although most aliens denied asylum by INS were then bound over to the Executive Office for Immigration Review (EOIR) for deportation proceedings, the Nicaraguans denied asylum received unique treatment. Former Attorney General

Edwin Meese established the Nicaraguan Review Program (NRP) in July 1987 to consider the cases of Nicaraguans denied asylum by INS. . . . The Reagan and Bush Administrations were reluctant to deport anyone to Nicaragua as long as the Sandinistas were in power, and reportedly only Nicaraguans known to be criminal aliens were likely to be returned. (1997, 7–8)

See Wasem (1997) for further details regarding administrative responses to immigration from El Salvador, Guatemala, and Nicaragua during the 1980s and 1990s.

3. In fact, during the 1980s, refugee rights groups in the United States devoted considerable effort to *moving* this line so that more theories of political persecution could be legally viable (Sklar, Hing, and Silverman 1985).

4. The claim that U.S. immigration law prohibits illegal immigration has also been challenged. Some scholars have concluded that, far from forbidding unauthorized presence, U.S. immigration authorities tacitly tolerate undocumented immigration (Bach 1978; Jenkins 1978; Portes 1978). According to this argument, laws that bar entry without inspection are primarily symbolic, designed to satisfy public concerns about illegal immigration without preventing employers from utilizing a desired (and more exploitable) labor force (Calavita 1990, 2005). The notion that U.S. immigration law fails to bar illegal presence is explicit in Congressman Hamilton Fish's (R-NY) rebuttal of the claim that granting Salvadorans temporary legal status would encourage more migration:

Isn't our current [1984] inability to identify and initiate action against the vast majority of Salvadorans illegally in the United States already a powerful magnet to those still in that country? And in view of the reality of the present situation, which presumably is well-known in El Salvador, isn't a formal policy of extended voluntary departure really likely to make very, very little difference? (House of Representatives 1984, 99)

Taking "tacit tolerance" arguments seriously suggests that, even as their presence was officially prohibited and even as thousands were deported, Salvadorans and Guatemalans were unofficially accepted as desired workers.

5. According to Gregg Beyer (1994), a "control" orientation characterized initial implementation of the 1980 Refugee Act. Examiners, who had no particular training in asylum or refugee law, were given responsibility for adjudicating affirmative asylum applications at district offices.

6. An attorney who was involved in that litigation described the theory of the case and the resources that were mobilized:

In 1980 when the Refugee Act was passed, they added a category to the act—membership in a particular social group. And there had never been any definition of what that was and we decided that basically this was what it was meant for, people who didn't necessarily have their own political opinions but the government suspected them of having a political opinion. And so we developed what was really an imputed political opinion theory but couched it in terms of young men of military age from El Salvador as a social group and who the government suspected of being guerrillas or guerrilla supporters. We decided to nationally put significant resources into this case. We raised money throughout the country. We did a mailing throughout the country for the case with the assistance of the sanctuary movement and with the national office of the National Lawyers Guild and to put on a test case that people would then be able to use throughout the country.

7. For a fuller account of these debates, see House of Representatives 1984.

8. Regarding the wisdom of this strategy, one interviewee commented:

If I was for combating building popular support to oppose U.S. intervention in El Salvador and I worked in the Department of Justice and I could choose what group I would arrest, I think I'd choose a middle-class church group full of nuns. And that's what they did. I don't think there were anti-interventionist moles in the Department of Justice. But you couldn't do anything more counterproductive to your political aims.

9. During the November 1989 final offensive, the Salvadoran guerilla forces demonstrated their continued military capability by occupying large sections of San Salvador. During the offensive, members of the Atlacatl Brigade of the Salvadoran Armed Forces assassinated six Jesuit priests, their housekeeper, and her daughter, provoking widespread international condemnation. See Byrne 1996, 152–53, and Montgomery 1995, 217–20, for accounts of the final offensive.

10. Bush's signing statement voices his reservations about the TPS portion of the legislation:

In signing this legislation, I am concerned with the provision of S. 358 that creates a new form of relief known as "temporary protected status." The power to grant temporary protected status would be, except as specifically provided, the "exclusive authority" by which the Attorney General could allow otherwise deportable aliens to remain here temporarily because of their nationality or their region of origin. I do not interpret this provision as detracting from any authority of the executive branch to exercise prosecutorial discretion in suitable immigration cases. Any attempt to do so would raise serious constitutional questions (Bush 1990, 1718).

11. In 1995, immigration officials adopted a "last-in, first-out" policy, and delayed issuing work permits to asylum applicants for 180 days after they applied. As a result, individuals who applied for asylum were scheduled for interviews during the 180-day period, did not obtain work permits, and were placed in deportation proceedings if their asylum cases were referred to court.

12. This ambiguity was captured by President Clinton's remarks to the Central American presidents:

Some of those immigrants [from Central America] are there [in the United States] legally, but not as legal immigrants. That is, there is a separate category of our immigration law which says if you're, in effect, fleeing political disruption in your own country, you can stay in our country but you don't become a legal immigrant with the right to apply for citizenship after 5 years. But many of them have been there quite a long while. Some of them are not legal under that status but they've been there quite a long while, and they did come because of the political upheaval. (Clinton 1997, 570–71).

13. In a March 10, 1999, speech to the Salvadoran Legislative Assembly, Clinton stated:

I believe fairness means treating people equitably, whatever their country of origin. Now, during the 1980s, many Central Americans fled oppression by both the right and the left. Some were hurt by soldiers, some harmed by rebels. All whose lives were shattered have a right to sympathy, safety and justice. Many who have been in the United States for a long time have established deep roots in our communities. At my request, following the Central American Summit in Costa Rica two years ago, our Congress passed legislation to help them. But it did so by establishing different treatment among groups of Central Americans, depending upon where they were from. I will do everything I possibly can to overcome that different treatment. And I will work with our Congress to write laws that are more even-handed. Our treatment of people from Central America should reflect what they suffered, rather than who caused the suffering. This is wrong and we should change it. (White House, Office of the Press Secretary, 1999)

3. Atención a la Comunidad en el Exterior (Attention to Salvadorans Living Abroad)

1. Vis-à-vis El Salvador, they thus occupy a position as insiders, yet outsiders, a position that has certain similarities to that of naturalized U.S. citizens. See Coutin 2003.

2. I do not mean to suggest that this was *merely* an argument. There is evidence that the FMLN did receive training, weapons, and other support from the Sandinistas. Byrne (1996, 77) states that "the FMLN possessed a base for command and control, logistics, and the transport of military and other supplies in Nicaragua; access to training and arms from Cuba, Vietnam, and other Soviet bloc countries; [and] financial support from these nations and some nonaligned states" (see also Arnson 1989). Receipt of such assistance does not mean that the FMLN was controlled by outside forces, however, or that there were not indigenous causes for the revolution.

3. This argument came to be known as the domino theory. The idea was that, like dominos standing in a line, if one country fell to Communism, its neighbors would fall.

4. According to a report published by the National Defense Research Institute at RAND, however, these national security concerns *limited* U.S. influence:

Salvadorans recognized . . . that the position of Republican presidents and their Democratic opponents in Congress was identical on the important issue concerning El Salvador: both were adamant, for domestic political and apparent geostrategic reasons, that El Salvador not fall to the FMLN. How, then, could the Salvadoran armed forces and far right be pressured to reform by threats to cease aid? (Schwarz 1991, 82).

5. In 1981 and 1989, FMLN forces launched major offensives designed to provoke a popular uprising. As Montgomery (1995) notes, the fact that this did not occur was cited by U.S. and Salvadoran officials as evidence that the population did not support the guerrillas. Byrne argues that "much of the population [was] not actively committed to either side" (1996, 105), whereas Montgomery contends that the guerrillas could not have survived without civilian support.

6. Montgomery (1995, 152) writes:

Colonel Jorge Adalberto Cruz Reyes, commander of the garrison in San Francisco Gotera, Morazán, justified attacks on civilians by citing the FMLN's presence in an area: "Civilians who don't want to cooperate leave the area and those who remain are collaborating." A few months later, Colonel Sigfrido Ochoa, who at the time was commander of the base at El Pariso, Chalatenango, told a Mexican reporter, "I can massively bomb the red zones because only subversives live in them."

7. FMLN forces also committed human rights violations, though these were fewer in number. The Commission on the Truth for El Salvador (1993) documented cases of summary executions of mayors, extrajudicial executions, and abductions by FMLN members. The FMLN also reportedly engaged in forced recruitment and forced requisition of food and other material goods. The Commission on the Truth for El Salvador nonetheless attributed 85 percent of human rights abuses committed during the civil war to the armed forces or to paramilitary death squads (Kaye 1997).

8. Likewise, guerrilla forces engaged in consciousness-raising activities designed to enlist popular support (Binford 1999).

9. A report by U.S. colonels on the civil defense patrols states, "In committing himself to protect his village through civil defense, the individual casts his lot in favor of the existing order and rejects revolution" (Schwarz 1991, 54).

10. Personal communication, Central American Resource Center (CARECEN) Los Angeles staff, 1993. For additional population estimates, see Aguayo and Fagen 1988, Montes Mozo and García Vasquez 1988, and Ruggles, Fix, and Thomas 1985.

11. Although the goals of individual groups differed, generally speaking the solidarity movement denounced human rights abuses committed by Salvadoran authorities, raised funds to support their organizational counterparts in El Salvador, argued that Salvadorans in the United States deserved refugee status, opposed U.S. military intervention in Central America, and sought to increase the legitimacy of the FMLN and related groups (C. Smith 1996). The U.S. government denounced solidarity work as "a determined propaganda campaign [that] has sought to mislead many in Europe and certainly many in the United States as to the true nature of the conflict in El Salvador" (Reagan 1982, 214) and subjected some groups, such as the Committee in Solidarity with the People of El Salvador (CISPES) to covert surveillance (Gelbspan 1991; Select Commission on Intelligence 1989).

12. In fact, the employer sanctions provisions of IRCA were seemingly designed to allow employers to continue to hire undocumented workers, as long as these workers presented work authorization documents that were not blatantly fraudulent. See Calavita 1990.

13. Note that the language used in other segments of these memoirs does *not* resemble that of the solidarity movement, e.g., "We insist on the tragedy that Central America

has lived, as the last scene of the cold war on the continent, war between great powers, in which the Central American countries became involved" (Calderón Sol 2002, 110).

14. Hurricane Mitch was not, directly, the reason for granting the presumption of hardship. An official involved in drafting the NACARA regulations explained, "Hurricane Mitch had an effect on the discussion of whether or not to grant a blanket finding of hardship. The feeling was that if that had been warranted, then temporary protected status would have been granted to Salvadorans because of Hurricane Mitch, but it wasn't. If TPS couldn't be granted due to Hurricane Mitch, then they couldn't justify a blanket finding of hardship because of Hurricane Mitch in the case of the NACARA eligible Salvadorans." A State Department official related that U.S. officials nonetheless cited the NACARA regulations as a means of providing relief to El Salvador in the wake of Hurricane Mitch (see also Rosenblum 2000): "They [U.S. officials] gave TPS to the Nicaraguans and to the Hondurans, but not to the Salvadorans, because there was less damage in El Salvador. But when it came to doing the regulations, they hoped to in part address the problem of Hurricane Mitch that way."

15. In fact, in 2002, various groups, including the City of San Salvador, ASOSAL, CARECEN (Central American Resource Center), Western Union, El Salvador País Joven, and *Prensa Gráfica*, sponsored a contest to rename this monument. The winning name was "Hermano, Bienvenido a Casa" (Ábrego 2004).

16. According to a Salvadoran economic official:

The law of investments says in certain parts that it considers and grants the status of foreign investor to the Salvadoran who has resided outside the country for more than a year. He can receive and enjoy all the privileges that the law awards to a foreign investor. What it does is establish international investment standards, as are used in any country, such as the free conversion of currency, the free transfer of profits, guarantees against expropriation.

17. See "Datos sobre la Distribución de Salvadoreños alrededor del Mundo" at http://www.comunidades.gob.sv/website/comunidades.html, accessed 29 August 2006.

18. See "Immigration by Region and Selected Country of Last Residence: Fiscal Years 1820 to 2005," available at www.uscis.gov/graphics/shared/statistics/yearbook/LPR05.htm, accessed 29 August 2006.

19. Speech, Wilshire Grand Hotel, Los Angeles, 16 August 2004.

20. In fact, TPS has now been extended until September of 2007. See *El Diario de Hoy* 2004.

21. According to the foreign policy plan developed during the 1999–2004 Flores administration, "The Salvadoran conflict located our country at the focal point of negative attention on the part of international public opinion. Nevertheless, the end of the armed conflict and the signing and successful execution of the Peace Accords and of the process of democratization . . . has made the Salvadoran experience an authentic international example" (Ministerio de Relaciones Exteriores n.d.[b]). Truth commission reports may help governments draw a line in the sand. By detailing past abuses, the reports can enable governments to argue that human rights abuses no longer occur (Hayner 2001; Kaye 1997).

22. See Casa Presidencial, "Transmisión de mando presidencial 2004: Gabinete de Gobierno 2004–2009," available at http://www.transmisonpresidencialelsalvador.com/gabinete.htm, accessed 18 August 2004.

4. En el Camino (En Route)

1. See Chavez (2001; 2007) for discussions of images of undocumented immigrants as invaders.

2. For instance, imagine how maps might be redrawn if the realities of unauthorized migration were taken into account. The U.S.-Mexico border, for instance, might be blurry or more of a zigzag, unauthorized routes might predominate over marked highways and ports of entry, and border sites—Tapachula, Tijuana, El Paso—would be more significant than sites in countries' interior.

3. The classified sections of Salvadoran newspapers advertised trips to the United States "with arrival guaranteed" within a specified period of time. Although I cannot verify that smugglers placed these ads, it does not seem likely that travel agencies catering to tourists would find it necessary to "guarantee" arrival. Moreover, Salvadorans told me that smugglers publicized their services in local papers.

4. Mexican anthropologist and human-rights advocate Victor Clark Alfaro reports that there are distinctions between local "polleros" (literally "chicken handlers" and a slang term for alien-smugglers) who are more reliable, and smugglers who belong to cartels (personal communication).

5. See www.elsalvador.org/home.nsf/infoconsular and www.embassyofmexico.org regarding visa requirements to travel within Central America and Mexico.

6. Legislation authorizing the construction of seven hundred miles of border fencing was signed into law in October 2006 (see Gaouette 2006b).

7. The California Rural Legal Assistance Foundation's Border Project tracks deaths along the U.S.-Mexico border. See www.stopgatekeeper.org. Accessed 10 March 2006.

8. This official commented that his office had passed out many "Stop Illegal Trafficking in Humans" bumper stickers, "but somehow we never see them on the cars!"

9. Moodie (2006) points out that bodies can become signs in national and international calibrations of suffering.

10. This interviewee may have been confusing two situations. There is a large Salvadoran community in Hempstead, New York, but the Arlandria section of Arlington, Virginia, has become known as "Chirilagua" due to the large number of residents from Chirilagua, El Salvador.

11. Personal communication and interview with official in Department of Homeland Security, 14 July 2004.

5. Las Remesas (Remittances)

1. I do not mean to suggest that, during the 1980s, Salvadorans immigrated to the United States primarily for economic reasons.

2. Montes, a Jesuit scholar who was assassinated in November 1989 during the "final offensive" of the Salvadoran civil war, surveyed Salvadorans in the United States and in El Salvador between 1987 and 1989, in order to describe the Salvadoran population in the United States, analyze the economic conditions of migrants and their families, identify ways that emigration was changing Salvadoran family structures, estimate the amount and uses of remittances, and consider the effects of remittances on El Salvador as a nation.

3. Athukorala disputes this claim, suggesting that there are two "informal" modes of remitting that do not show up as "official remittances" but which do appear in other

columns. One is the transfer of goods brought into the country, and the other is currency brought home and then given to someone—these are called "pocket transfers." Athukorala explains, "Personal imports become a debit entry (as part of total merchandise imports) in the balance of payments account, but the related credit entry comes under 'errors and omissions,' rather than under migrant remittances. Foreign money, when converted into local currency, would show up in the balance of payments account under tourist expenditure, thus leading to an under-recording of migrant remittances" (515). Athukorala identifies leakages as follows: (1) depositing savings in foreign banks outside of the home country; (2) bringing currency into the country and then exchanging it on the black market ("the problem is that the government has no control over these funds and hence their utilization may not bring maximum benefit to the nation") (515); (3) use of a courier—a migrant gives the courier money in the host currency, then the courier delivers it to a relative in the migrant's home country but in the currency of that country.

4. In the wake of the attacks of September 11, 2001, there have been increased concerns that the informal mechanisms used to transfer remittances may also be used by terrorists. See de Goede 2003.

5. See also Montes Mozo and García Vasquez (1988) for an account of the effects of remittances on Intipucá.

6. I'm grateful to Beth Baker-Cristales for emphasizing this point to me.

7. Chami et al. (2005) characterize the possibility that states would rely on immigration and remittances for financial stability as a moral hazard problem.

8. For more detailed descriptions of hometown associations, see Baker-Cristales 2004; Fox and Rivera-Salgado 2004; Hamilton and Chinchilla 2001; Lungo et al. 1996; E. Popkin 1995, 1999; R. Smith 1998.

9. In contrast, hometown association members complained that their ambulances were detained in Customs at the border of El Salvador. Members felt that they should not have to pay taxes on what was, after all, a donation.

10. Officials also praised local expertise, however. For instance, in a video presented during the signing of an agreement between the Salvadoran government and several hometown associations, the director of the FISDL stated, "Unidos por la Solidaridad (United in Solidarity) is not to come to ask [you] for money. On the contrary, it is to offer you money, to offer you money to be invested in the projects that you want to realize . . . because we know that you also know what it is that your communities need."

11. Note that hometown associations requested such government assistance, particularly, matching funds and tax-exempt status for their donations.

6. Productos de la Guerra (Products of War)

Epigraph translation: We are the result of a dark past in El Salvador.

1. On ways that political or legal statuses and processes come to be inscribed in bodies, see Aretxaga 1995, Coutin 2005a, Foucault 1977, Goldstein 2003, Jenkins and Valiente 1994, Scarry 1985, and Yngvesson and Coutin 2006.

2. Querying the distinction between direct and indirect forms of violence, Jenkins (1998, 124; see also Dickson-Gómez 2004) writes, "The systematic deployment of terror as a means of coercion defies distinction between actual violence and the threat of im-

manent violence. Is not the display of mutilated bodies more than the result of violence or the threat of violence, but a form of violence itself?"

3. Amid rising fears that terrorists are abusing U.S. immigration policies, restrictions on asylum have been increasing. According to IIRIRA, immigrants must apply for asylum within one year of entering the United States, unless they can demonstrate changed circumstances in their country of origin (see U.S. Department of Justice 2000). The 2005 REAL ID Act raised the level of proof required to obtain political asylum (see chapter 7, note 12).

4. Similarly, recent legal campaigns on behalf of asylum applicants who were victims of female genital mutilation seek to open the door to similarly situated individuals. See Lewis (2005) regarding this issue and see Bhabha (1996) and McKinley (1997) for discussions of gender-based asylum claims.

5. The term "refugee" can also have racial connotations, as Jesse Jackson pointed out in relation to the media's use of the term "refugee" to refer to victims of Hurricane Katrina. See CNN 2005.

6. Of course, homicides, kidnappings, robberies, and assaults occurred as part of the violence associated with the civil war, but in the postwar period these were described as criminal rather than as political in nature, and also as random and unpredictable.

7. Moodie (2006, 86) observes that in the postwar period "war death and war-death imagery have been divested of much of the public value they once had. Despite dominant efforts at erasure, they continue to haunt Salvadoran imagination."

8. Of course, by the time that the war ended many had developed lives in the United States and were therefore reluctant to return. Note that grants of political asylum do not require recipients to leave when conditions in their homeland change, but rather permit recipients to remain in the United States and to qualify for legal permanent residency and eventually U.S. citizenship.

9. By 2002, the homicide rate had declined to sixty per one hundred thousand residents (Dalton 2002a).

10. Analysts debate the degree to which the growth of gangs in El Salvador is attributable to deportation from the United States. Gangs existed in the El Salvador during the 1980s, but rising gang membership in the 1990s is associated with the Mara Salvatrucha and 18th Street, both of which originated in the United States. A recent survey of gang members incarcerated in El Salvador suggested that "even though just half (52.2%) said they knew fellow gang members in North America, the vast majority (85.8%) said they had no contact with fellow gang members outside the country and only between 5.7 and 8.5% had even traveled to the U.S. or Mexico" (Washington Office on Latin America 2007, 6).

11. Despite these alarming figures, I do not mean to imply that El Salvador is an unsafe place to live or to visit. El Salvador is a beautiful country with a rich cultural heritage, and, as officials often point out, crime is a common occurrence in many places, including major urban areas in the United States.

12. Ramos (2000, 9) states, "In the second half of the '90s, the official figures regarding criminal action struck an average of 8,000 criminal homicides, with rates that were located between 120 and 140 homicides for every 100,000 inhabitants. Facts that, upon remaining constant, would leave more mortal victims in the '90s than the twelve-year armed conflict."

13. Interviewees who discussed crime—and I should note that this topic arose primarily in interviews with members of Salvadoran NGOs—tended to locate the source

of delinquency in Salvadoran society rather than in the perpetrators themselves. When conducting interviews for this project, I did not anticipate that I would be writing about delinquency, so I generally did not pose questions about this topic. Many interviewees nonetheless raised this issue, drawing my attention to crime as a symptom of government shortcomings, as a product of emigration and particularly of deportation, and as a reason for continued emigration.

14. A 2005 report on crime in El Salvador notes that the Salvadoran government attributes homicides to increases in gang violence: "This [government] discourse attributes the majority of homicides committed in the country, in percentages that have ranged from more than 50% to 80%, to these groups. Nonetheless, on being confronted with statistical data regarding possible perpetrators or victims of homicides, the people involved in gangs, though a significant portion, do not make up the majority of these acts" (Fundación de Estudios 2005, 1). The Washington Office on Latin America reports that "perceptions about the growth and seriousness of the [gang] problem are fed by frequently sensationalized and unfounded reports of the transnational spread of youth gang violence, and of ties between gangs and organized crime such as narcotraffic, terrorism, human trafficking and arms dealing. However, current research shows that while a growing and complex problem, the transnational and criminal nature of youth gangs is quite limited" (2007, 1). WOLA nonetheless concludes that "youth gangs are a serious public security problem in El Salvador, Honduras and Guatemala" (2007, 1). A USAID report also suggests that while gangs contribute to crime and public insecurity, their impact is exaggerated: "While the media bombards the public with news accounts of gangs involved in criminal activity, there is little analysis of the origins and proliferation of the gang phenomenon. Instead, gangs are often the scapegoat for all social ills, which limits the public's deeper understanding of gangs and other issues affecting the country" (2006, 5).

15. Teresa Caldeira (2000, 79) points out that those who are, in some sense, "outsiders" are often associated with criminality. Similarly, in El Salvador, the common conflation of "gang members" and "deportees" contributes to defining both criminals and the gang problem as having origins outside El Salvador.

16. I do not mean to suggest that gang or other criminal activity is somehow a form of resistance. My point is rather that crime cannot be dissociated from the social and historical processes within which it is situated. Thus, financial fraud may be facilitated by social relations that create financial opportunities for powerful individuals, domestic abuse is made possible by gender inequalities, and youth violence may thrive in contexts of social exclusion. Further, not all of these crimes are equally stigmatized. Judging from the amount of press attention devoted to each of these topics, gang violence seems to provoke greater social concern than either domestic violence or financial fraud (see also Calavita et al. 1997).

17. I am grateful to Daniel Goldstein for drawing my attention to this point.

18. Súper Mano Dura—literally Super Firm Hand—has also been translated as "iron fist" and as zero tolerance. See Godoy 2005, Zilberg 2004.

19. According to Fundación de Estudios (2004), this plan was a continuation of an existing trend toward mass police detention of gang members, rather than an entirely new policy.

20. In 2004, the slogan "un gobierno con sentido humano" appeared in speeches, announcements, and advertisements, such as the FISDL's advertisement, "Participación

Desarrollo Combate a la Pobreza" ("Participation in Development Combats Poverty"), which appeared in the *Diario de Hoy*, 9 September, 2004, 5.

21. The measures announced in this speech included the creation of specialized units to operate in areas of high criminal activity, the creation of special antigang prosecutors, increased police operations in areas controlled by gangs, the creation of anti-drug units to combat gang's drug-dealing activities, specialized police units to break up the distribution of stolen goods, efforts to fight contraband and white-collar crime, a prison task force to prevent crime from occurring in or operating out of prisons, police patrols in unmarked cars in areas of high criminal activity, and improved methods of searching for fugitive gang members.

22. See advertisement published by the Ministerio de Gobernación in *La Prensa Gráfica*, 8 September 2004, 21.

23. The stigmatization of gang members may be part of a broader criminalization of youth occurring in the United States and elsewhere. See Ferrell and Sanders (1995) for discussions of the criminalization of youth culture.

24. The latter practice was prohibited by the 1992 peace accords, which redefined the mission of the armed forces as national defense rather than internal security (Studemeister 2001). Costa (2001, 22) points out that "in Latin America, public security has traditionally been the task for the military, and until relatively recently, the functions of the military and police were difficult to separate. Armies guaranteed external and internal security at the same time. The involvement of Latin American militaries in counter-subversion since the 1960s and their more recent participation in counter-narcotics activity has helped blur the line between police and military action even more."

25. Angelina Godoy (2004, 641) also draws attention to connections between neoliberalism and efforts to strengthen the rule of law:

> To suggest that the solution to the widespread exclusion of marginalized populations is to grant them access to the institutions of state law . . . while at the same time reducing state spending for social policies and limiting the opportunities for political mobilization, is to propose a law-centered vision of social and political change.
>
> It is, on closer inspection, a vision that coincides neatly with the same neoliberal vision of governance espoused by the very lending institutions who often bankroll "rule of law" reforms. This is a vision in which problems like poverty and social exclusion are to be resolved through market mechanisms, not remedied by redistributive state policy. The formal legal system remains available to redress egregious wrongs, of course; but it is not intended, nor even empowered, to promote an activist vision of social change.

7. ¡Sí, se puede! (Yes, it can be done!)

1. A similar initiative was approved by Arizona voters in 2004. See State of Arizona 2004 Official Canvass.

2. One feature of Proposition 187 that was allowed to stand was the determination that undocumented immigrants and those with temporary legal status could not be considered legal residents of the State of California and therefore had to pay out-of-state

tuition at public universities. This financial constraint made higher education impossible for many students. California Assembly Bill 540, approved in 2001, now permits eligible undocumented immigrants to pay in-state tuition (see Immigrant Legal Resource Center n.d.; Krueger 2005). Similar legislation, known as the Dream Act, has been proposed at a federal level. See http://www.ilrc.org/ab540.html.

3. In the article "Immigrants Keep U.S. Economy Supple," Associated Press reporter John McAuley writes that in February 2000 "Greenspan said in his semiannual congressional testimony that 'imbalances in the labor market may have more serious implications for inflation pressures,' especially because 'there is an effective limit to new hiring, unless immigration is uncapped.' " See also U.S. Federal Reserve 2000.

4. Pete Wilson, a Republican and governor of California from 1991–99, and a presidential aspirant, earned the ire of many Latino voters by supporting Proposition 187, the "Save Our State" initiative, which required doctors, teachers, and social service workers to report suspected undocumented immigrants to U.S. immigration authorities. Although Proposition 187 won passage, many of its provisions were subsequently declared unconstitutional. Many analysts, such as the interviewee quoted, suggest that Wilson's prominent opposition to illegal immigration alienated Latino voters and thus doomed Wilson's political career and hurt the Republican Party in California.

5. Wasem (2002, 5) writes that "in an October 26 letter to congressional leaders, President Clinton led his list of reasons he would veto the CJS appropriations bill with failure to include LIFA."

6. Wasem points out that if both of these measures were approved, many of the Central Americans who would benefit from NACARA parity would also be eligible under the change in registry date, so these estimates "are not cumulative" (2002, 4).

7. Some would argue that this "dependency" results from employers' desire to hire employees who are more vulnerable and who can therefore be expected to work for lower wages and in worse conditions. According to this argument, if employers complied with existing labor laws and paid living wages, they would not need to "depend" on immigrant workers (see, e.g., Jenkins 1978). Based on a survey of undocumented immigrants, Chiswick (1988) concluded that "there is no denying that illegal aliens are paid low wages relative to the average U.S. worker. But the low wages of illegal aliens do not appear to be the result of employer exploitation. Rather, they appear to be the result of low skill levels" (143). See also U.S. General Accounting Office 1988.

8. These three agencies are the Citizenship and Immigration Services (USCIS), Immigration and Customs Enforcement (ICE), and U.S. Customs and Border Patrol. In 1891, the Office of the Superintendent of Immigration was established in the Treasury Department. In 1903, what had then become the Bureau of Immigration was transferred to the Department of Commerce and Labor. The Immigration and Naturalization Service was created in 1933, and, in 1940, it was moved from the Department of Labor to the Department of Justice (M. Smith 2006). Calls for restructuring the INS by dividing its enforcement and service functions into separate agencies predated September 11, 2001.

9. This segment of the act targets asylum and judicial review of removal orders as areas of vulnerability. Other measures outlined in Title I of the REAL ID Act include enabling judges to determine whether an asylum applicant ought to have been able to provide particular evidence in support of a claim, enabling judges to use any statement asylum applicants ever made when assessing credibility, broadening the definition of

terrorist organizations and of terrorist activity as grounds for deportation, and limiting judicial review of orders of removal. (REAL ID Act of 2005. Public Law 109–13–May 11, 2005. 119 Stat. 302)

10. Note that in *Hamdi v. Rumsfeld*, the U.S. Supreme Court ruled that the executive branch could detain U.S. citizens as enemy combatants, but that such individuals had the right to a hearing at which they could present evidence disputing this designation.

Conclusion

1. My understanding of ethnographic accounts is indebted to conversations and collaborations with Barbara Yngvesson.

2. The sense that new perspectives produce new accounts may be one of the justifications for the current fascination with interdisciplinary research and the fatigue with traditional disciplines—the sense that they have been exhausted and new combinations are needed in order for new knowledge to be produced (Strathern 2004).

3. For example, in *Argonauts of the Western Pacific*, Malinowski (1922, 4) opens his account as follows, "Imagine yourself suddenly set down surrounded by all your gear, alone on a tropical beach close to a native village, while the launch or dinghy which has brought you sails away out of sight." I am grateful to Tom Boellstorff for drawing my attention to the relevance of this passage.

Epigraph

1. These lines are taken from a sermon that Salvadoran archbishop Oscar Romero preached on March 23, 1980, the day before he was assassinated.

2. Elana Zilberg reports, "The word in the original transcript is *tabiando*. However, given Bullet's English translation 'doing time,' it's quite likely that the word is actually *tapiando*. The verb *tapiar* is translated 'to wall or block up (as in a window or a door).' "

3. *Guanacos* is a slang term for Salvadorans. *Pipiles* are a group of people indigenous to El Salvador.

4. "Immigration" here refers to La Migra, that is, U.S. immigration authorities, not to the process of migrating

5. "Radical society" does not connote left- or right-wing politics.

6. Meaning, I think, "We shouldn't say otherwise."

Index

Page numbers in italics refer to tables and figures.